The Civil War
as a Theological Crisis

The Steven and Janice Brose Lectures
in the Civil War Era

William A. Blair, editor

The Civil War
as a
Theological Crisis

by
Mark A. Noll

The University of North Carolina Press

Chapel Hill

Set in Trinité by Tseng Information Systems, Inc.
Manufactured in the United States of America

The paper in this book meets the guidelines
for permanence and durability of the Committee
on Production Guidelines for Book Longevity
of the Council on Library Resources.

Library of Congress Cataloging-in-Publication Data
Noll, Mark A., 1946–
The Civil War as a theological crisis / by Mark A. Noll.
p. cm. – (The Steven and Janice Brose lectures in the Civil War era)
Includes bibliographical references and index.
ISBN-13: 978-0-8078-3012-3 (cloth : alk. paper)
ISBN-10: 0-8078-3012-7 (cloth : alk. paper)
1. United States – History – Civil War, 1861–1865 – Influence. 2. United States –
History – Civil War, 1861–1865 – Religious aspects. 3. Slavery and the church –
United States – History – 19th century. 4. Slavery – Moral and ethical
aspects – United States – History – 19th century. 5. United States –
Church history – 19th century. I. Title. II. Series.
E468.9.N65 2006
277.3′081 – dc22
2005034944

10 09 08 07 06   5 4 3 2 1

To Gene Genovese

Proverbs 27:17

Contents

Acknowledgments

This book is a revision and expansion of my Steven and Janice Brose Lectures, which were given at the George and Ann Richards Civil War Study Center of Penn State University on April 10-12, 2003. A combination of warm personal hospitality and bracing intellectual discussion made my time at Penn State a thorough delight. One of the reasons for expanding the lectures is to answer questions from some in attendance who wanted to know more about how African Americans put the Bible to use on the controversies surrounding slavery in the years before the Civil War. I would like to offer special thanks to William Blair, director of the Richards Center, for the chance to participate in the lively activities of his pathbreaking program.

Another reason for expanding the lectures involves another heartfelt word of thanks, this time to the staff of the John W. Kluge Center of the Library of Congress. The opportunity to hold the Ann and Cary Maguire Chair of American History and Ethics during the 2004-5 academic year offered an excellent opportunity to flesh out a number of themes that I could only sketch at Penn State, especially concerning foreign comment on religious aspects of the Civil War. The library's unmatched resources and the superlative assistance provided to visiting scholars by Kluge Center personnel made for an ideal place to finish this book.

It does remain, however, the printed version of lectures, which means that more room is afforded the personal voice and a certain measure of speculation beyond exhaustive documentation than would be appropriate in a full-scale monograph.

The invitation to deliver the Sprunt Lectures at Union Seminary in Richmond, Virginia, in January 2005 was also much appreciated since it offered an opportunity to try out some of my ideas in a more extended form. For the hospitality of Louis Weeks and Mark Valeri, I am especially appreciative. I would also like to thank other hosts who patiently provided a willing ear and helpful criticisms in responding to presentations drawn from material in this book: the Reformed Institute of Metropolitan Washington, D.C. (and Bruce Douglass); the University of Wisconsin, Madison (and Charles Cohen with Ronald Numbers); the University of Wisconsin, Green Bay (and Harvey Kay); North Park Theological Seminary (and Stephen Graham); the Cincinnati Summit on Racism (and Pastor Ray MacMillian); and the Institute for the Study of Christianity and Culture, East Lansing, Michigan (and Malcolm Magee).

Responsibility for translations of European sources is my own, but I would like to thank Mary Noll Venables for help with a couple of sticky German passages and Maria Walford for even more of that kind of assistance with the Italian from *La Civiltà cattolica*. Some years ago, Peter Wallace and David Bebbington generously assisted me by gathering sources, for the United States and Britain respectively, and I would like to thank them for the benefits their efforts continue to afford. Similarly, I am grateful to David Livingstone and the late George Rawlyk for pointing me to relevant depositories of nineteenth-century periodicals in, respectively, Belfast and Ontario. I am grateful to the late Peter D'Agostino, John McGreevy, and John Quinn for their kindness in reading chapter 7 and providing useful suggestions for its improvement. Kurt Berends, Beth Barton Schweiger, and Harry Stout also provided much-appreciated help along the way.

Finally, the dedication expresses sincerely a very deep but also complex intellectual debt.

The Civil War
as a Theological Crisis

Chapter 1

Introduction

In the uncertain days of late 1860 and early 1861, the pulpits of the United States were transformed into instruments of political theology. Abraham Lincoln, the president-elect, continued to insist that he would follow through on the platform of the Republican Party to prohibit forever the spread of slavery into new United States territory. On December 20, delegates to a special convention in Columbia, South Carolina, voted to secede from the Union. The other states of the Deep South seemed sure to follow, and those of the Upper South and border South likely to do so. In such dire circumstances, Americans looked to their preachers for instruction from God.

Ministers throughout the United States responded confidently. The will of God, as revealed first in the Scriptures and then through reflection on the workings of divine providence, was clear. Or at least it was clear to the ministers as individuals, many of whom were eager to raise a trumpet for the Lord. As a group, however, it was a different story, for the trumpets blown so forthrightly were producing cacophony. On no subject was the cacophony more obvious, and more painful, than on the question of the Bible and slavery. On no subject did the cacophony touch such agonizing depths as on the question of God's providential designs for the United States of America.

The Bible and Slavery

Whether the Union should be preserved was everywhere acknowledged to be the political question of the hour, but only inference or deduction could discern a message in the Bible concerning the specific fate of the United States of America. By contrast, on slavery, which everyone knew was the economic, social, and moral issue on which the political question turned, it was a dif-

ferent matter. The Bible, or so a host of ministers affirmed, was clear as a bell
about slavery.

The Bible, for example, was clear to Henry Ward Beecher, the North's most
renowned preacher, when he addressed his Plymouth Congregational Church
in Brooklyn, New York, on January 4, 1861, a day of national fasting called
to have the people pray for the country's healing. In Beecher's view, the evil
for which the United States as a nation most desperately needed to repent,
"the most alarming and most fertile cause of national sin," was slavery. About
this great evil, the Bible could not speak with less ambiguity: "Where the
Bible has been in the household, and read without hindrance by parents and
children together – there you have had an indomitable yeomanry, a state that
would not have a tyrant on the throne, a government that would not have a
slave or a serf in the field."[1]

But of course the Bible spoke very differently to others who also rose to
preach in that fateful moment. Six weeks earlier at a day of fasting called
by the state of South Carolina, the South's most respected minister, James
Henley Thornwell, took up before his Presbyterian congregation in Columbia the very same theme of "our national sins" that Beecher would address
before the Congregationalists of Brooklyn. To Thornwell, slavery was the
"good and merciful" way of organizing "labor which Providence has given
us." About the propriety of this system in the eyes of God, Thornwell was so
confident that, like Beecher, he did not engage in any actual biblical exegesis;
rather, he simply asserted: "That the relation betwixt the slave and his master is not inconsistent with the word of God, we have long since settled. . . .
We cherish the institution not from avarice, but from principle."[2]

The fact that Beecher in the North and Thornwell in the South found contrasting messages in Scripture by no means indicates the depth of theological crisis occasioned by this clash of interpretation. Since the dawn of time,
warring combatants have regularly reached for whatever religious support
they could find to nerve their own side for battle. Especially in our postmod-
ern age, we think we know all about the way that interests dictate interpretations. It was, therefore, a more convincing indication of profound theological crisis when entirely within the North ministers battled each other on
the interpretation of the Bible. In contrast to the struggle between Northern
theologians and Southern theologians, this clash pitted against each other
ministers who agreed about the necessity of preserving the Union and who

also agreed that the Bible represented authoritative, truth-telling revelation from God.

Thus only a month before Beecher preached to the Brooklyn Congregationalists about the monstrous sinfulness of slavery, the Reverend Henry Van Dyke expounded on a related theme to his congregation, Brooklyn's First Presbyterian Church, just down the street from Beecher's Plymouth Congregational. But when Van Dyke took up the theme of the "character and influence of abolitionism," his conclusions were anything but similar to Beecher's. To this Northern Presbyterian, it was obvious that the "tree of Abolitionism is evil, and only evil – root and branch, flower and leaf, and fruit; that it springs from, and is nourished by, an utter rejection of the Scriptures." [3] So clear to Van Dyke were the biblical sanctions for slavery that he could only conclude that willful abolitionists like Beecher were scoffing at the Bible's authority.

An even more interesting contrast with Beecher's confident enlistment of the Bible against slavery was offered by Rabbi Morris J. Raphall, who on the same day of national fasting that provided Beecher the occasion for his sermon, addressed the Jewish Synagogue of New York. Like Van Dyke's, his sermon directly contradicted what Beecher had claimed. Raphall's subject was the biblical view of slavery. To the learned rabbi, it was imperative that issues of ultimate significance be adjudicated by "the highest Law of all," which was "the revealed Law and Word of God." Unlike the addresses from Thornwell and Beecher, Raphall's sermon was filled with close exegesis of many passages from the Hebrew Scriptures. Significantly, this Northern rabbi was convinced that the passages he cited taught beyond cavil that the curse pronounced by Noah in Genesis 9 on his son Ham had consigned "fetish-serving benighted Africa" to everlasting servitude. Raphall was also sure that a myriad of biblical texts demonstrated as clearly as demonstration could make it that slavery was a legitimate social system. Those texts included passages from Exodus, Leviticus, and Deuteronomy.[4] Raphall's conclusion about the scriptural legitimacy of slavery per se reflected his exasperation at anyone who could read the Bible in any other way: "Is slaveholding condemned as a sin in sacred Scripture? . . . How this question can at all arise in the mind of any man that has received a religious education, and is acquainted with the history of the Bible, is a phenomenon I cannot explain to myself."[5] As we shall see, Raphall had more things to say on the subject because he contended that much in the Bible argued against slavery *as it was practiced in the United States*; but on the issue of the legitimacy of the institution, narrowly defined, the New York rabbi was definite.

One of the many Northerners with a good religious education who knew the Bible very well, yet in whose mind questions did arise about the intrinsic evil of slaveholding, was Tayler Lewis, a Dutch Reformed layman and since 1838 a professor of Greek and oriental studies, first at New York University and then at Union College. In an essay that was originally published as a direct rejoinder to the Presbyterian Van Dyke and the Jew Raphall, Professor Lewis complained that "there is . . . something in the more interior spirit of those [biblical] texts that [Van Dyke] does not see; he does not take the apostles' standpoint; he does not take into view the vastly changed condition of the world; he does not seem to consider that whilst truth is fixed, . . . its application to distant ages, and differing circumstances, is so varying continually that a wrong direction given to the more truthful exegesis may convert it into the more malignant falsehood."[6] Given the extreme emotions of the day, Lewis was relatively charitable about what he considered Rabbi Raphall's misreading of the Hebrew Scriptures. He was more concerned to show the errors in Van Dyke's use of the Christian New Testament to defend slavery. Stated in its simplest form, Lewis's contention was that "there is not a word in the New Testament about buying and selling slaves."[7] And since buying and selling slaves was intrinsic to the American slave system, the New Testament obviously condemned that system.

So it went into April 1861 and well beyond. The political standoff that led to war was matched by an interpretive standoff. No common meaning could be discovered in the Bible, which almost everyone in the United States professed to honor and which was, without a rival, the most widely read text of any kind in the whole country.

Providence

Clashes over the meaning of the Bible on slavery were matched during the era of the Civil War by an equally striking division in what the nation's most widely recognized religious thinkers concluded about the workings of divine providence. Confident pronouncements about what God was "doing" in and through the war arose in profusion from all points on the theological compass. Yet as with debates over the Bible and slavery, interpretations of divine providence differed materially depending on the standpoint of the one who identified how God was at work.

An extreme example of such difference is provided by a pair of discourses from April 1861 and April 1862, which were similar in their learning, conviction, and religious passion, but otherwise strikingly at odds in opinions about what God intended for the slave system of the United States. In the *Southern Presbyterian Review* of April 1861, John H. Rice offered a comprehensive explanation for the existence of the Southern states that was based almost exclusively on the workings of providence. To Rice, it was obvious that the slave system – which he described as foisted on the Southern colonies by New England's mercantile greed and Britain's callous imperialism – had entered on hard times after the Revolutionary War and was by about 1815 nearing a crisis. Because the crisis was caused by the presence of a large and restive black slave population, it "could not be solved by any scheme of abolition, emancipation, or colonization." At that bleak hour, "the providence of God opened the door of safety, by the operation of causes originating at points distant from each other by the whole length of the continent and the width of the broad Atlantic." The "almost simultaneous" invention of the cotton gin in Connecticut and the spinning jenny in Britain, along with the opening of fertile cotton-producing land in America's new Southwest, was manifestly God's way of overcoming the crisis. After that remarkable conjunction of events, the South had flourished, with the only threat to its prosperity occasioned by "the foolish and wicked meddling of men" who attacked those "to whom God in His providence, has committed [the institution of slavery for] its guidance and control." From this history, according to Rice, the South had taken the lesson "never to consent that her social system . . . be confined and restrained by any other limits than such as the God of nature interposes." Slavery, in a word, had developed under "certain providential conditions" that Rice discerned as clearly as he saw "the wonderful providence of God" that had led first to the European colonization of America and then to the unexpected victory of American patriots in the War of Independence.[8]

One year later, Daniel Alexander Payne, presiding bishop of the African Methodist Episcopal Church, preached a sermon in Washington, D.C., in order to celebrate the Union legislation that ended slavery in the federal district but also to urge his fellow African American Methodists to make the best of their newfound freedom. To Payne, it was as clear as it had been to Rice what God was about, although *what* he saw was the opposite of Rice's perception. "Who has sent this great deliverance?" was Payne's query. "The answer shall be, the Lord; the Lord God Almighty, the God of Abraham and Isaac and Jacob." Only "thou, O Lord, and thou alone couldst have moved the heart of this Nation to have done so great a deed for this weak, despised and needy people!"[9]

The manifest contradiction in these two interpretations of providence, which was multiplied on every hand during the war years, was not the most telling feature of the appeal to providence. Rather, that most telling feature was the confident assurance with which those appeals were made. This widely shared confidence was, ironically, a major reason for the shallowness of providential reasoning during the war. It was also a feature suggesting that providential reasoning marked a crucial turning point in the broader history of American thought.

As with the question of the Bible and slavery, the American perception of providence also has a history. Unpacking that history is the best way to make sense of how providential reasoning worked during the war and then of why the exercise of such providentialism factored so significantly in the later intellectual history of the United States.

The Shape of This Book

The purpose of this book is to explain why clashes over the meaning of the Bible and the workings of providence, which grew directly out of the nation's broader history before the Civil War, revealed a significant theological crisis. Although I hope that the book will indicate why serious attention to religion can add greatly to an understanding of the origin, the course, and especially the intensity of the Civil War, my main purpose is to show how and why the cultural conflict that led to such a crisis for the nation also constituted a crisis for theology.

The inability to find a univocal answer in Scripture to the pressing question of slavery troubled Americans for more than thirty years—from, that is, at least the early 1830s, when the rise of a more radical abolitionism precipitated a responding defense of slavery as a positive good, to the end of the war in 1865, when the success of Union arms rendered further exegetical debate pointless. Why this clash over the interpretation of Scripture – a clash that helps explain the intense religious fervor displayed on both sides – was so important in the broader sweep of American religious history is the issue I address in chapter 3. In chapter 4 this theme is carried further in order to explore the specific confusion that resulted when what the Bible said (or did not say) about race was subordinated to what it said about slavery. Then in chapter 5 the question turns to why widespread American belief in divine providence – the belief that God ruled manifestly over the affairs of people and nations – added fuel to the crisis, particularly as interpretations about God's actions in and through the Civil War came to clash as fundamentally as did interpretations of God's written Word, the Scriptures.

These discussions of the Bible and of providence expand on arguments I have made before.[10] Chapters 6 and 7, by contrast, push into terrain that is mostly new to me and, it appears, to other historians of the Civil War. In an effort to probe wider dimensions of the American theological crisis, I have tried to discover what opinion from outside the United States concluded about the state of American religion as reflected in the War between the States. In this effort I am trying to gain for American history of the mid-nineteenth century some of the benefits that have accrued so richly to historical study of the colonial and revolutionary periods from viewing the New World in constant conjunction with the Old. This investigation has revealed two divergent streams of foreign commentary. The first, from European and Canadian Protestants, as well as from Europe's liberal Roman Catholics, featured intense religious conviction about the evils of slavery and the urgent need to end the slave system in the United States. It is a noteworthy literature for revealing much stronger opinions *against* slavery than *for* the North. It is also noteworthy for providing almost no evidence, even from the most theologically conservative sources, that these non-Americans endorsed what so many American Protestants believed concerning the Bible's legitimization of slavery.

The second strand of foreign commentary, from conservative European Catholics, is in some ways more interesting. It features wide-ranging comparisons between societies built on Protestant foundations and those in which Catholicism prevailed. It is noteworthy both for asserting forthrightly that the Bible does sanction slavery and for bluntly challenging commonly accepted American ideals of individual liberty. What is also striking about such commentary is that it challenges common American opinion of the mid-nineteenth century by learnedly defending the Catholic Church as the guardian of true liberty. Because this strand of foreign Catholic opinion supplied significant intellectual resources for American Catholics as they responded to the era's crisis, chapter 7 broadens slightly to include a review of the recent scholarship that has so splendidly illuminated American Catholic attitudes before and during the Civil War.

The payoff from even a preliminary assessment of foreign religious commentary is to add intriguing, but usually neglected, voices to the moral battles that raged as fiercely as the era's political and military conflicts. Even more, it is to gain a number of perceptive interpretations of American religious life and religious thought that, because they did not share convictions common to most Americans, offered unusually provocative assessments of where that life and thought were headed. As with the examination of domestic attitudes about Scripture and divine providence, so too the examination of foreign religious opinion on the American conflict is designed to probe religious reasoning about the War between the States with the same seriousness that legions of Civil War scholars have brought to bear on other aspects of the conflict, and with such striking success.

Foreign observers saw more clearly than most Americans what was at stake when interpretations of Scripture and understandings of providence divided this particular people beyond hope of resolution. American national culture had been built in substantial part by voluntary and democratic appropriation of Scripture. Yet if by following such an approach to the Bible there resulted an unbridgeable chasm of opinion about what Scripture actually taught, there were no resources within democratic or voluntary procedures to resolve the public division of opinion that was created by voluntary and democratic interpretation of the Bible. The Book that made the nation was destroying the nation; the nation that had taken to the Book was rescued not by the Book but by the force of arms.

BY WAY of further introduction, it is important to make preliminary comments about the study of religion in Civil War history, about the state of religion itself in the United States during the middle decades of the nineteenth century, and about how the theological history of the Civil War compares to the theological history of other military crises in modern Western history.

From these path-clearing discussions, the book turns in chapter 2 to outline the historical contexts that explain why the conflict concerning Scripture and providence revealed such a large-scale crisis. Debates in the 1860s over what the Bible taught and what God was doing in history always also concerned how Scripture and providence had been perceived in the decades before the war.

Studying Religion in the Era of the Civil War

On the question of how the Civil War influenced the general course of American intellectual life, a number of historians have made particularly significant contributions. Yet most of that good work has concentrated on how a relatively few Northern intellectuals or members of the upper classes were pushed by the war toward exchanging traditional religious convictions for more secular perspectives. Thus as long ago as 1965 George Fredrickson showed how among these elites the war hastened the acceptance of rational business planning over decentralized local autonomy, promoted pragmatic and practical views of the self over Emersonian transcendentalism, and led to the prestige of scientists over the authority of clergymen.[11] Similarly, in 1992 Anne Rose concluded that for a significant group of well-born men and women whom she called "Victorians," "the Civil War was a cornerstone in [their] redefinition of sacred values in secular terms."[12] More recently, Alfred Kazin has suggested that Abraham Lincoln's Second Inaugural Address in 1865 marked the "culmination" of the "age of belief" in the United States, which very soon thereafter began to recede.[13] Louis Menand has also argued that for Oliver Wendell Holmes Jr. and a rising cadre of Northern intellectuals, the war precipitated "a failure of ideas" that undermined the confident "beliefs and assumptions of the era that preceded it" as thoroughly as similar beliefs were later undermined by World War I and the war in Vietnam.[14]

Such provocative studies shed little direct light on the nature of religious thought among people for whom the war did not secularize traditional beliefs, but rather intensified them or left them undisturbed. Yet here we are talking about the vast majority of Americans, at least as indicated by those who expressed in some public way their opinions concerning the meaning of the conflict. Their standpoint is the focus of this book. To see why examining the thought of traditional religious believers is critical for understanding the

Civil War as a whole, it is useful to sketch the general situation of religion in mid-nineteenth-century America.

After a long period of unwarranted neglect, the nation's majority religious populations circa 1860 are now being examined in a gratifying surge of serious scholarly work. Major histories of the Civil War by, for example, Phillip Paludan and Allen Guelzo, have included full treatment of religious developments during the conflict.[15] Although James McPherson neglected religious matters in his monumental *Battle Cry of Freedom*, a book that was superb in every other respect, he has more recently published significant materials supporting his own view that "Civil War armies were, arguably, the most religious in American history."[16]

On several fronts, a growing number of historians are pursuing the broader challenge that McPherson posed when he wrote, "Religion was central to the meaning of the Civil War, as the generation that experienced the war tried to understand it. Religion should also be central to our efforts to recover that meaning."[17] Many of the recent contributions to the never-ending river of Civil War-era biographies, for example, give religious matters an emphasis that is proportionately much closer to the place it occupied in the subjects' lives.[18] Welcome, too, is the serious biographical attention now being paid to at least some of the era's major religious figures, including due justice to their part in the sectional conflict.[19] After decades in which the close scrutiny of religion in the Civil War was limited to only a few lonely scholars like Lewis Vander Velde, James Silver, James Moorhead, and Gardiner Shattuck,[20] recent years have witnessed a flourishing of religious themes in studies written or coordinated by, among others, John McGivigan, Mitchell Snay, Randall Miller, Harry Stout, Charles Reagan Wilson, Steven Woodworth, and Kent Dollar.[21]

Close-grained attention to the war years has been wonderfully supplemented by major studies documenting the central role of religion in developments during the antebellum period that led to secession and the outbreak of armed conflict. Among such works, pride of place must be given to the magisterial study of religion and antebellum politics by Richard Carwardine, but works of nearly similar scope have appeared from, among others, McGivigan, Snay, Eugene Genovese, Elizabeth Fox-Genovese, Drew Gilpin Faust, Kenneth Startup, John Daly, and Michael O'Brien.[22] Also of note are studies of Civil War-era sermons produced by David Chesebrough[23] and ones that have appeared in several responsible popularizations for a broader read-ing public.[24] This quick bibliographical celebration does not take into con-sideration the great boost that is being given to debate over the religious meaning of the war by very new works, including Harry Stout's moral his-tory of the Civil War and the long-awaited study of the South's slaveholding classes from Elizabeth Fox-Genovese and Eugene Genovese.[25]

A different kind of stimulus was provided by the movie *Gods and Generals*, which came out in 2003. If it could be charged with romanticizing the bru-tality of combat and ignoring the larger moral questions that brought on the war, the film nonetheless did capture some religious aspects of the conflict more accurately and more extensively than any big-budget Hollywood film has ever done before.[26]

This brief survey has not mentioned many of the other relevant works in the flood of Civil War literature that continues to pour from the presses.[27] But it should indicate that serious consideration of theology in the Civil War is now riding the crest of a historiographical wave.

Religion in the Era of the Civil War

It is important to be clear about why this recent burst of scholarship meets a fundamental historical need. The United States in 1860 was not uniquely religious, but it was nonetheless, and by almost any standard of compari-son, a remarkably religious society. Comparisons are imperative for making this point. In 1860 between a third and two-fifths of Americans were formal members of churches. By itself, that number is not overly impressive since today about two-thirds of Americans claim church membership.[28] Much more impressive about that earlier period, however, is that the rate of adher-ence – of people participating regularly in church life – was probably double the rate of membership.[29] Today, by contrast, only a little more than half of the Americans who claim membership in a religious body regularly attend their places of worship.

Two especially significant realities about American religion in 1860 are also best defined comparatively. First is the fact that religion was then much more important than any other center of value at work in the country; second is the fact that American religion was still mostly Protestant. On the first point, churches, church attenders, and religious societies were not, proportionately considered, all that much more numerous or widespread than they are now. But almost all other institutions and agencies of culture with which we are now familiar were much smaller than they have become. Richard Carwardine put the matter well in his study of religion and politics before the Civil War when he concluded that during the mid-1850s "over 10 million Americans, or about 40 percent of the total population, appear at that time to have been in close sympathy with evangelical Christianity. This was the largest, and most formidable, subculture in American society."[30]

Other comparisons that highlight the great significance of religion in the 1860s risk mindless statistical overkill, but they are nonetheless intriguing.[31] Consider, as an example, the scale of organized religion vis-à-vis the scale of the federal government.

- In 1860 about 4.7 million American men voted in the decisive presidential election, but during that same year at least three (and maybe even four) times that many men, women, and children were regularly in church on any given Sunday. In the 2004 presidential election, about 115 million adult Americans went to the polls, which was roughly the same number of Americans who attended a religious service on any given day of worship.
- In 1860 there were about as many Methodist clergy as U.S. postal workers. Today the ratio of postal workers to Methodist clergy is about nine to one.
- In 1860, before mobilization for the Civil War, the number of active duty U.S. military personnel was about half the number of the nation's active clergymen. In the early twenty-first century, before mobilization for war with Iraq, the ratio of military to clergy was about three to one.
- In 1860 the income of the nation's churches and religious voluntary societies came quite close to matching the total receipts of the federal government. Today the ratio of annual federal income to annual religion-related giving is about twenty-five to one.

Mention of the federal budget opens up considerations of other economic matters.

- In 1850 the total value of all church property in the country was pegged by the census at over $87 million, and in 1860 at over $169 million. Of all American industries, only the railroads enjoyed greater capital investment.

‣ In 1860 there were in the United States thirty-five churches for each banking facility; today there are four churches for each banking facility.

The central role of religion for both intellectual and popular culture offers more to consider.

‣ In 1840 each person in the United States received on average six pieces of mail through the postal system, which was about one-third the total number of sermons that each person, again on average, heard during the year.[32]

‣ In 1860 there were about 400 institutions of higher learning in the country, all but a bare handful of them run by religious organizations.

‣ Only a few years earlier, the Methodist *Christian Advocate* was pleased to tell its readers that of the fifty-four oldest colleges in the United States, fifty-one were presided over by clergymen. They were somewhat less pleased to report that forty of the fifty-one clergymen were Presbyterians or Congregationalists.[33]

‣ In 1860 the only well-organized postgraduate education that extended its concerns beyond narrow professional qualification was provided by the nation's theological seminaries.

In short, the importance of religion for American society in 1860 lay partly in its wide dispersion. Even more, it resided in its overwhelming presence when compared with other institutions of government, culture, education, and the media that have grown so vast in American society since the close of the Civil War. As a promoter of values, as a generator of print, as a source of popular music and popular artistic endeavor, and as a comforter (and agitator) of internal life, organized religion was rivaled in its impact only by the workings of the market, and those workings were everywhere interwoven with religious concerns.[34]

The second important point about religion in the mid-nineteenth century concerns its makeup, which in 1860 was still overwhelmingly Protestant. To be sure, the religious pluralism for which the United States is justly renowned was already in place, no less among Protestants as in the rapidly growing number of Roman Catholics, Mormons, Jews, and other non-Protestant groups. But we need to bear in mind how very Protestant most religion remained in the United States at the start of the Civil War.

The 1860 census reported that there were seventy-seven Jewish places of worship in the United States, which represented a doubling from only ten years earlier. The number of Roman Catholic places of worship had risen even faster, from about 1,200 in 1850 to over 2,500 in 1860. Nevertheless, the nation's formal religious life was dominated by Protestant institutions, with over 83 percent of the value of church property, over 92 percent of the seating accommodations in houses of worship, and over 95 percent of the churches themselves (about 50,000 of them). A finer-grained analysis shows that the main denominational families of Baptists, Congregationalists, Methodists, and Presbyterians—that is, the largest representation of evangelical, British-descended Protestantism—accounted for about 55 percent of the value of all church property, nearly 72 percent of all the seats available in churches, and almost 75 percent of the churches themselves.[35] Pluralism, both intra-Christian and among religions more generally, was definitely on the rise in 1860. But the reality on the ground in most regions of the country was still overwhelmingly Protestant, and Protestant of a readily identifiable evangelical type.

Given this Protestant demography, and given intense Protestant engagement with the moral arguments that led to war, it is hardly surprising that the fortunes of war deeply affected Protestant thinking. What did not occur during the American Civil War, however, was what had in fact occurred at a number of other times and places in Western history when traumatic conflict was joined to intense religious commitment.

Warfare and Theological Depth

Warfare—and the more cataclysmic the better—has sometimes been the mother of theological profundity. As a prime example, more than a millennium of European history was decisively influenced by Augustine's *City of God*, a book prompted by the broodings of a Roman colonial over the sack of the Eternal City. A surprisingly large number of other great theological enterprises also received critical impetus from the tumults of war. Thomas Aquinas, for one, was spurred to his monumental labors against the backdrop of the thirteenth century's ideological and military conflicts with Islam. John Calvin published successive editions of the *Institutes of the Christian Religion* directly in response to conditions created by the French civil wars of the mid-sixteenth century. Many of the theological standards of the Reformation era – including, the Lutherans' Augsburg Confession, the Catholics' Canons and Decrees of the Council of Trent, the Helvetic Confessions of the Swiss Reformed churches, the Scots' Confession, and the Westminster Confession of the English Puritans – arose directly out of armed, as well as doctrinal, controversy. One of the most widely distributed Protestant confessions, the Heidelberg Catechism, was commissioned to resolve doctrinal, rather than military, strife, but it entered into the depths of the Dutch psyche during a dreadful period of all-out war with Habsburg Spain. In the twentieth century, there would have been no dialectical theology of neo-orthodoxy from Karl Barth without World War I and no "theology come of age" from Dietrich Bonhoeffer without the Hitler terror.

If cataclysmic military conflict has played a direct role in producing theology of high quality for intellectual elites, it has also sometimes produced profound Christian reflection among the people at large, especially in hymns that, through arising from specific circumstances of wartime devastation, nonetheless feature compelling general commentary on the nature of existence under God. A range of still vital hymnody from the crusading era – like Bernard of Cluny's "Jerusalem the Golden" (twelfth century) – illustrates this potential for popular theology. It is most clearly seen, however, in the literary harvest of the Thirty Years' War (1618-48) with hymns like Martin Rinkart's "Now thank we all our God" (1636), Georg Neumark's "If thou but suffer God to guide thee" (1641), and Paul Gerhardt's "Holy Ghost, dispel our sadness" (1648) – all of which were composed against the backdrop of unspeakable military devastation.[36]

To these generalizations about the theological fecundity of warfare, the most cataclysmic war in the history of the United States is an exception. The Civil War and the political-social-religious conflicts that preceded it do not seem to have stimulated deep theological insights from either elites or the masses. Hymns arising from the time of national conflict can indeed still warm the heart – like James Russell Lowell's "Once to Every Man and Nation" (1844), George Duffield's "Stand Up, Stand Up, for Jesus" (1858), Julia Ward Howe's "Battle Hymn of the Republic" (1862), or Henry Wadsworth Longfellow's "I Heard the Bells on Christmas Day" (1864). Before their cause went down, Southerners were similarly moved by hymnlike songs such as Henry Timrod's "Ethnogenesis" (1861). But such hymns never appealed to believers outside the nation (or region) in which they were written, and they possess scant theological gravitas.

In the composition of elite theology, a similar situation prevails. The Civil War provoked incredible religious energy, with virtually all the nation's foremost theological minds toiling diligently to fathom both the ultimate meaning of the conflict and, more grandly, Ultimate Meaning itself as illuminated by the light of exploding shells and the flames devouring towns, fields, and factories. In surprisingly large measure, however, the religion with which theologians emerged from the war was essentially the same as that with which they entered the war. Despite the conflict's horrific character and the way it touched personally many of America's greatest religious thinkers, the conflict seems to have pushed theologians down the roads on which they were already traveling rather than compelling them to go in new, creative directions.[37]

It is remotely possible that theology only appears thin during the Civil War because of a lack of attention by historians. Neither of two closely related questions has ever been studied with anything like the seriousness each deserves: First, how was the Civil War interpreted as a theological event at the time? Second, what contribution did the Civil War make to the history of theology more generally? The paucity of interest in these issues is astounding in light of the overwhelmingly Christian population of both North and South, the centrality of religious argument in justifying the existence and the actions of both the Union and the Confederacy, and the substantial Christian presence that remains in the United States to this day. Regrettably, what historian Richard Wolf wrote many years ago is still true: "No comprehensive treatment of 'Christian' interpretations of the Civil War has yet appeared, much less a theological analysis in depth of the national crisis."[38] Work has hardly even begun on the more comprehensive question of how the immense quantity of theological reflection brought on by the war related to the more general history of American religious thought. Despite the absence of serious historical investigation, however, we can surmise that lack of attention to theological profundity in the Civil War is almost certainly related to the fact that there simply existed so little theological profundity. This book is an effort to explain why.

Chapter 2

Historical Contexts

The most important first step toward understanding the Civil War as a theological event is to recognize how reasoning about the war reflected long-standing habits of mind.[1] For more than a century before 1860, American theologians had been uniting historical Christian perspectives with specific aspects of American intellectual experience. The ubiquitous Christian reflection on the war followed trails blazed in the late eighteenth century and then set firmly in place by a confluence of intellectual forces during the early years of the Republic. A culturally powerful combination of intellectual ingredients gave American theologians their categories for apprehending sectional controversy and the war itself. For the most numerous and most public American religious groups, biblical Protestantism of a primarily evangelical cast provided the religious content of the synthesis. Despite tumultuous conflicts with each other, these Protestants shared a number of fundamental convictions that grew directly out of their American experience.

Religious Habits of Mind

The convictions can be summarized succinctly, though each was deeply rooted in a thick network of historical events and time-tested ideology. Evangelical Protestants of British background agreed in their practice on a very great deal:

- They exalted the Bible instead of tradition or clerical elites as the basic religious authority.
- They were skeptical about received religious authority.
- They emphasized both the activity of grace in their lives and the need for lives of gracious activity.

- They practiced discipline of self and others.[2]
- They regarded Roman Catholicism not as an alternative Christian religion but as the world's most perverse threat to genuine faith. To most American Protestants, Catholicism seemed as alien to treasured political values as it was antithetical to true Christianity.[3]
- They were culturally adaptive. Since most American Protestants treated ideas and institutions as possessing primarily instrumental value, by comparison with the ultimate realities of the gospel, they felt free to take up, modify, discard, or transform inherited ideas and institutions as local circumstances dictated.[4]

American theologians never talked about these practices in naked religious terms. Rather, the evangelical Protestantism that dominated public life at midcentury had gained its place because it successfully clothed the Christian faith in the preeminent ideological dress of the new Republic. In particular, it had vivified, ennobled, and lent transcendent value to republican political assumptions, democratic convictions about social organization, scientific reasoning pitched to common sense, and belief in the unique, providential destiny of the United States.

More particularly, America's leading Protestant theologians first argued convincingly that the people of the United States stood in a covenantal relationship with God. For most of them, a vocabulary of corporate repentance and renewal, handed down from the Puritans, remained an appropriate vocabulary for addressing the American public about its privileges and duties before God. An indication of the enduring power of covenantal reasoning was public acceptance of the numerous fast days proclaimed in both the North and the South. Although Northern Democrats came to protest Abraham Lincoln's proclamations calling for such days as partisan Republican propaganda, they were otherwise well received.[5] Ironically, in the South, where a tradition designated as "the spirituality of the church" had frowned on the mixture of politics and religion, the similar days proclaimed by President Jefferson Davis were even more eagerly embraced. For both North and South, the template for these national religious observances was the time-honored pattern of covenant, as taken over from a reading of the Old Testament: repent and God may reverse evil days; give thanks and He may allow the propitious times to continue.

Second, with other American intellectuals, theologians assumed that a republican calculus could account for the relationship between private character and public well-being. No matter how plastic moral categories became, theologians took for granted that connections between virtue and liberty, on the one side, and vice and tyranny, on the other, were fixed, determinative, enduring, and – of greatest significance – transparent.[6]

Third, and most important for understanding patterns of biblical interpretation, religious thinkers also shared in the American appropriation of the Enlightenment. In particular, they assumed that perceiving the causes and effects of political developments was a simple matter, once distracting traditions had been set aside. In keeping with Enlightenment confidence, they also assumed that human beings of the right sort possessed a nearly infallible ability to perceive clear-cut connections between moral causes and public effects.[7]

During the years of conflict, countless believers illustrated such convictions by assuming that moral or spiritual perception could be crystal clear and that the means of moral action lay entirely within the grasp of well-meaning individuals. Thus in 1860 the Kentucky Presbyterian Robert Breckinridge told readers how they could discover the essence of a Christian church: "If the world, and more especially the children of Christ, would follow simply and earnestly the light of reason . . . and the teachings of that divine word, which he has given to be a map unto our feet . . . , it is not easy to imagine how the least obscurity could hang over such a question."[8] In 1861 the Brooklyn Presbyterian Henry Van Dyke expressed bewilderment when he pondered how abolitionists could read the Bible as they professed to read it: "When the Abolitionist tells me that slaveholding is sin, in the simplicity of my faith in the Holy Scriptures, I point him to this sacred record, and tell him, in all candor, as my text does, that his teaching blasphemes the name of God and His doctrine."[9] That very year, however, the abolitionist Gerrit Smith thought it was just as uncomplicated to come to the opposite conclusion: "The religion taught by Jesus is not a letter but a life. So simple is it that the unlearned can both understand and teach it. . . . The true religion is too simple to make the training of a theological seminary necessary for those who teach it. We should allow the wisdom and goodness of God to assure us that the religion which He has given to the world must correspond in its simplicity with the simplicity of the masses."[10] From the South in that same year the

Baptist Thornton Stringfellow expressed the opinion that since God's intentions were clearly expressed in the Bible, they were readily available to all;
benevolence to Stringfellow was, in Drew Faust's summary, "a 'simple' matter of explicating the Bible and guiding men in following its dictates."[11] In
December 1864 the Presbyterian *Independent* of New York felt that the problem of caring for liberated slaves could be easily solved: "In effect the problem is simple, and its solution comparatively easy. The question of labor is
settled at once by the excess demand over supply. The question of individual
regeneration is determined by those familiar appliances which have raised
the American character in the Free States to its present altitude."[12] The implicit trust that the Bible was a plain book whose authoritative deliverances
could be apprehended by anyone who simply opened the covers and read was
expressed by Phoebe Palmer, the holiness evangelist, like this in 1865: "The
Bible is a wonderfully simple book; and, if you had taken the naked Word of
God as . . . your counsel, instead of taking the opinions of men in regard to
that *Word*, you might have been a more enlightened, simple, happy and useful Christian."[13]

Nowhere was the Christian-Enlightenment marriage more clearly illustrated than in the pervasive belief that understanding things was *simple*. The
significance of this marriage was far-reaching. On the one side, it bestowed
great self-confidence as Americans explained the moral urgency of social attitudes and then of national policy. On the other, it transformed the conclusions reached by opponents into willful perversions of sacred truth and natural reason. The combination of biblical faith and Enlightenment certainty
imparted great energy to the builders of American civilization. It also imparted a nearly fanatical force to the prosecution of war.

With respect to one other important dimension of antebellum life, most
American believers also accommodated themselves to the assumptions of a
market economy. To be sure, numerous Southern ministers questioned the
free rein given to markets, and not a few in the North were cautious about
their workings as well.[14] In general, though the bond between religion and
the market was strong, it was probably not as strong as the alliance between
religious values and Enlightenment, covenantal, and republican values.

Theological reasoning during the Civil War rested on this grand intellectual alliance. Yet a significant weakness of the remarkable synthesis was revealed when it proved unable to unify the nation's sectional interests. So it

came about that the Civil War precipitated intellectual-religious, as well as domestic, fratricide. Several decades ago, Perry Miller rightly perceived the "unity amid diversity which sustained the majority of American Protestants" in antebellum decades, but which also "makes the Civil War the more poignant, for it was fought, not by Puritans against Cavaliers nor by republicans against royalists, but among the rank and file, all children of the Revival."[15] More recently, the Canadian philosopher and social critic Charles Taylor has highlighted the same conflict: "This is a country whose common values were from the beginning organized around certain defined ideas, understandings of freedom: what has been described as a 'public philosophy.' It is a country, moreover, where the crucial inner battles, in particular the literal and bloody struggle of the Civil War, were fought in the name of interpretations of this philosophy."[16] The story of theology in the Civil War was a story of how a deeply entrenched intellectual synthesis divided against itself, even as its proponents were reassuring combatants on either side that each enjoyed a unique standing before God and each exercised a unique role as the true bearer of the nation's Christian civilization.

An even larger problem than the division of the United States' Christian-intellectual heritage against itself, however, was the confidence of religious thinkers in claiming to describe the simplicity of God's action in the world. The particular difficulty posed by this confidence was its timing in relationship to broader developments in Western intellectual history. American religious thinkers were expressing such confidence, that is, precisely at the moment when Western culture was being pushed powerfully away from the habits of the evangelical-Enlightenment synthesis. By clinging so tightly to the shared values hammered out in the new nation's cultural history, religious thinkers made it all the more difficult to adjust to the changes brought on by new intellectual developments at midcentury and in the following decades. Large claims for evolution, critical contentions about ancient biblical texts, and the dynamics of a burgeoning industrial economy soon pressed hard on all religious believers. In the 1850s and early 1860s, however, most Americans of faith were far less concerned about adjusting to impending intellectual change than they were about dealing with contradictory biblical conclusions arising from a common application of the interpretative methods they had embraced in earlier American history.

The Structure of Biblical Interpretation

In the United States in 1860, debates over the interpretation of the Bible took on an immense significance. It was not only that so much of the religious ground was occupied by Protestants, with their inherited loyalty to Scripture as ultimate religious authority, but also that this ground was occupied by the specific type of Protestants that had flourished in the new American nation.

Conflict over the interpretation of the Bible was vitally important in 1860 – both for the public at large and for the fate of theology – because of how American culture had been shaped from the time of the Revolution onward. When, that is, Henry Ward Beecher, James Henley Thornwell, and their ministerial colleagues squared off over the meaning of the Bible, the stakes were anything but merely academic or privately sectarian. Rather, their clash presented a radical challenge to one of the fundamental supports of American civilization. This support was trust in the Bible as a divine revelation that, besides fulfilling traditional religious functions, also enjoyed a critical public presence. By 1860 a substantial majority of articulate Americans had come to hold a number of corollary beliefs about the Bible – specifically, that besides its religious uses, it also promoted republican political theory, that it was accessible to every sentient person, that it defined the glories of liberty, that it opposed the tyranny of inherited religious authority, that it forecast the providential destiny of the United States, and that it was best interpreted by the common sense of ordinary people. The ideological journey from 1776 to 1861 was complicated, but even a brief sketch of it will suggest why, on the eve of sectional warfare, conflict over Scripture was so politically, socially, morally, and culturally – as well as religiously – explosive.

Anti-traditionalism. The United States was brought into existence by men who deliberately rejected the authority of tradition in forming the new country. It was not precedent, history, or inherited dicta that pointed the way to an independent nation, but "truths [considered] to be self-evident." Churches that clung to the past, like the Episcopalians in their fastidiousness about tradition or even the Congregationalists in their hankering for church-state establishment, rapidly lost ground to the churches that celebrated the new nation's birthright of liberty. By the 1860s other religious bodies with a higher respect for tradition, including Catholics, Lutherans, and Jews, had established a foothold in America, but most of them still spoke with a foreign accent that rendered their public presence incommensurate with their actual numbers.

Republicanism. As deliberately as they rejected political traditions, the founding fathers also committed themselves to republican ideals of political life. Republicanism was always easier to evoke than to define, but for most Americans through the time of the Civil War, it usually meant, on the one side, virtuous character and action linked with political liberty and the flourishing of society and, on the other side, vice (usually defined as luxury, indolence, or deceit in high places) linked with corruption in government, tyrannical politics, and the collapse of social order. In the crucible of heated imperial conflicts that led up to the War of Independence, colonial Protestants reversed the settled judgments of their European ancestors, who regarded republicanism as tantamount to religious heresy, and embraced a republic vision of politics. After this nation-defining war, the American denominations that expanded most rapidly were the ones that most successfully presented themselves as both traditionally Christian and faithfully republican.

Written instruments of government. As they went about creating a new nation, the founding fathers put their trust in written instruments of government, especially the new U.S. Constitution. Where in Europe fundamental authority and political stability had been supplied by hereditary power, monarchy, and the aristocratic ordering of society, in the United States authority and stability came from constitutional principle. Correspondingly, in religious life, the groups that flourished after the unstable years of the 1780s and early 1790s were those that trusted the Bible rather than hereditary ritual, top-down ecclesiastical authority, or aristocratic control over the interpretation of religious experience. In regard to the connection between political trust in a written Constitution and religious trust in the Bible, it is pertinent to note that James Henley Thornwell was not only the South's most effective defender of slavery on the basis of the Bible but also one of the South's most powerful defenders of secession as a strictly constitutional step.[17]

Ideological evolution. In a series of interwoven ideological moves, the Protestant churches that after 1800 burgeoned in the American landscape, and

that after 1830 came to exert such a pull on public life, adjusted their inherited theological convictions to what might be called the new rules for
public discourse in the infant American nation. In ethics, they traded the traditional Augustinian view, which considered true virtue as a gift of God limited to the regenerate, for a view associated in the eighteenth century with
Francis Hutcheson of Scotland, which considered virtue as a live possibility
for all peoples on the basis of natural endowments from God. On the question of human capacity specifically, there was a change of equal magnitude.
The movement was *away from* a conservative definition of human freedom as
constrained by human character, such as articulated in the mid-eighteenth
century by both the Anglican Arminian Samuel Johnson and the Congregational Calvinist Jonathan Edwards. The movement was *toward* a belief that
in moral choices, as one theologian put it, humans always had a "power to
choose and refuse," or as phrased by Charles Finney, the nineteenth-century's
best-known revivalist, "The moral government of God everywhere assumes
and implies the liberty of the human will, and the natural ability to obey
God."[18]

As Protestant instincts evolved, they became much more democratic.[19] The
Baptists, the Methodists, and the Restorationists – that is, the denominations that led all the rest in mass public appeal – forthrightly championed
their populist character, excelled at empowering the laity, and stimulated
continuing resentment at anyone else's efforts to manage religion or politics from on high. Other groups, like the Quakers and the Congregationalists, who were less resolutely democratic in practice, nonetheless went even
further than their antiformalist contemporaries in propounding democratic
theory, with the result that by the 1830s Quakers and Congregationalists were
leading all denominations in opening space for women to exercise public
religious authority.[20] Catholics, Lutherans, Mormons, and even Presbyterians, who remained in principle opposed to simple democracy, nonetheless
found their practices pulled along by the democratic tide.

Finally, while other ideological changes were taking hold, the entire religious population of the United States wholeheartedly embraced the Enlightenment spirit I have described above. While for the most part rejecting Enlightenment notions when they were linked to David Hume's skepticism, the
deism of French philosophes, or William Godwin's social radicalism, American believers nonetheless came to share the Enlightenment confidence that

they could explain connections between public states of affairs and the virtues and vices that propelled public action. Soon romantic notions would come to influence America as well, but in their belief that the workings of the world – both physical and moral – were wide open to the definitive assignment of cause and effect, and also that it was an essentially simple matter to figure out such relationships, America's religious spokespersons long remained fully convinced of the truths of the Enlightenment.[21]

The cumulative effect of these subtle ideological changes was to convince an ever-broadening number of Christians in the United States that they had the power within themselves to discover the true meaning of sacred texts, the power to see things in general as they really were, the power to act effectively against those in the wrong, and the power to choose righteously when faced by moral dilemmas – if, that is, they would only put their minds to the task.

Creation of an American culture. The American Constitution, in the memorable phrase of John Murrin, created "a roof without walls." It set up a national government but did little to nurture a national culture. Even with the Constitution in place, Murrin suggests, "American national identity was . . . an unexpected, impromptu, artificial, and therefore extremely fragile creation."[22] The eventual construction of a national identity, or a national culture, involved many factors, but one that contributed almost nothing was the religion practiced by the founding fathers themselves. Their ideal for providing the morality required by a republican project was religion defined as judicious, refined, restrained, and (at least for Thomas Jefferson and John Adams) Unitarian. In addition, the founders thought the action (or nonaction) of government would play a large role in building national culture. Federalists believed that direct governmental programs could do the job, while Democratic-Republicans held that preventing the government from acting would accomplish the same purpose.

In the event, what actually happened was that citizens, without paying much attention to government at all, went about creating a national culture for themselves. Long before political parties became effective as national, democratic institutions, Methodists, Baptists, and Presbyterians were building the nerve system of a national culture. Their labors were strengthened immeasurably by the creation of voluntary societies, most of them religious in nature, that began to proliferate from the first decade of the nineteenth century. Market economics moved with similar dynamism at the grass roots. With the confluence of economic and religious forces, Americans were developing what we call today "civil society." They were themselves establishing structures that mediated between, on the one hand, individuals and local communities and, on the other, the nation. It was a bottom-up process in which direction from presidents, bishops, or even presbyters was not needed.

In retrospect, we can see that the ability of religious denominations to help form a national culture depended on the separation of church and state, the unprecedented step that had looked so risky to so many in the 1790s. The strongest churches of prerevolutionary times, Congregationalist and Anglican, had been supported by colonial governments, and only because of the need for compromise at the Constitutional Convention did disestablishment begin to carry the day in the new nation. But once begun, disestablishment unleashed tremendous energy. The churches that most eagerly embraced the separation of church and state – again, Baptist, Restorationist, and Methodist – expanded rapidly and set a tone for the whole nation. The churches that gloried in disestablishment were the ones that benefited most from the libertarian legacy of the Revolution. They were the ones best able to exploit commonsense forms of reasoning in the vacuum created by discredited intellectual traditions. They were the ones best equipped to meet the religious needs of a population fanning out into the incredibly vast spaces of the American interior. Disestablishment, in other words, represented the negative means that allowed voluntary religious organizations to shape culture in the free spaces of the New World, just as the positive practice of establishment had allowed the state-churches of Europe to shape culture in the traditional spaces of the Old World.

In 1838 a veteran Methodist, Nathan Bangs, with long experience as an itinerant, an editor, and a denominational organizer, paused to reflect on what Methodists – and, by extension, the whole phalanx of voluntary free churches – had achieved in the United States. Bangs asserted, correctly, that Methodists had really not been much interested in politics, and yet he thought he could see in their history an inadvertent political effect of great consequence: "The extensive spread [of Methodism] in this country, the hallowing influence it has exerted in society in uniting in one compact body so many members, through the medium of an itinerant ministry, interchanging from north to south, and from east to west, has contributed not a little to the union and prosperity of the nation."[23] Bangs, if anything, understated his case.

Evangelical revival.   Neither ideological evolution nor the separation of church and state nor the sanctifying of American republicanism would have made evangelical Protestants important at the time of the Civil War if the United States had not witnessed from 1790 to 1860 an unprecedented dynamism within the churches considered primarily as religious institutions. Because the churches flourished in this period as purveyors of religion, as they never did before or thereafter, they exerted an unusual impact on public life. It was religion, narrowly considered, that drove an unprecedented ecclesiastical expansion – from about 700 Methodist churches in 1790 to nearly 20,000 in 1860; from fewer than 900 Baptist churches to more than 12,000; from no Campbellite or Restorationist or Disciples churches to over 2,000; from about 700 Presbyterian churches to well over 6,000. In the helter-skelter of the new nation's experience, messages from the churches made sense. Preeminently from evangelical churches, but then with rapidly accelerating influence from Catholic, Mormon, Adventist, Jewish, and sectarian communities as well, came persuasive accounts of God, the human condition, and the means for finding reconciliation with God and neighbor. During this period the evangelical churches, and then others, altered the course of American politics because they gave direction, purpose, meaning, and stability to so many American lives. And they did so North and South, for blacks and whites, for men as well as women. Only because they were so important religiously did the churches also become so important politically.

Broken churches, broken nation.   One momentous by-product of religious expansion was the fact that the institutional life of the major Protestant churches worked an echoing effect on the body politic.[24] So it was that from quite different perspectives John C. Calhoun and Henry Clay offered identical testimony about the great schisms experienced by the Baptists and the Methodists, both in 1844. As these two great national churches split into Northern and Southern fragments, Clay opined that "this sundering of the religious ties which have hitherto bound our people together, I consider the greatest source of danger to our country."[25] Calhoun's similar forecast from

1850, in his last major speech before the U.S. Senate, was long remembered: that when the national bonds represented by the great Protestant denominations would all break, "nothing will be left to hold the States together except force."[26]

THE HISTORY that I have sketched so rapidly in this chapter structured the national crisis, as well as the theological crisis, that had been reached by December 1860. During the years immediately after the Revolution, America's own church leaders wondered if they could ever recover from the shocks of war. Overseas, most European observers believed that it was impossible to maintain even a semblance of orthodox Christianity if churches were disestablished and if their leaders embraced the worldly principles of republican politics. But in the actual course of events, American churches promoting reasonably orthodox beliefs and reasonably traditional practices flourished precisely *because* they adapted so energetically to the republican freedoms won in the War of Independence, guaranteed by the U.S. Constitution, and then expanded considerably with the opening of the new country. The positive connection between evangelical religion and republican public life had been observed already by Alexis de Tocqueville in the mid-1830s: "America is . . . the place in the world where the Christian religion has most preserved genuine powers over souls; and . . . the country in which [the Christian religion] exercises the greatest empire is at the same time the most enlightened and most free."[27]

Although Tocqueville in the 1830s was struck by how well the American experiment in Protestant republican Christianity was turning out, the situation in 1860 was more ominous. Both North and South, evangelical Protestants, who believed that the Bible was true and who trusted their own interpretations of Scripture above all other religious authorities, constituted the nation's most influential cultural force. By 1860 religion had reached a higher point of public influence than at any previous time in American history. Moreover, religion had become vitally important because the nation's evangelical churches and its evangelical voluntary associations had contributed so much to the construction of national culture. They had achieved such prodigies, in large part, by relying on Scripture as the highest and most compelling authority.

Yet in American society as a whole, there was no recognized authority greater than the individual interpretation of Scripture to deploy for the purpose of understanding the Scriptures. And in 1860 fundamental disagreement existed over what the Bible had to say about slavery at the very moment when disputes over slavery were creating the most serious crisis in the nation's history. The same level of disagreement existed among evangelicals about how to interpret the providential actions of the God they worshiped in nearly identical terms.

If we keep in mind that it was never only a matter of interpreting individual biblical texts, but always a question of putting actively to use the authoritative Book on which the national culture of the United States had been built, then we are in a position to understand why in 1860 battles over the Bible were so important, why divergent views of providence cut so deeply, and why foreign commentary on the Civil War illuminated so much about the general character of religion in America.

Chapter 3

The Crisis over the Bible

By 1860 Americans who believed in the Scriptures as unquestioned divine revelation should have been troubled by the growing number of their fellow citizens who seemed willing to live without that belief. The most prominent among those coming to doubt the all-sufficiency of Scripture were savants like Oliver Wendell Holmes Jr., elite literati like William Dean Howells, and practitioners of realpolitik like William Henry Trescot, who were turning aside from all a priori authorities, including the Bible. Instead, they were looking to scientific, legal, literary, business, or governmental substitutes to provide the necessary ballast required by what they hailed as an increasingly secular, consumer-oriented, and religiously pluralistic society.[1] However important this shift in American perspective represented by such postreligionists actually was, it would be more noticed after the sectional conflict than before or during.

At the time of the Civil War, the party of abolitionists, for whom nothing matched the imperatives of personal freedom, was much more worrisome to traditional believers. Foremost in this group was William Lloyd Garrison, who in 1845 paid homage in the *Liberator* to Thomas Paine for providing him with intellectual resources for getting beyond the Bible. While Garrison never became as thoroughly skeptical about the miracle stories of Scripture as had Paine, and while he always retained belief in God as moral arbiter of the universe, he no longer looked upon the Scriptures as indisputable revelation from God: "To say that everything contained within the lids of the bible is divinely inspired, and to insist upon the dogma as fundamentally important, is to give utterance to a bold fiction, and to require the suspension of the reasoning faculties. To say that everything in the bible is to be believed, simply because it is found in that volume, is equally absurd and pernicious."

So inclined, Garrison no longer had any difficulty with biblical passages that seemed to countenance the legitimacy of slavery: "To discard a portion of scripture is not necessarily to reject the truth, but may be the highest evidence that one can give of his love of truth."[2]

Garrison's move was audacious and courageous, but his willingness to jetson the Bible if the Bible was construed as legitimating slavery was too radical for most of his fellow Americans. In fact, the willingness of Garrison and a few others to favor abolitionism *in place of* Scripture actually worked to the advantage of those who defended slavery on the basis of Scripture. With increasing frequency as the sectional conflict heated up, biblical defenders of slavery were ever more likely to perceive doubt about the biblical defense of slavery as doubt about the authority of the Bible itself. In the words of Henry Van Dyke on December 9, 1860, from his pulpit in Brooklyn, "Abolitionism leads, in multitudes of cases, and by a logical process, to utter infidelity. . . . One of its avowed principles is, that it does not try slavery by the Bible; but . . . it tries the Bible by the principles of freedom. . . . This assumption, that men are capable of judging beforehand what is to be expected in a Divine revelation, is the cockatrice's egg, from which, in all ages, heresies have been hatched."[3] In short, the radicalism of all-out abolitionists like Garrison made it much harder for anyone who wanted to deploy the Bible in order to attack American slavery. Garrison's stance was more important for how it alienated those who continued to trust in the Bible than it was for attracting sympathizers.

In order to show how this situation developed, the present chapter first lays out the standard biblical defense of slavery as it had been developed in the two generations before the start of the war. It then examines various attempts made by orthodox Christians to take back the Bible for the fight against slavery. The question of how attitudes toward race entered into the use of the Bible with regard to slavery is so involved that it is reserved for separate treatment in the next chapter.[4]

Debates over Scripture and slavery, which combined passionate moral reasoning, careful attention to the particulars of exegesis, and intense argument about the general meaning of the Bible, pointed toward a twofold theological crisis. The first-order crisis was manifest: a wide range of Protestants were discovering that the Bible they had relied on for building up America's republican civilization was not nearly as univocal, not nearly as easy to interpret, not nearly as inherently unifying for an overwhelmingly Christian people, as they once had thought. But the second-order crisis, which was not as obvious, was even worse: although legions of faithful believers struggled long and hard to discern what the Bible said about slavery, far fewer turned seriously to Scripture to find an authoritative message concerning race or the transformation of the American economy, even though race and economic transformation had become the most pressing dangers threatening America's biblical civilization.

The Biblical Defense of Slavery

The power of the proslavery scriptural position—especially in a Protestant world of widespread intuitive belief in the plenary inspiration of the whole Bible—lay in its simplicity. The standard procedure was exemplified in one of the first modern defenses from the early 1770s.[5] Thomas Thompson published *The African Trade for Negro Slaves, Shewn to Be Consistent with Principles of Humanity, and with the Laws of Revealed Religion* at a time when long-standing antislavery agitation by relatively marginal Quakers was broadening out to include well-placed Englishmen, like the member of Parliament William Wilberforce, who were more politically central than the Quakers had ever been. Thompson's defense could not have been more direct. In effect: open the Bible, read it, believe it. After conceding that in ancient times God had set strict limits to Hebrew enslavement of other Hebrews, he then quoted Leviticus 25:45–46a: "Moreover of the children of the strangers that do sojourn among you, of them shall ye buy, and of their families that are with you, which they begat in your land: and they shall be your possession. And ye shall take them as an inheritance for your children after you, to inherit them for a possession; they shall be your bondmen for ever." Then, after acknowledging New Testament injunctions to piety, charity, and respect for others, Thompson turned to the book of Philemon, the brief letter of St. Paul in which the apostle instructed an escaped slave, Onesimus, to return to his master. Thompson's message was straightforward: if God through divine revelation so clearly sanctioned slavery, and even the trade in "strangers," how could genuine Christians attack modern slavery, or even the slave trade, as an evil?

This mode of argument became more elaborate and more definite when other Bible believers took up Scripture to attack slavery. Crucially, as Larry

Tise and others have pointed out, biblical defenses of slavery were once wide-spread throughout the Western world; they were put forward by both Catho-lics and Protestants, both Europeans and North Americans.[6] Nonetheless, by the mid-nineteenth century, the force of the biblical proslavery argument had weakened everywhere except in the United States. There, however, it re-mained strong among Bible believers in the North as well as among Bible believers in the South.

It was no coincidence that the biblical defense of slavery remained strong-est in the United States, a place where democratic, antitraditional, and indi-vidualistic religion was also strongest. By the nineteenth century, it was an axiom of American public thought that free people should read, think, and reason for themselves. When such a populace, committed to republican and democratic principles, was also a Bible-reading populace, the proslavery bib-lical case never lacked for persuasive resources. Precedents provided by the books of Leviticus and Philemon were only part of the picture. Protestants well schooled in reading the Scriptures for themselves also knew of many other relevant texts, among which the following were most important:

- Genesis 9:25-27: "And he [God] said, Cursed be Canaan; a servant of ser-vants shall he be unto his brethren. And he said, Blessed be the Lord God of Shem; and Canaan shall be his servant. God shall enlarge Japheth, and he shall dwell in the tents of Shem; and Canaan shall be his servant." (For the sin of Ham, who exposed his father Noah's nakedness, Ham's descen-dants through his son Canaan were to be owned as slaves by descendants of Noah's two other sons.)

- Genesis 17:12: "And he that is eight days old shall be circumcised among you, every man child in your [Abraham's] generations, he that is born in the house, or bought with money of any stranger, which is not of thy seed." (God sanctioned and regulated the slaveholding of the patriarch Abraham, father of all believers.)

- Deuteronomy 20:10-11: "When thou goest forth to war against thine ene-mies, and the Lord thy God hath delivered them into thine hands, and thou hast taken them captive . . ." (God sanctioned the enslavement of Israel's enemies.)

- While Jesus abrogated many of the regulations of the Old Testament – for example, those allowing for polygamy and easy divorce – he never said a word against slaveholding.

- 1 Corinthians 7:21: "Art thou called being a servant? Care not for it: but if thou mayest be made free, use it rather." (While a Christian slave may welcome emancipation, that slave should not chafe if emancipation is not given.)
- Romans 13:1, 7: "Let every soul be subject unto the higher powers. For there is no power but of God: the powers that be are ordained of God. . . . Render therefore to all their dues: tribute to whom tribute is due; custom to whom custom; fear to whom fear; honour to whom honour." (The Apostle Paul urged Christian believers to conform to the Roman imperial system, which practiced a harsh form of slaveholding.)
- Colossians 3:22, 4:1: "Servants, obey in all things your masters according to the flesh; not with eyeservice, as menpleasers; but in singleness of heart, fearing God: . . . Masters, give unto your servants that which is just and equal; knowing that ye also have a Master in heaven." (The apostle regulated the master-slave relationship, but did not question it.)
- 1 Timothy 6:1-2: "Let as many servants as are under the yoke count their own masters worthy of all honour, that the name of God and his doctrine be not blasphemed. And they that have believing masters, let them not despise them, because they are brethren; but rather do them service, because they are faithful and beloved, partakers of the benefit. These things teach and exhort." (The apostle explicitly taught that the conversion of slaves did not provide cause for even Christian masters to emancipate those Christian slaves.)

Between the publication of Thomas Thompson's book in the early 1770s and the intensification of American debate over slavery six decades later, circumstances in the North Atlantic world shifted significantly. In Britain, with Bible-believing evangelicals in the lead, scruples supporting a scriptural defense of slavery were largely overcome as the Parliament first outlawed the slave trade, in 1807, and then banned slavery in all British territories, in 1833. More generally, Western attachment to ideas of basic human rights, which ironically had been greatly stimulated by the founding of the United States of America, made it increasingly difficult to imagine how slavery could exist in a modern civilized polity. More recent sentiments about the inviolability of the human personality that were associated with romantic movements pushed in the same direction. Christian humanitarianism was trumping biblical traditionalism.

Yet countercurrents also worked against these trends that were making it harder to imagine slavery as a just form of social organization. Heightened abolitionist attacks on slavery, slaveholders, and slave society angered those who were under assault. Especially when such attacks were expressed with the antibiblical rhetoric that William Lloyd Garrison employed, they deeply troubled religious believers of almost all sorts. By defining slaveholding as a basic evil, whatever the Bible might say about it, radical abolitionists frightened away from antislavery many moderates who had also grown troubled about America's system of chattel bondage, but who were not willing to give up loyalty to Scripture. With these ideological currents were also mingled political and economic developments that ever more clearly differentiated "the South" as a distinctive society, a distinctive moral culture, and a distinctive political power. And in the North as well as the South, critics of the nation's expanding commercial capitalism were becoming more insistent that this economic system was fraught with moral problems.

The general result was that by the 1840s American debates over the Bible and slavery had assumed a critical new gravity. In particular, those who saw in Scripture a sanction for slavery were both more insistent on pointing to the passages that seemed so transparently to support their position and more confident in decrying the wanton disregard for divine revelation that seemed so willfully to dismiss biblical truths.

Two Defining Publications

The force that biblical proslavery arguments were exerting can be suggested by two important works published by leading moderates, Francis Wayland and Moses Stuart, in the years before sectional antagonism passed beyond the point of no return. When the triennial gathering of the American Baptist Missionary Union resolved in 1844 that it would not appoint slaveholders as missionaries, this action precipitated the establishment of the Southern Baptist Convention the following year. It also led the Reverend Richard Fuller of Beaufort, South Carolina, to write a letter to the editors of the *Christian Reflector* to defend the legitimacy of slavery. Fuller's letter, in turn, prompted a lengthy response from Francis Wayland, president of the Baptist Brown University in Providence, Rhode Island, which then elicited a further rejoinder from Fuller.[7] This exchange was one of the United States' last serious one-on-one debates where advocates for and against slavery engaged each other directly, with reasonable restraint, and with evident intent to hear out the opponent to the extent possible. The argument between Wayland, a careful reasoner and a careful biblical exegete defending an antislavery (but not abolitionist) stance, and Fuller, a resolute defender of slavery who nonetheless admitted that Southern slavery contained substantial abuses, represented a signal moment in American moral history.

For our purposes, it was most important for illustrating forcefully how secure the biblical defense of slavery had become in the minds of its advocates. Fuller, in his initial letter, and after praising Wayland's earlier writings on the subject, succinctly summarized the dilemma he was convinced that Bible believers of Wayland's emancipationist convictions could not avoid: "His position is this: the moral precepts of the gospel condemn slavery; it is therefore criminal. Yet he admits that neither the Saviour nor his apostles commanded masters to emancipate their slaves; nay, they 'go further,' he adds, 'and prescribe the duties suited to both parties in their present condition;' among which duties, be it remembered, there is not an intimation of manumission, but the whole code contemplates the continuation of the relation." Fuller was relentless in drawing his conclusion: "Here, then, we have the Author of the gospel, and the inspired propagators of the gospel, and the Holy Spirit indicting [i.e., recording] the gospel, all conniving at a practice which was a violation of the entire moral principle of the gospel!"[8] By admitting that slavery as practiced in the South entailed practices that were explicitly condemned in Scripture, Fuller only felt that he was turning the screw even tighter. Had not the Roman system of slavery, which the New Testament writers everywhere simply took for granted, also contained practices explicitly condemned by that same New Testament? He was left with only one conclusion: "The matter stands thus: the Bible did authorize some sort of slavery; if now the abuses admitted and deplored by me be essentials of all slavery, then the Bible did allow those abuses; if it be impossible that revelation should permit such evils, then you must either reject the Scriptures, as some abolitionists are doing, or concede that these sins are only accidents of slavery, which may, and perhaps in cases of many Christians, do exist without them."[9]

Wayland's response to Fuller's arguments—which required more than ten pages for every one that Fuller took to state his case—was learned, calm, and

intensely biblical. In the course of that response Wayland raised many of the
objections that will be canvassed later in this chapter. But whether in the interpretive climate that then prevailed in the United States, Wayland's elaborate response carried more conviction than the simple statement of Fuller's
position must be doubted.

Five years after the Fuller-Wayland exchange, Moses Stuart of Andover
Seminary in Massachusetts published a major tract on the same issue, *Conscience and the Constitution*.[10] Stuart, who was widely recognized as the nation's
most learned biblical scholar, entered the lists after he was attacked for com-
mending Daniel Webster when the senator supported the Compromise of
1850. Webster had followed the lead of Henry Clay, who engineered admission of California as a free state but also agreed to a strict law for the capture
and return from the North of fugitive slaves, a concession that incensed abolitionists everywhere.

Stuart did take the last twenty pages of his tightly packed monograph
to indicate why he felt biblical principles should move Southerners, especially Southern Christians, to give up slavery voluntarily. But because he
was angered by charges from Webster's (and his) abolitionist opponents that
slavery must be regarded by all honorable Christians as a self-evident moral
evil, Stuart began with a lengthy consideration of that very question. In a
curious mixture of painstaking biblical exegesis and rough-hewn political
polemics, Stuart took readers over familiar ground. He quoted Leviticus 25;
he pointed out that neither Jesus nor Paul had condemned slavery as such;
and he cited frequently referenced passages like Ephesians 6:5 ("Servants, be
obedient to them that are your masters according to the flesh, with fear and
trembling, in singleness of your heart, as unto Christ"). In summing up his
biblical conclusions, this learned and pious Northern emancipationist followed Richard Fuller rather than Francis Wayland: "Not one word has Christ
said, to annul the Mosaic law while it lasted. Neither Paul nor Peter have
uttered one. Neither of these have said to Christian masters: 'Instantly free
your slaves.' Yet they lived under Roman laws concerning slavery, which were
rigid to the last degree. How is it explicable on any ground, when we view
them as humane and benevolent teachers, and especially as having a divine
commission—how is it possible that they should not have declared and explicitly [so] against a *malum in se* [something evil in itself]?" Stuart did not
feel it would help the abolitionist cause "to dodge the question." For him,

as well as for Fuller, the alternatives were stark: abolitionists "must give up the New Testament authority, or abandon the fiery course which they are pursuing."[11]

Stuart's defense of the moral legality of slavery, however, differed strikingly from many others of the period. While he strenuously resisted efforts to label slavery a simple moral evil, he also expounded at length on the general biblical teachings that he felt should lead to a gradual, peaceful, and voluntary elimination of the institution. In this part of his argument, Stuart sounded much more like Francis Wayland. He pointed especially to abuses in the Southern system of bondage – like the breaking up of marriages and the sexual predation practiced by white masters on their female slaves – that violated biblical morality. He also insisted on labeling ideas of Caucasian superiority over Africans as an "anti-biblical theory."[12] At the same time, because of the views on states' rights and on limits of federal authority that he shared with Daniel Webster, Stuart did not think there was anything he and other non-Southerners could do to restrict or eliminate the slave system. Stuart's interpretation of the Bible convinced him of the need for gradual emancipation. But that same interpretation led him to view the threat from Bible-denying abolitionism as greater than the South's failure to move toward voluntary emancipation.

This was the situation with respect to biblical interpretation that prevailed in 1850, that would only strengthen throughout the whole country up to the outbreak of hostilities in 1861, and that would remain exceedingly powerful in the South long after most Northerners had reconfigured the War for the Union as also a War for Emancipation. It was the interpretative history that, as we have seen, allowed James Henley Thornwell to say on the eve of the conflict that "we have long since settled" the issue of biblical sanction for slavery.[13] It was the background that permitted the Southern Methodist minister J. W. Tucker to tell a Confederate audience in 1862 that "your cause is the cause of God, the cause of Christ, of humanity. It is a conflict of truth with error – of Bible with Northern infidelity – of pure Christianity with Northern fanaticism."[14] It was this argument that into the early years of the war itself left many moderate and conservative Christians in the North convinced against themselves that Thornwell and Tucker were probably right.

Opposition: Scriptural Principle and Republican Certainty

The primary reason that the biblical defense of slavery remained so strong was that many biblical attacks on slavery were so weak. To oversimplify a complicated picture, the most direct biblical attacks on slavery were ones that relied on common sense, the broadly accepted moral intuitions of American national ideology, and the weight of "self-evident truth." They were also the easiest to refute. More complicated, nuanced, and involved biblical attacks against slavery offered more formidable opposition. But because those arguments did not feature intuition, republican instinct, and common sense readings of individual texts, they were much less effective in a public arena that had been so strongly shaped by intuitive, republican, and commonsensical intellectual principles.

Like the biblical defenses of slavery, the attacks on the system had a lengthy history. In America these attacks typically arose from an alliance between scriptural principle and republican certainty. In a pioneering tract from 1776, Samuel Hopkins of Newport, Rhode Island, who had been a student and close friend of Jonathan Edwards, concluded that "the whole divine revelation" spoke against slavery.[15] Less than two decades later, but now disillusioned by the failure of an independent United States to move rapidly against slavery, Hopkins returned to the subject. This time he insisted, with a combination of republican and Christian language, that "tyranny and slavery" were "evils" that "the gospel" thoroughly opposed.[16] Hopkins did pay some attention to individual passages like Leviticus 25 and the book of Philemon, but for him grasping the broad sweep of Scripture and applying the most basic meaning of American experience were more important.

Likewise, a rousing polemic from 1815 by George Bourne, *The Book and Slavery Irreconcilable*, dealt at length with individual texts of Scripture, even as it leaned even harder on what Bourne obviously considered the humanitarian agreement of biblical and republican principles. Thus he made much of texts like Exodus 21:16 that in his view should have convinced all believers to oppose the slave trade and slavery itself ("And he that stealeth a man, and selleth him, or if he be found in his hand, he shall surely be put to death"). But the burden of Bourne's argument was carried by grand reasoning from first principles: "Every man who holds Slaves and who pretends to be a Christian or a Republican, is either an incurable Idiot who cannot distinguish good from evil, or an obdurate sinner who resolutely defies every social, moral, and divine requisition. . . . Every ramification of the doctrine, *that one rational creature can become the property of another,* is totally repugnant to the rule of equity, the rights of nature, and the existence of civil society."[17] Once established, this principled approach to Scripture became the staple of abolitionism.

In October 1845 two able casuists took up the fight in a public debate in Cincinnati that went on for eight hours a day through four long days of public declamation.[18] The thrust and parry of face-to-face confrontation between two Presbyterian ministers did not allow the abolitionist Jonathan Blanchard and the moderate emancipationist Nathaniel Rice to attain the level of sophistication reached by Francis Wayland and Richard Fuller in their written exchange of the same year, but this Cincinnati spectacular was still memorable. Blanchard, who had been a student of Moses Stuart at Andover Seminary, defended the abolitionism that Stuart would later attack in his 1850 monograph. Rice, who had studied at Princeton Theological Seminary, where Stuart's general theology was considered suspect as a deficient form of Calvinism, defended Stuart's position that, although the Bible pointed toward the eventual, voluntary elimination of slavery, it nowhere called slavery evil as such.

Although this debate is worth studying for many reasons, it is pertinent here for how Blanchard advanced the most popular form of the biblical antislavery argument. As Rice methodically tied Blanchard in knots over how to interpret the proslavery implications of specific texts, Blanchard returned repeatedly to "the broad principle of common equity and common sense" that he found in Scripture, to "the general principles of the Bible" and "the whole scope of the Bible," where to him it was obvious that "the principles of the Bible are justice and righteousness."[19] Early on in the debate, Blanchard's exasperation with Rice's attention to particular passages led him to utter a particularly revealing statement of his own reasoning: "Abolitionists take their stand upon the New Testament doctrine of the natural equity of man. The one-bloodism of human kind [from Acts 17:26]:—and upon those great principles of human rights, drawn from the New Testament, and announced in the American Declaration of Independence, declaring that all men have natural and *inalienable* rights to person, property and the pursuit of happiness."[20] Blanchard's linkage between themes from Scripture and tropes from American republicanism was repeated regularly by abolitionists. But this use of the Bible almost never found support in the South and only rarely among Northern moderates and conservatives. In general, it was a use that suffered particular difficulties when, as in the ground rules laid down for Blanchard and Rice in their Cincinnati debate, disputants pledged themselves in good Protestant fashion to base what they said on the Bible as their only authoritative source.[21]

Harriet Beecher Stowe's lightning-rod novel, *Uncle Tom's Cabin*, provided one of the era's most powerful examples of the abolitionist appeal to the general spirit of the Bible. The question of the Bible and slavery appeared repeatedly in this novel, which was serialized in 1851 and then published to great acclaim (and scorn) the next year. Stowe, herself a dedicated if romantic partisan for the Bible, nonetheless subtly queried widespread American notions about the self-interpreting power of Scripture. For example, she had one of her slave-owning characters, Augustine St. Clare, suggest that scriptural interpretation was driven more by interest than intellect: "Suppose that something should bring down the price of cotton once and forever, and make the whole slave property a drug in the market, don't you think we should have another version of the Scripture doctrine? What a flood of light would pour into the church, all at once, and how immediately it would be discovered that everything in the Bible and reason went the other way!"[22]

Stowe also intimated the cynical conclusion, which would become more common among secularists after the Civil War, that the Bible was easily manipulated to prove anything with regard to a problem like slavery that readers might desire. "Honest old John Van Trompe," with an instinctive objection to slavery, long had kept himself at arms' length from church because of ministers who claimed that Scripture sanctioned the institution. But when he found experts on the other side who could use Greek and Hebrew to attack slavery as effectively as others had used such knowledge to defend it, Van Trompe, in Stowe's dialogue, "took right hold, and jined the church."[23] At another place in the novel, Stowe had passengers on a steamboat, which was carrying slaves down the Ohio River, exchange biblical texts with each other like bird shot. On the one side: " 'It's undoubtedly the intention of Providence that the African race should be servants—kept in a low condition,' said a grave-looking gentleman in black, a clergyman, seated by the cabin door. ' "Cursed be Canaan: a servant of servants shall he be," the scripture says.' " On the other side: "A tall, slender young man, with a face expressive of great feeling and intelligence, here broke in, and repeated the words, ' "All things whatsoever ye would that men should do unto you, do ye even so unto them." I suppose,' he added, '*that* is scripture, as much as "Cursed be Canaan." ' "[24] In each case, Stowe's own sentiments obviously lay with the antislavery use of the Bible, but her portrayal of a divided usage could not have reassured those who paused to reflect on how this novel might awaken uncertainty about the supposedly perspicuous authority of the Bible.

By contrast, Stowe's most extensive incident featuring an appeal to Scripture conveyed a less ambiguous message. After the slave Eliza escapes over the ice-clogged Ohio River with her young son, she comes, exhausted, to the home of Senator and Mrs. Bird just as they have finished discussing the senator's support for Ohio's version of the Fugitive Slave Law. When Mary Bird surprises her husband by attacking all such laws as "shameful, wicked, [and] abominable," John Bird replies with arguments paralleling the biblical defense: "But, Mary, just listen to me. Your feelings are all quite right, dear, and interesting, and I love you for them; but, then, dear, we mustn't suffer our feelings to run away with our judgment." To arguments in favor of fugitive slave laws, which regularly included a proslavery use of the Bible, Mary Bird blows away the equivalent of chapter and verse argumentation with a larger gestalt of scriptural sentiment:

> "Now, John, I don't know anything about politics, but I can read my Bible; and there I see that I must feed the hungry, clothe the naked, and comfort the desolate; and that Bible I mean to follow."
>
> "But in cases where your doing so would involve a great public evil –"
>
> "Obeying God never brings on public evils. I know it can't. It's always safest, all round, to *do as He* bids us."
>
> "Now, listen to me, Mary, and I can state to you a very clear argument, to show –"
>
> "O, nonsense, John! You can talk all night, but you wouldn't do it, I put it to you, John – would *you* now turn away a poor, shivering, hungry creature from your door, because he was a runaway? Would you now?"[25]

At that very point the fugitive slave Eliza arrives at their door, and the senator proves his mettle by setting aside his "arguments" and moving Eliza in the dead of night away from danger to the home of John Van Trompe.

The significance of Stowe's *Uncle Tom's Cabin* for the biblical debate over slavery lay in the novel's emotive power. More effectively than debaters like Jonathan Blanchard or Francis Wayland, Stowe exemplified – rather than just announced – the persuasive force of what she regarded as the Bible's overarching general message.

The fact that a novelist brought off this task more effectively than the exegetes did not stop abolitionist scholars and preachers from continuing the battle in their chosen media. On the eve of conflict, George Cheever, a Congregationalist minister from upstate New York, published one of the era's most elaborate biblical attacks on slavery. Cheever labored diligently, if not too convincingly, to show that Old Testament "bondmen" and New Testament "servants" were not slaves at all. He certainly scored points in using biblical prohibitions against "manstealing" when he excoriated the internal trade in slaves and, by implication, all slaveholding.[26] Yet over and again he appealed to the inconsistency between slavery and "the benevolence commanded in the Scriptures." At the end he brought his book to a climax by moving from the biblical "letter" to a much broader basis: "The moral argument from Scripture on the subject appeals to the common conscience of all mankind, and at every step enlists the common sense of humanity in its behalf."[27]

So also did Henry Ward Beecher reason in his climactic public statement on the eve of conflict. Maybe, he conceded, a defense of slavery could be teased out of obscure, individual texts of Scripture, but surely the defining message of the Bible was something else entirely. In his fast day sermon of January 4, 1861, Beecher strenuously appealed to the general meaning of the Bible as opposed to the pedantic literalism that undergirded the proslavery view: " 'I came to open the prison-doors,' said Christ; and that is the text on which men justify shutting them and locking them. 'I came to loose those that are bound;' and that is the text out of which men spin cords to bind men, women, and children. 'I came to carry light to them that are in darkness and deliverance to the oppressed;' and that is the Book from out of which they argue, with amazing ingenuity, all the infernal meshes and snares by which to keep men in bondage. It is pitiful."[28]

Such use of the Bible doubtless carries more weight today than it did in 1860, when the way that Beecher reasoned disturbed broad reaches of American religious opinion. At the time, however, the conviction that he could easily separate the Bible's antislavery "spirit" from its proslavery "letter" was not only a minority position; it was also widely perceived as a theologically dangerous position.

A devastating theological weakness of this position made many, who were otherwise sympathetic, shy away. As early as 1846, the Connecticut Congregationalist Leonard Bacon, who very much wanted to oppose slavery as a sin, nonetheless hung back. His analysis of the "spirit" over "letter" argument caught the dilemma exactly: "The evidence that there were both slaves and masters of slaves in the churches founded and directed by the apostles, cannot be got rid of without resorting to methods of interpretation which will get rid of everything." In Bacon's view, the well-intentioned souls who "torture the Scriptures into saying that which the anti-slavery theory requires them to say" did great damage to the Scriptures themselves.[29] To Bacon and many others who were tempted to make a move from the Bible's "letter" of sanction for slavery to its "spirit" of universal liberation, the facts of American experience may have been the great stumbling block. Precisely by following the Bible strictly, by tending to its "letter" when heretics of various kinds were running after its "spirit," the churches had prospered, and the balm of the gospel had reached unprecedented numbers of spiritually needy men and women.

This consideration did not deter abolitionists like Cheever and the Beechers. Yet the stronger their arguments based on general humanitarian principles became, the weaker the Bible looked in any traditional sense. By contrast, rebuttal of such arguments from biblical principle increasingly came to look like a defense of Scripture itself.

Opposition: Historical Contexts and Prudential Reasoning

Bacon and those who like him wanted both to preserve traditional biblical authority and to oppose slavery still had one more argument to advance. They could concede that the Bible never did in fact condemn slavery per se, but they could also contend that, when properly interpreted, Scripture did condemn *the kind of slavery practiced in the American South*. With a substantial history behind it, this was an argument of some subtlety, and one that Bacon himself, along with a sizable number of other earnest Bible believers, tried to make in the years before war broke out.[30]

In 1808 one of the first and best biblical arguments against the Southern system of slavery was published by David Barrow.[31] His *Involuntary, Unmerited, Perpetual, Absolute, Hereditary Slavery, Examined; on the Principles of Nature, Reason, Justice, Policy and Scripture* featured arguments denying that the descendants of Canaan were Africans. More generally, he held that the precedents for slavery found by paying close attention to Abraham's life and Mosaic law were, for American experience, irrelevant. If all cotton growers and owners of rice plantations were Hebrews, if they could locate Canaanites for slaves, and if they would then transport their operations to the Middle East, then Barrow would concede a biblical warrant for slavery.

By the 1840s, such quick resolutions would no longer suffice, however effective they might once have seemed. Much of Francis Wayland's lengthy response to Richard Fuller went over Barrow's argument, only with more erudition and with more detail from the Hebrew language and Old Testament history. To Wayland, in an argument that also loomed large in African American biblical exegesis (as we shall see in the next chapter), the fact that Abraham circumcised his slaves (Genesis 17:12), and so included them in all the blessings God promised to "his people," set up a very different situation than prevailed in the South. So it was as well with the Mosaic legislation that provided for manumission if a master harmed a slave in any way (such as knocking out a tooth, Exodus 21:27) or if a slave escaped to a Hebrew town (Deuteronomy 23:15–16). Wayland did not believe that Old Testament slavery provided a legitimate rationale for slavery in other times and places. But even if it did, he held that to follow the Bible meant that Americans would have to abandon the slave system that then existed in their land: "Suppose . . . that whatever was sanctioned to the Hebrews is sanctioned to all men at all times, . . . I do not see in what manner it could justify slavery in the United States. It is, I presume, conceded that a permission of this kind is to be understood according to the utmost strictness of application. If slavery be justified by the law of Moses, it is, of course, only justified *in the manner* and *with the restrictions* under which it was placed by that law."[32]

A few years later a Baptist preacher with far less of a reputation made Wayland's points even more sharply, and he did so in Kentucky, where such opinions could be dangerous. James M. Pendleton was a hard-nosed defender of the Bible's inerrancy as well as of Baptist distinctives, but that cast of mind did not prevent him from mounting a strong case against slavery as practiced in Kentucky at a time when possible legislation concerning slavery was being considered by a state constitutional convention.[33] Pendleton turned to the standard passages about Abraham and his slaves and observed "that there are points of material dissimilarity between that system and our system of slavery." Unlike owners in the Southern states, where it was usually illegal for slaves to be armed, Abraham gave weapons to his slaves, and Abraham was prepared, before his son Isaac was born, to make a slave his heir. The only conclusion that Pendleton could draw was that "it does not follow necessarily that Abraham's servants were slaves in the American acceptation of the word."[34] In a clever but also bitterly expressed play on categories widely used at the time, Pendleton made his case as forcefully as he could:

> Hence when the position is established that "slavery is not of necessity sinful," that it "is not a sin in the abstract," pro-slavery men most ridiculously transport their idea of the innocence of slavery in the abstract to slavery in the concrete. Because they can conceive of circumstances in which a master may hold a slave without doing wrong, they infer that there is nothing wrong in the system of slavery in Kentucky. They reason from what *might be* to what is. For example, they would say something like this: The slavery which sacredly regards the marriage union, cherishes the relation between parents and children, and provides for the instruction of the slave, is not sinful. Therefore the system of slavery in Kentucky, *which does none of these things*, is not sinful. Is this logic? Is it not rather a burlesque on logic?[35]

The kind of biblical reasoning proposed by Pendleton and his predecessors still loomed large, at least among learned advocates, on the eve of conflict. In the first chapter we heard from Rabbi Raphall and Professor Tayler Lewis, who vigorously opposed abolitionist attempts to describe slavery as a simple sin. But in their fuller expositions, both Raphall and Lewis went on to mount strong arguments against slavery as it existed in the United States.

After his scathing attack on abolitionists that we have quoted from his sermon of January 4, 1861, Rabbi Raphall turned to argue against the hard-nosed defenders of American slavery as a positive good. The crux of his argument echoed much of the Catholic commentary that is examined in chapter 7. In particular, unlike ancient systems, American slavery dehumanized the slave: "The slave is a *person* in whom the dignity of human nature is to be respected; *he has rights*. Whereas, the heathen view of slavery which prevailed at Rome, and which, I am sorry to say, is adopted in the South, reduces the slave to a *thing*, and a thing can have no rights."[36]

Tayler Lewis made an even more extensive case in response to proslavery use of the Bible. He began by arguing that "the Patriarchal Servitude" in ancient times was very different from the slavery found in the American South. And he echoed Rabbi Raphall in asserting that, regardless of the social system in place, Scripture never spoke of servants as mere property. Lewis then expounded at length on what he held to be a key feature of Old Testament teaching—yes, there was divine approval for buying non-Jews as slaves, but never for selling them. More important, since this provision for servitude depended on the distinction in ancient Israel between the people of God and "the heathen," it was imperative to recognize the great change inaugurated by the coming of Jesus Christ. If, as Christians believe, Jesus opened the doorway of salvation to all people everywhere, who then were "the heathen" of modern times? In Lewis's words, "We still speak of heathen, using the term geographically, and, to some extent, ethnologically; but theologically, ecclesiastically, Christianly, there are no heathen." Rather, because the work of Christ accentuated what Lewis called "the blood unity of the race," it was necessary to recognize that there were no longer any "heathen" whom it was acceptable for the people of God to enslave. To drive his point home, he asked why, if proslavery advocates were so faithful in believing the Bible, slaves who became Christians (who, that is, stopped being "heathen" even in the illegitimate sense in which the term was still being used) were not manumitted immediately. Finally, Lewis returned at the end of his long argument to repeat that the slave system practiced in the United States could not by any means be considered the same as anything practiced in the ancient world. In his view, even the brutal Roman system was not as degenerate by biblical standards as the American: "No Roman court ever made a decision so casting a man out of the state, and out of the pale of humanity, as the Dred Scott [case]."[37] In sum, Lewis argued that the Bible nowhere legitimated racially defined slavery and everywhere condemned social systems beset with the evils that in fact attended the practice of slavery in the United States.

Taking Stock

Promising as the arguments made by Professor Lewis might now seem, they failed in late 1860 to make much headway in American public debate. Three reasons explain why this nuanced biblical attack on American slavery was so relatively ineffective. The first was that biblical defenders of slavery found it easy to lump Lewis's kind of nuanced biblicism with the arguments of radical abolitionists who claimed that the Bible condemned slavery per se as a sin. Since these radical arguments seemed so obviously to lead to the overthrow of the Bible, the more nuanced position probably did too.

The other two reasons for the failure of a nuanced biblical antislavery concerned the weighty issues of race and common sense. As indicated in Professor Lewis's arguments, an inability to countenance "the blood unity of the race" provided strong support for biblical defenses of slavery. How Bible believers, both white and black, tried to counteract that inability is the subject of the next chapter.

On the other front, nuanced biblical attacks on American slavery faced rough going precisely because they were nuanced. This position could not simply be read out of any one biblical text; it could not be lifted directly from the page. Rather, it needed patient reflection on the entirety of the Scriptures; it required expert knowledge of the historical circumstances of ancient Near Eastern and Roman slave systems as well as of the actually existing conditions in the slave states; and it demanded that sophisticated interpretative practice replace a commonsensically literal approach to the sacred text. In short, this was an argument of elites requiring that the populace defer to its intellectual betters. As such, it contradicted democratic and republican intellectual instincts. In the culture of the United States, as that culture had been constructed by three generations of evangelical Bible believers, the nuanced biblical argument was doomed.

The question of Scripture and slavery constituted a great problem in 1860 because a biblically inspired people had done so much to construct the country they were now pulling apart. The interpretative practices that had grown up with the great antebellum denominations favored democratic, republican, antitraditional, and commonsensical exegesis. Against this historical background, the biblical proslavery argument seemed very strong, the biblical antislavery argument seemed religiously dangerous, and the nuanced biblical argument against slavery in its American form did not comport well with democratic practice and republican theory. Yet many in the North who because of their commonsensical interpretation of the Bible opposed any use of Scripture to attack slavery were nonetheless uneasy with the system. They were joined by at least a few from the South. Though conservative in their attachment to traditional views of the Bible, they continued to struggle against the all-out proslavery biblicism of the South's great champions.

On the eve of the Civil War, interpretations of the Bible that made the most sense to the broadest public were those that incorporated the defining experiences of America into the hermeneutics used for interpreting what the infallible text actually meant. In this effort, those who like James Henley Thornwell defended the legitimacy of slavery in the Bible had the easiest task. The procedure, which by 1860 had been repeated countless times, was uncomplicated. First, open the Scriptures and read, at say Leviticus 25:45, or, even better, at 1 Corinthians 7:20-21. Second, decide for yourself what these passages mean. Don't wait for a bishop or a king or a president or a meddling Yankee to tell you what the passage means, but decide for yourself. Third, if anyone tries to convince you that you are not interpreting such passages in the natural, commonsensical, ordinary meaning of the words, look hard at what such a one believes with respect to other biblical doctrines. If you find in what he or she says about such doctrines the least hint of unorthodoxy, as inevitably you will, then you may rest assured that you are being asked to give up not only the plain meaning of Scripture, but also the entire trust in the Bible that made the country into such a great Christian civilization.

With debate over the Bible and slavery at such a pass, and especially with the success of the proslavery biblical argument manifestly (if also uncomfortably) convincing to most Southerners and many in the North, difficulties abounded. The country had a problem because its most trusted religious authority, the Bible, was sounding an uncertain note. The evangelical Protestant churches had a problem because the mere fact of trusting implicitly in the Bible was not solving disagreements about what the Bible taught concerning slavery. The country and the churches were both in trouble because the remedy that finally solved the question of how to interpret the Bible was recourse to arms. The supreme crisis over the Bible was that there existed no apparent biblical resolution to the crisis. As I have written elsewhere, it was left to those consummate theologians, the Reverend Doctors Ulysses S. Grant and William Tecumseh Sherman, to decide what in fact the Bible actually meant.[38]

Chapter 4

"The negro question lies far deeper
than the slave question"

In April 1861, just as the guns were speaking at Fort Sumter, the *Mercersburg Review* published a long article on slavery by the émigré theologian and church historian, Philip Schaff. Schaff, a native Swiss who had studied at Germany's finest universities before accepting a call to the German Reformed seminary in Mercersburg, Pennsylvania, was the nation's most versatile religious scholar. He was also one of the era's shrewdest interpreters of American religion to European audiences.[1] Schaff's learned article upheld the conservative position in almost its Southern form with detailed exegesis of the many biblical texts that, in his view, legitimated slavery. Toward the end of his essay, he turned from the general topic of the Bible and slavery to address the particular American situation. In this analysis, Schaff argued that slavery would one day be recognized as "no doubt an immense blessing to the whole race of Ham," but he also anticipated that "Christian philanthropy" would bring about the gradual, voluntary end of the American slave system. It was for its time and Schaff's place not an unusual performance, with one exception. That exception was Schaff's frank conclusion about the relationship of race to slavery: "*The negro question*," as he put it in italics, "*lies far deeper than the slavery question.*"[2]

Schaff's lengthy article in the spring of 1861 did not live up to the promise of his own insightful observation, since it did not even raise the question whether the general sanction for slavery he found in the Bible could be applied unambiguously to the black-only form of slavery that existed in the United States. Yet with this elision of questions concerning slavery and questions concerning the enslavement of only African Americans, Schaff was again representative of his age.

What Schaff saw when he defined "the negro question" and "the slavery question" as two distinct matters and what Schaff practiced in assuming that they could be treated as one problem constituted a theological crisis. The crisis created by an inability to distinguish the Bible on race from the Bible on slavery meant that when the Civil War was over and slavery was abolished, systemic racism continued unchecked as the great moral anomaly in a supposedly Christian America. This crisis reflected a greater difficulty than when a large Protestant population drew incommensurate theological conclusions from a commonly exalted sacred text that it approached with common hermeneutical principles.

The crisis identified by Schaff involved two badly handled questions. The first concerned how to regard African Americans and their relationship to Caucasians. This issue pointed to foundational theological difficulties since most of America's white Bible-believing Christians addressed the issue with commonsense solutions derived neither from the Bible nor from the historical storehouse of Christian moral reflection.

The second mishandled question was the issue of what the Bible had to say about the general economic organization of the United States and its practices, potential, and problems. This issue also betrayed theological difficulties because, while oceans of ink were spilled in trying to decide whether the Bible legitimated slavery, far less biblical analysis was devoted to the broader American economy of which slavery was a part and to principles of economic justice. David Brion Davis once highlighted the underpinnings of the confusion involved here: "In the United States . . . the problem of slavery . . . had become fatally intertwined with the problem of race. Race had become the favored idiom for interpreting the social effects of enslavement and emancipation and for concealing the economy's parasitic dependence on an immensely profitable labor system"[3] – and for concealing as well the challenge posed to capitalist individualism by the patriarchal communalism of the slave South. Buying and selling slaves so monopolized theological attention that little energy remained for evaluating American systems of buying and selling in general.

To be sure, as a number of historians have convincingly demonstrated, Southern defenders of slavery did, in fact, raise serious questions from Scripture about the moral order of an individualistic and profit-mad economy, which they saw as the North's aggressive alternative to a slave order. In

Eugene Genovese's words, the threat was of "a materialistic, marketplace society that promoted competitive individualism and worshiped Mammon." Or, as Kenneth Startup has put it, the "economically, socially rooted affirmation of slavery was . . . complemented by the Southern ministers' attempt to link abolitionism with Northern greed and selfishness and with a peculiar, destructive distortion of Northern economic sensibility."[4] Southern critics were joined in their worries by a few political economists from the North like Francis Wayland.[5] But since most Southern thinking on the economy came to be anathematized because of the prominence it gave to racial slavery, and since Northerners like Wayland, as if in exhaustion, gave up theological analysis of the economy once slavery had been eliminated, Christian attention to the larger economic questions tailed off dramatically after the end of the Civil War.

For the religious history of the 1860s, the restriction of serious theological analysis to slavery alone, at the expense of theological attention to the economy as a whole, was less important than the confusion between slavery as such and America's system of black-only slavery. But if this book were extended to the postbellum period, it would be pertinent to ask if "victory" in the constitutional elimination of slavery – accompanied as it was by a general retreat from theological analysis of economic issues – did not contribute to the parlous economic-religious history of the latter nineteenth century. In an oversimplified picture, those were years when a commercial capitalism far larger and more all-encompassing than ever imagined by the probusiness Whigs of the antebellum era came to exert an unprecedented influence in American society; when many of the Protestants who had once guided national life retreated from efforts at shaping society in order to cultivate private gardens of inward spiritual development; and when potentially innovative religious convictions among newer immigrant groups (Catholic, Lutheran, Jewish) were only inching toward broad public commentary on economic issues.[6]

In that postbellum climate, Southern Christian defenses of patriarchal communalism were fatally compromised by their association with slavery, and Northern Christian assessments of economic principle ran out of steam after human bondage was brought to an end. The result was theological weakness in the face of pressing economic circumstances: while there was a heightened capacity to produce wealth, there was also a heightened capacity to produce alienation and vast economic inequality. These issues were eventually addressed practically by pietists like the Salvation Army and theoretically by leaders of the Social Gospel, yet theological incoherence in the face of modern economic realities has remained a major problem for Christian thinking ever since the Civil War.

During the years of the Civil War and before, however, confusion between race and slavery was a more pressing concern than the dynamics of the economy. In this chapter, therefore, we look first at several clear statements from white commentators to show that the confusion between slavery in the abstract and the enslavement of only African Americans was apparent to at least some contemporary observers. Then an attempt is made to explain why considerations of slavery at the time so systematically took for granted – rather than confronted – issues of race. Finally, it is important to ask how Bible-believing African Americans brought Scripture to bear on these questions. Not surprisingly, what they found in the Bible was very different from the scriptural word proclaimed by the defenders of slavery, though the word they found was just as clear and reassuring.

Black Slavery, White Slavery

One of the strongest indications of the prevailing racism of the mid-nineteenth century was that Bible expositors could not get Americans to take as seriously what Scripture said about the color of biblical slaves as what it said about slavery itself. Some secular thinkers, like George Fitzhugh and James Hammond, were, in fact, aware that proving slavery by the Bible might be proving too much.[7] More so than most religious figures, they were open to the idea of enslaving whites as well as blacks. But the possibility that Scripture might sanction slavery for whites, unlike the general defense of slavery from the Bible, got nowhere with the general public.

Debate in Kentucky over a new state constitution in 1849 allowed two opponents of slavery in that state to make a forceful case for the Bible's color-blindness. James M. Pendleton, whose efforts at differentiating "slavery in the abstract" from "slavery in the concrete" we observed in the last chapter, also attacked the axiomatic link between slavery and black-only American slavery. When responding to an opponent who claimed that the slave system as it existed in the United States promoted the "holiness and happiness" of slaves, Pendleton played what he considered the unbeatable race card: "If then it could be established that slavery promotes the holiness and happiness of slaves, it would follow that as it does not promote the holiness and happiness of the white population it would be well for white people to be enslaved in order to their holiness and happiness."[8]

Even stronger arguments were heard during that same Kentucky debate from John G. Fee, an independent-minded minister who was among the South's most forceful opponents of the slave system. In his battle to convince Kentuckians that "caste" (that is, race) was the deeper evil that propped up slavery itself, Fee pushed well beyond other Kentucky emancipationists like Robert Breckinridge, a Presbyterian controversialist who took much heat for his lifelong opposition to slavery, but who also favored the colonization scheme as a way of avoiding the "amalgamation" of the races.[9]

In a series of pamphlets from the mid-1840s, Fee offered a full arsenal of biblical antislavery armament. In fact, he provided so many arguments, and of so many kinds, that his sharp analysis of the racial situation seems to have been lost in the tussle. As an example, in 1851 he published a substantial pamphlet that included the bold declaration that American slavery, "by whomsoever caused, is always sinful," and he did not hesitate to claim that "the plain principles of the Bible (justice, mercy, impartial love) are opposed to slavery." Amid this fusillade of argumentation more characteristic of radical abolitionists who played fast and loose with Scripture, strict attention was paid to race. Thus Fee argued that if the slavery of African Americans was defended because as a race they were less intelligent or had darker skin, the logic led to an absurd conclusion: "The fact that one man, or race of men, may have more intellectual capacity than another man, or race of men, gives no just ground for enslaving the inferior; otherwise the most intellectual man that exists may have a right to enslave every other man – white and black. . . . Otherwise, he who has a fairer skin . . . than you or I, may have a right to enslave us; and the fairest man in the world may enslave every other man."[10]

Most pointed of all was Fee's direct reasoning from the Bible. Let us grant, he supposed, that the New Testament never condemned the enslavement by Rome of those it conquered in Germany, Gaul, Spain, Greece, Egypt, and so forth. "What," he asked, "was the complexion of these nations?" His answer was that "most were as white or whiter than the Romans themselves." Consequently, if in general "the apostles' teaching and practice sanctioned slavery, it sanctioned *the slavery of the age* – the slavery amongst which the apostles moved. N.B. THIS SLAVERY WAS WHITE SLAVERY . . . the large portion of those enslaved were *as white, and many of them whiter than their masters.*"[11]

However slight was the hearing gained by Pendleton and Fee through such polemics, at least one ex-Kentuckian was able to use the Bible in a similar way during the course of later political strife. In a speech in Cincinnati in the late summer of 1859, Abraham Lincoln continued his ongoing exploration of the era's political crises by responding to what Senator Stephen A. Douglas had only shortly before told an audience in the same city. Lincoln acknowledged that some in Kentucky were "trying to show that slavery existed in the Bible times by Divine ordinance." He paused to pay a back-handed compliment to Senator Douglas for not picking up on this argument. "Douglas knows that whenever you establish that Slavery was right by the Bible, it will occur that that Slavery was the Slavery of the *white* man – of men without reference to color."[12] As it happened, however, that thought did not "occur" to many of those who, in the North as well as in the South, interpreted the Scriptures as justifying American slavery.

Had white Protestants been following the Bible as carefully as they claimed, they could not have so casually dismissed the biblical interpretations advanced by Pendleton and Fee and mentioned by Lincoln. The inability to propose a biblical scheme of slavery that would take in all races reveals that factors other than simple fidelity to Scripture were exerting great influence as well. Personal interest, as satirized by Harriet Beecher Stowe, was certainly a factor. Even more important was the unbiblical assumption that slavery could only mean black slavery.

Experience, Common Sense, and Race

No biblical warrant existed for the assumption that slavery could only mean black slavery except the often refuted application of the "curse of Ham" that, according to Genesis, chapter 9, doomed Ham's progeny, Canaan, to servitude.[13] Rather, it was acceptance of black racial inferiority that supplied the missing term to many of the arguments that defended American slavery by appeal to Scripture. Especially in an age like our own that has become sanctimonious about its ability to discern the evils of race, class, and gender stereotyping, it is important to attend carefully to the texts of an earlier era when different presuppositions prevailed. What such attention reveals is that opponents of slavery often had the same difficulty as its defenders in recognizing the large role that extrabiblical racial axioms played in their arguments, even when they professed to be arguing from the Bible alone. Laura Mitchell has put the matter well in her study of religious responses to the Compromise of 1850. As she describes them, antebellum Bible readers encountered difficulty when they attempted scriptural interpretations of American events because the Old and New Testaments "describe specific situations whose applicability to the antebellum United States was complicated and imperfect. The passages raised many questions that could not be answered within the body of the text." First among the difficulties was race. In Mitchell's terms, "Even the most committed abolitionists often had trouble perceiving blacks as 'beloved' brothers."[14]

Among early antislavery advocates in the late eighteenth century, there may have been more awareness than among antebellum Americans of the weight that preconceptions about race exerted on arguments about slavery. Two of America's most active early opponents of slavery were Benjamin Rush, a Philadelphia physician and all-purpose polemicist, and Samuel Hopkins, the student of Jonathan Edwards who at the time of the American War of Independence was a Congregationalist minister in Newport, Rhode Island. In carefully argued works published when protests against "British tyranny" were coming to a climax in the colonies, Rush and Hopkins both turned to the Bible as much to justify the full human dignity of Africans as to refute the biblical defense of slavery. Together they acknowledged that God, for his own purposes, had allowed the ancient Hebrews to make slaves of non-Hebrews. But they also held that this was only a temporary expedient designed to preserve the Israelites from intermarriage, which would have thwarted the good that God intended to bestow on all humanity through the promised Jewish messiah, Jesus Christ.

In the Christian era, however, these authors held that such racial discrimination was no longer appropriate. On the subject of race, Rush contended that Africans "are equal to the Europeans, when we allow for the diversity of temper and genius which is occasioned by climate." Any vices that seemed to be more prevalent among African Americans than among whites had resulted from "the genuine offspring of slavery" itself.[15] For Hopkins, the Bible as a whole spoke against any special designation of blacks as due subjects for slavery or of Europeans as their due masters. Moreover, the fact that Jews once held non-Jews as slaves offered just as strong a rationale for modern blacks to enslave whites as vice versa.[16]

It may be true, as David Brion Davis has suggested, that Rush, Hopkins, and other early opponents of slavery made a fatal concession when they acknowledged that Israel's need for racial purity justified slavery in the ancient world. A practice once acknowledged as historical precedent might be revived for modern use.[17] But Rush and Hopkins insisted so stoutly on both the uniqueness of Jewish experience and the racial equality of contemporary blacks and whites that if they offered any support for later biblical defenses of slavery, it was very slim indeed.

An indication of how the landscape shifted in the decades that followed is provided by the instructive case of Moses Stuart. Stuart's reputation as America's most competent Bible scholar, which was based on a parade of learned grammars, commentaries, and treatises published from the 1810s into the 1850s, was well earned. That reputation wore a special luster because great learning had not turned him away from the practical piety he had maintained as a loyal son of New England's revival tradition. As we have seen, Stuart's 1850 monograph, *Conscience and the Constitution*, was notable for its combination of exegetical rigor (defending the divine permission of slavery) and pastoral unction (urging the South to follow scriptural principle and start to dismantle the slave system). Its treatment of one of the most important passages to figure in debate over fugitive slave provisions in the Compromise of 1850 was also noteworthy for what it assumed about race.

The passage was Deuteronomy 23:15-16: "Thou shalt not deliver unto his master the servant which is escaped from his master unto thee. He shall dwell with thee, even among you, in that place which he shall choose in one of thy gates, where it liketh him best; they shalt not oppress him."[18] Opponents of fugitive slave laws claimed that the Bible at this place stood unequivocally on their side. Stuart begged to differ.

To Stuart, this injunction from Deuteronomy took for granted that the escaped servant (or slave) had to have come from outside Israel, from "a heathen master."[19] Otherwise, if it had been a slave escaped from a Hebrew master, "restoration, or restitution, if we may judge by the tenor of other property-laws among the Hebrews, would have surely been enjoined." Stuart held that

God's treatment of Israel, as his "chosen people," was singular by being designed to preserve them from "all tangling alliances and connections with the heathen." Thus when a slave escaped from one of Israel's neighbors, it was a humanitarian gesture not to return the slave, and it amounted also to an evangelistic gesture since the slave could come to know the true God. Such an escaped slave might even be circumcised and so come to enjoy all the benefits of solidarity with the chosen people.

If, however, the slave had escaped from a fellow Hebrew, everything was different. Since Jewish slave laws were relatively mild, since property laws among the Jews were strict, and since the slave of a Hebrew was already being instructed in God's law, any slave escaped from a fellow Hebrew had to be returned to his or her rightful owner.

As Stuart then turned to the American situation, exegesis receded and assumptions advanced. He first declared that the United States was "one nation — one so-called Christian nation" and that "Christianity is a national religion among us." Of course, not everyone in the country was personally a Christian believer, but almost all of the American people "profess to respect Christianity, and appeal to its precepts as a test of morals, and as furnishing us with the rules of life." The fact of American national Christianity meant that Northerners could not look upon slave masters in the South "as heathen in our sight." Because there were so many true believers in the South, "a bondman, fleeing from them to us, is a case of just the same kind as would have been presented among the Hebrews, if a Hebrew bond-man had fled from the tribe of Judah to that of Benjamin." In that case, the response was clear: the slave must be returned, since "we do not send back the refugee from the South to a heathen nation or tribe." At this point, Stuart's sturdy federalism joined his sharp sense of American chosenness to drive home a firm conclusion:

> But be the master as he may, since we of the North are only other tribes
> of the same great commonwealth, we cannot sit in judgment on cruel
> masters belonging to tribes different from our own, and having, by
> solemn compact, a separate and independent jurisdiction in respect to
> all matters of justice between man and man, with which no stranger
> can on any pretence whatever intermeddle. . . . The Mosaic law does not
> authorize us to reject the claims of our fellow countrymen and citizens,

for strayed or stolen property—property authorized and guarantied as such by Southern States to their respective citizens. These States are not *heathen*. We have acknowledged them as *brethren* and *fellow citizens* of the great community. A fugitive from them is not a fugitive from an idolatrous and polytheistic people.[20]

The force of Stuart's application of this passage from Deuteronomy 23 to the United States in 1850 depended on two premises imported into his argument. Each of these premises contradicted what Stuart, as a formidable Calvinist theologian, otherwise held concerning God's work in history.

The first imported premise was the belief that the American states were analogous to the tribes of Israel. Although this notion was widespread at the time, standard Reformed theology taught that God's purposes for Israel had been fulfilled in his creation of the Christian church for all times and places. Israel had indeed borne the promise of God uniquely for many centuries, but then the appearance of Christ broadened out those promises to all who turned to Christ in faith. As Samuel Hopkins had written in his own pamphlet on the subject of slavery in 1776: "This distinction [between Israel and other nations] is now at an end, and all nations are put on a level; and Christ, who has taken down the wall of separation, has taught us to look on all nations as our neighbours and brethren, without any respect of persons, and to love all men as ourselves, and to do to others as we would they should treat us; by which he most effectually abolished this permission given to the Jews."[21]

Stuart himself, in a commentary on the book of Romans that long represented the American ideal for close scriptural exegesis, concluded just about the same when he considered the Jews and Gentiles whom Paul treated in Romans 9 through 11. In the Christian dispensation, God regards all nationalities the same, "without any respect of persons" (on Romans 9:25); again, "the goodness of God is not limited to the Jewish nation, but equally proffered to all" (on Romans 10:12); and, in conclusion, "the apostle has shown once more . . . that the Gentiles stand on an equal footing with the Jews, as to gospel privileges, and that God may, in perfect consistency with his ancient promises and declarations, cast off the Jews, when they persist in unbelief, and receive believing Gentiles as his people in their stead" (on Romans

10:21).[22] By the light of Stuart's own Calvinism, therefore, the analogy between American states and Hebrew tribes was impossible.

The second imported premise was that the federal union (even with its shaky analogy to Old Testament Israel) created a higher organic bond than the bond constituted by the unity of all Christian believers in the church. Early in the development of British antislavery, some evangelicals had contended that converted slaves must be treated as full members of the Body of Christ, his church, and thus as full fellow members of Spiritual Israel. This Spiritual Israel, in turn, deserved a higher loyalty than the loyalty appropriate for any man-made entity, including the nation-state. Proslavery advocates had turned aside this argument, in part because leading early evangelicals like George Whitefield had denied that Christian conversion should affect the status of slaves.[23] But they had not succeeded in silencing those who felt that biblical teaching about oneness in Christ superseded the sanction Scripture offered to modern tribal nationalism.

Stuart, however, did not seem to feel that escaped slaves—considered as either Christians or potential Christians—had a higher claim on fellow believers than did Southern slaveholders considered as fellow American citizens. Rather, by overriding his commitment to standard Reformed theology, Stuart's strong sense of American national messianism constrained his interpretation of Scripture. Even for this rightly honored defender of strict biblical exegesis, race exerted a powerful sway. White fellow Americans counted for more than black fellow Christians. Analogical Israel meant more than Spiritual Israel. A dubious theological warrant (treating America as the chosen people) exerted more force than a strong theological warrant (including blacks in the fellowship of the church).

The bearing of racist thinking on biblical defenders of slavery who did not share Stuart's desire to promote voluntary emancipation was much stronger. Thornton Stringfellow, a Virginia Baptist who published several of the era's most influential treatises laying out the biblical sanction for slavery, offers an instructive example.[24] At least some of his books depended as much on his experience with African Americans as on his reading of Scripture. Thus, in a work titled *Slavery, Its Origin, Nature, and History Considered in the Light of Bible Teachings, Moral Justice, and Political Wisdom* (1861), Stringfellow moved unself-consciously between dictates of Scripture and conclusions from experience. While the Bible was the prime authority to defend the legitimacy of slavery, it was otherwise when Stringfellow showed why blacks, and blacks only, were the proper subjects of enslavement. Unlike white children, who eventually grew out of a state of dependency, or white convicts, who by their own actions put themselves into penal servitude, the members of "the African race" were suited to "domestic slavery for life," Stringfellow thought, "because they are not qualified to use political freedom, and because they receive the full due for this [slave] service and labor, and that in a form accommodated to the service they pay for it." Stringfellow was sure about this conclusion, but not because he found it in the Bible: "The African race is constitutionally inferior to the white race. Experience proves this in all the conditions and countries they have ever occupied."[25]

For other biblical defenders of slavery, like James Henley Thornwell, "common sense" supplied the premises that Thornton Stringfellow found in "experience." Thornwell, an exemplary Southern theologian, was also exemplary in the clarity of his prose. In 1861 when he was asked by the newly organized Southern Presbyterian church to address European Christians on reasons for secession, Thornwell began with a profession to reason by Scripture alone. That pledge deserves full quotation as one of his era's strongest statements of its type:

> As a Church, let it be distinctly borne in mind that the only rule of judgment is the written word of God. The Church knows nothing of the intuitions of reason or the deductions of philosophy, except those reproduced in the Sacred Canon. She has a positive Constitution in the Holy Scriptures, and has no right to utter a single syllable upon any subject, except as the Lord puts words in her mouth. She is founded, in other words, upon express *revelation.* Her creed is an authoritative testimony of God, and not a speculation; and what she proclaims, she must proclaim with the infallible certitude of faith, and not with the hesitating assent of an opinion.[26]

A few pages further on, however, when Thornwell took up treatment of African American slaves, biblical warrant faded into the background. As was then customary, he first simply took for granted that the only slaves would be Africans. Then he offered a series of conclusions based on anything but the explicit guidance of Scripture.

▶ Justification for enslaving blacks only rested on Thornwell's own judgment: "As long as that race, in its comparative degradation, co-exists side
by side with the whites, bondage is its *normal* condition."

▶ Thornwell's conclusion that, in the scale of races, African slaves were "at
the bottom of the line" and did not deserve what was "out of proportion
to [their] capacity and culture" rested on his assessment of the past. People
"are distributed into classes, according to their competency and progress.
For *God is in history.*"

▶ Finally, in defending Southern slavery, Thornwell said that he would need
"some eternal test" to justify the system. At this point, especially after the
profession of sole scriptural authority that began his argument, one would
expect to find a biblical text. But, no, it was rather to "*an inward necessity of
thought,* which in all minds at the proper stage of maturity, is absolutely
universal" that he appealed. And he concluded, "*Whatever is universal is natural.* We are willing that Slavery should be tried by this standard."[27]

Thornwell's letter was a breathtaking performance in an era filled with
such pyrotechnics. It was matched in its bold biblicism and self-contradict-
ing audacity only by Henry Ward Beecher's claim, made just a few months
earlier, that slavery had no chance to survive in those civilizations where the
Bible was read freely without prelate or priest.

WITH ONLY a few exceptions, during the antebellum era confusion beset
whites who turned to Scripture for guidance on slavery. The exceptions included bold, but ignored, figures like John G. Fee who insisted on taking the
Bible *very* seriously: if the United States were to sanction slavery on the basis
of Scripture, then let it be slavery without distinction of color as was the
slavery of biblical times. Fee's argument was logical. But because it appeared
amid the standard repertoire of abolitionist denunciations of bondage per se,
majority religious opinion dismissed it with the same nervousness that it
dismissed the claim that the Bible ruled out slavery without qualification.
Much more common was the not so logical argument that since the Bible allowed slavery, it provided sanction for American slavery. Had American Bible
believers faced squarely the illogic of this reasoning, especially where it confused slavery with black-only slavery, there is no telling what would have
happened. Too many interests, political entanglements, economic commit-

ments, and sectional tensions existed for any painless solution. The one certainty is that the use of Scripture would have become more complicated. If white Americans, North and South, could have recognized the disjunction between what the Bible taught about slavery and what experience together with common sense taught about race, they could not have been as convinced that they had discovered the mind of the Lord.

But, of course, whites were not the only ones looking to Scripture for a sure word.

African Americans, the Bible, and Slavery

By the time of the Civil War, there existed a substantial history of African American biblical commentary on slavery. Considering the circumstances, in which opportunities for both education and church leadership were limited, it was also a history rich in specific theological argument. The pervasive biblicism of black spirituals and black preaching provides solid evidence for how deeply Scripture had entered into African American consciousness.[28] The record is equally clear from written sources. For example, the *Christian Recorder*, a weekly paper of the African Methodist Episcopal Church that began publication in the mid-1850s, was as evangelically Scripture-saturated as any comparable periodical in the English-speaking world. Without exception, each issue showered readers with the Scriptures: Bible-based homilies, injunctions to piety from Scripture, reports on Bible distribution at home and abroad, and frequent articles directly supporting the supernatural character and divine authority of the sacred text. Among countless instances was the issue of April 13, 1861: on the same page the editors turned to "the Holy Word of God" to take the measure of "the present crisis" and defended Scripture as the "doctrinal basis of Christianity" by saying that "errors of faith always lead to errors of life . . . unbelief in the doctrines of the Bible will sooner or later lead to a rejection of Christianity."[29] In fact, so securely did the Bible become *the* book for black Americans that in the years before the Civil War there seems to have been a diminishing need to rehearse arguments from the Bible against slavery. As was true for much of white Protestant Christendom outside the United States, scriptural antislavery had simply become instinctive.

Yet if African Americans ever felt the need for arguments to match those of the learned exegetes who found sanction for slavery in the Bible, they were ready to hand.[30] Beginning in the early years of the century, black ministers and other careful Bible readers had responded critically and creatively to biblical interpretation moving the other way. A panoply of such arguments can be found scattered in several works that I draw on here, which were spread throughout the antebellum period:

- Daniel Coker's *Dialogue between a Virginian and an African Minister* (1810) advanced at least seven biblical arguments against slavery as it then existed in the United States. Coker was one of Richard Allen's first colleagues as a minister in the African Methodist Episcopal Church.[31]
- In an unusually full sermon from 1813, Lemuel Haynes, a Congregational minister in Vermont, set out a picture of human relationships, including slavery, that drew on the theological principles he had learned from the works of Jonathan Edwards.[32]
- In 1829 David Walker, a free black in Boston, published the era's most widely noticed attack on the slave system by an African American. His *Appeal . . . to the Coloured Citizens of the World* was unusual for both its militancy and its explicit Christian argumentation. The work's most striking feature was Walker's prediction, based on scriptural precept, that the United States would soon be destroyed because of its sins as a slaveholding nation.[33]
- Only a few years after the appearance of Walker's tract, Daniel Ruggles of New York City used Scripture as the foundation for a scathing indictment of the sexual license that accompanied American slavery.[34]
- Better known was the work of Frederick Douglass, who in his newspapers regularly published biblical articles from others and who himself in March 1861 drew on the Bible when he attacked "the pro-slavery mob and the pro-slavery ministry."[35]
- At about the same time, the *Christian Recorder* was running a long series titled "Chapters on Ethnology," in which reflection on biblical accounts of early humanity was prominent.[36]

With even this limited range of sermons, tracts, dialogues, and periodical articles, the diversity of biblical argumentation was striking.

As might be expected, the abolitionist claim that the "spirit" or general principles of the Bible condemned slavery was prominent in works by African Americans. Daniel Coker, for example, emphasized "the unreasonableness of perpetual unconditional slavery" in light of "the righteous and benevolent doctrines and duties, taught in the New Testament." To Coker, passages like Matthew 7:12 ("Whatsoever ye would that men should do to you, do ye even so to them; for this is the law and the prophets") pointed to only one conclusion: "It is very evident, that slavery is contrary to the spirit and nature of the Christian religion."[37] Frederick Douglass was characteristically more impassioned, but less precise, when he made roughly the same point in 1861: "It would be insulting to Common Sense, an outrage upon all right feeling, for us, who have worn the heavy chain and felt the biting lash to consent to argue with Ecclesiastical Sneaks who are thus prostituting their Religion and Bible to the base uses of popular and profitable iniquity. They don't need light, but the sting of honest rebuke. They are of their father the Devil, and his works they do, not because they are ignorant, but because they are base."[38] To African Americans it seemed clearer than to all others that slavery contradicted the Scriptures in general.

Arguments from broad biblical principle were not, however, as frequent as interpretations pointed specifically to concrete features of the American slavery system. Thus much of this black writing simply bypassed the general question of the legitimacy of slavery as such in order to focus on anti-Christian aspects of the system in practice. This was the entire burden of Daniel Ruggles's pamphlet on the immoralities occasioned by American slavery. Ruggles took Psalm 50:18 as his text: "When thou sawest a thief, then thou consentedst with him, and hast been partaker with adulterers." His indictment was based on "four of the principal facts connected with the condition of female slaves": the rise in the number of mulattoes who "incontestably demonstrate the wide spread and incessant licentiousness of the white population"; the inability of black women to resist the advances of white males since "there is no law to preserve them, and no protecting authority to which they can appeal"; the manifest temptation from "pecuniary advantage" to slave owners who tried to breed as many slaves as possible; and the fact that in American slavery "the matrimonial connection among the slaves is altogether nullified."[39] In light of these conditions, Ruggles urged Christian believers to recognize the existence of a spiritual crisis and to meet that crisis with "evangelical weapons."[40] One such weapon proposed by Ruggles was for "female members of our Northern Christian churches" to rise up and "slay this hydra-headed monster of corruption and wo [sic]." Ruggles appealed particularly for them to denounce "slaveholding" as such, but his reasoning homed in on practices associated with the American system. Women church members should especially demand that "perpetual and impenitent transgressors of the seventh [adultery] and eighth [stealing] commandments" be ejected from the churches.[41] By describing slavery as it actually existed, Ruggles felt he could exploit explicit biblical commands against adultery and stealing to demand an end to the system.

Other black authors rang the changes on a full catalog of practices prohibited by Scripture that they saw as intrinsic to American slavery. Daniel Coker, for example, complained that slaves were regularly "deprived of instruction in the doctrines, and duties of religion."[42] David Walker was even more aggressive. In his view, Roman slavery "was, comparatively speaking, no more than a *cypher*, when compared with ours under the Americans." Walker cited many aspects of American slavery that he contended the Scriptures condemned. Especially galling to him was the treatment of slave children, which he felt involved constant violation of Jesus' command from Matthew 18:6: "Whoso shall offend one of these little ones which believe in me, it were better for him that a millstone were hanged about his neck, and that he were drowned in the depth of the sea." Walker had only scorn for disregard of such passages: "Now the avaricious Americans think that the Lord Jesus Christ will let them off, because his words are no more than the words of a man!!!" Such rhetoric struck fear into some white hearts, in part because of its vehemence, but also because of how effectively Walker evoked the Scriptures: "Will not those who were burnt up in Sodom and Gomorrah rise up in judgment against Christian Americans with the Bible in their hands and condemn them?"[43]

As might be expected, black opponents of slavery did not limit themselves to biblical arguments; they ranged widely in making their case. As white antislavery advocates had been doing since the Revolution, black abolitionists cited inconsistencies between the United States' stated republican ideals and the practice of slavery. In 1813 Lemuel Haynes praised George Washington for recognizing that religious virtue was required for a republic to flourish. He then pointed to slavery as illustrating how Washington's dedication to both religion and republicanism was not being honored by the Virginians who came after him. In referring to Washington's last will and testament, Haynes proclaimed, "He was an enemy to slaveholding, and gave his dying testimony against it, by emancipating, and providing for those under his care. O that his jealous surviving neighbors would prove themselves to be his legitimate children, and go and do likewise!"[44] Fifteen years later, David Walker made a similar point dramatically: "Can there be a greater absurdity in nature [than slavery], and particularly in a free republican country! . . . Americans! I ask you candidly, was your suffering under Great Britain, one hundredth part as evil and tyrannical as you have rendered ours under you?"[45]

Other pragmatic arguments were more religious, as in the repeated refrain about the damage done by slavery to American missionary efforts. Daniel Coker recounted the story of a band of Native Americans who, upon being approached by American missionaries, took counsel together before concluding: "The white people made slaves of the black people, and if they had it in their power, they would make slaves of the Indians; they therefore wanted no such religion."[46] Such reasoning was a staple.[47]

Although they skillfully presented other arguments, black Christians returned consistently to reasoning from Scripture. The grounding of American slavery in race prejudice was, not surprisingly, a regular theme. David Walker and Frederick Douglass underscored this point vehemently, while the *Christian Recorder* made it with subtlety. Walker appealed to the "Great Commission" from Matthew 28:18-20, where the resurrected Christ sends out his followers to "teach all nations . . . to observe all things whatsoever I have commanded you." Walker berated his white readers with a challenge: "You have the Bible in your hands with this very injunction – Have you been to Africa, teaching the inhabitants thereof the words of the Lord Jesus?" No, it was just the reverse. Americans "entered among us, and learnt us the art of throat-cutting, by setting us to fight, one against another, to take each other as prisoners of war, and sell to you for small bits of calicoes, old swords, knives, etc. to make slaves for you and your children." To Walker, such behavior was a direct contradiction of Scripture: "Can the American preachers appeal unto God, the Maker and Searcher of hearts, and tell him, with the Bible in their hands, that they made no distinction on account of men's colour?"[48]

Frederick Douglass said about the same when in early 1861 he spotlighted race as the keystone of American slavery: "Nobody at the North, we think, would defend Slavery, even from the Bible, but for this color distinction. . . . Color makes all the difference in the application of our American Christianity. . . . The same book which is full of the Gospel of Liberty to one race, is crowded with arguments in justification of the slavery of another. Those who shout and rejoice over the progress of Liberty in Italy, would mob down, pray and preach down Liberty at home as an unholy and hateful thing."[49]

In contrast to Walker and Douglass, the anonymous scholar who in 1861 contributed the "Chapters on Ethnology" to the *Christian Recorder* developed his subject with patient care. Yet his conclusion was the same: distinctions among the races of the sort that allowed for American slavery had no basis in reliable history or proper biblical authority. Against the rising scholarly notion that humankind had descended from many sources, the *Christian Recorder* responded that "the Jewish and Christian Scriptures . . . plainly teach, that mankind, of whatever race, family, or tribe, have descended from a single pair of progenitors." Details about early humans were not taught in the New Testament, except that nothing could be "more pointed and striking than the language of the Apostle Paul to the Athenians at Mars Hill, when he said: 'God hath made of one blood all nations of men for to dwell on all the face of the earth, and hath determined the times before appointed, and the bounds of their habitation' " (Acts 17:26).[50]

In the arsenal of African American biblical antislavery were also several instances of sophisticated interpretive reasoning. Daniel Coker offered one of the earliest and most theologically profound. His text was Genesis 17:13, where Abraham is commanded to circumcise his slaves ("He that is born in thy house, and he that is bought with thy money").[51] Proslavery Bible readers often used this text to argue that since God regulated slaveholding by Abraham, the father of all believers, slaveholding was legitimate for other believers in other times and places. Coker, however, went further by expanding on the second part of the same verse: "and my covenant [says God] shall be in your flesh for an everlasting covenant." He pointed out that "this law of circumcision" was a central part of biblical religion and that circumcision was "a token of that covenant, by which . . . the land of Canaan, and various privileges in it, were promised to Abraham and to his seed, and to all that were included in the covenant." To Coker, this last provision was critical. God's covenant promises were meant for "all . . . to whom circumcision (which was the token of the covenant) was administered." This inclusion extended to the one who "was bought with money." Therefore, all the benefits of God's covenant promises were extended to slaves whom Abraham purchased and whom he then, on God's command, circumcised. But once they were circumcised, "these persons bought with money, were no longer looked upon as uncircumcised and useless; as aliens and strangers; but were incorporated with the church and nation of the Israelites, and became one people with them." Consequently, once purchased slaves had been circumcised, they were part of Israel. And so the children of such circumcised slaves "were the servants of the Lord, in the same sense as the natural descendents of Abraham were" – which meant that, as naturalized Israelites, these children of circumcised slaves could not be sold as slaves themselves (Coker quoted Leviticus 25:42 and 54, with the prohibitions against Jews' enslaving other Jews). To Coker, the conclusion was inescapable: "The passage of scripture under consideration was so far from authorizing the Israelites to make slaves of their servants [sic] children, that they evidently forbid it; and therefore, are so far from proving the lawfulness of your enslaving the children of the Africans, that they clearly condemn the practice as criminal."

Coker's argument required concentration to follow since he was enlisting passages from several parts of the Pentateuch and then linking them into a single chain of reasoning. Yet it was a theologically powerful argument. In particular, he was taking seriously the principles of theological inclusion that would later prove so difficult for Moses Stuart. For Coker, once an Old Testament slave had been circumcised, enslavement of that circumcised slave's children was impossible, because circumcision represented God's incorporation of the slave into Israel. By implication, when in the modern era Africans were enslaved and, in consequence of that enslavement, brought under the preaching of the Christian gospel, their situation became analogous to the slaves of the Old Testament. As "spiritual Israel," Christianity bestowed on those grafted in as converts all the privileges that it offered to those who were raised in Christian homes.

Coker's voice is so clear in its reasoning that it is worth hearing him further when, at the end of his discussion of Genesis 17, he summarizes what was different about Old Testament history: "The Israelites were not sent by a divine mandate, to nations three hundred miles distant, who were neither doing, nor meditating any thing against them, and to whom they had no right whatever, in order to captivate them by fraud or force; tare [sic] them away from their native country, and all their tender connections; bind them in chains and fetters; croud [sic] into ships, and there murder them by thousands, for want of air and proper exercise; and then doom the survivors and their posterity to bondage and misery forever."[52]

Only shortly after Coker, the African Methodist Episcopal itinerant from Virginia, published his dialogue against slavery, Lemuel Haynes, the regular Congregationalist minister from Vermont, preached a doctrinally rich sermon, "Dissimulation Illustrated," at a commemoration of George Washington's birthday on February 22, 1813. Haynes's text, Romans 12:9 ("Let love be without dissimulation"), gave him full scope to criticize the dissimulation, or deceitful hypocrisy, that he saw in both President Madison's conduct of the War of 1812 and the American support for slavery. Near the start, he paused to lay a theological foundation, which he took from Jonathan Edwards's theory of true virtue.[53] To Edwards, virtue had meant treating any object in accord with its quality of being. Since God was ultimate Being, God deserved to be approached with ultimate love. And since humans were made in God's image, they deserved to be approached with proportionate love. Without this "regard" for "beings according to their magnitude and importance," as Haynes put it, the result would be only "pretences of love to mankind, and to our country." The spiritual truth Haynes wanted to teach was that if people attempted to love their fellow humans (lesser beings) without honoring God first (highest Being), "it [would be] highly preposterous."[54]

The reverse relationship allowed Haynes to make political points related to the War of 1812. He asked his listeners to judge whether "the warm zeal, party spirit, war and blood-shed" that then prevailed in the United States reflected the sort of benevolence to lesser beings that true love to God as highest Being required. Haynes obviously felt that President Madison's dragooning of New England into war with Britain failed this test of benevolence: "Benevolent affection will dispose men to make a proper estimate, or set a suitable value on things; men's lives are not to be trifled with, or vainly thrown away." Haynes, quoting the Apostle Paul's description of rulers in Romans 13, urged proper regard for proper government. But "unbounded" power was something else – it revived "the old tory spirit that was among us in our old revolutionary war."[55]

Almost as if in passing, Haynes then turned his combination of Edwardsean theology, republican ideology, and dissatisfaction with Madison into an assault on slavery. First, he expressed his sympathy for impressed sailors whose liberty was forfeited and who (in republican parlance) were languishing "in slavery" to the British. But then Haynes twisted the dagger: "Our president . . . can talk feelingly on the subject of impressment of our seamen. I am glad to have him feel for them. Yet in his own state, Virginia, there were, in the year 1800, no less than three hundred forty-three thousand, seven hundred ninety-six human beings holden in bondage for life!" His conclusion tied antislavery back to the theme of his sermon: "Partial affection, or distress for some of our fellow-creatures, while others, even under our notice, are wholly disregarded, betrays dissimulation."[56] From his objections to Madison's war effort and as guided by the theology of Jonathan Edwards, Haynes fashioned a sophisticated theological weapon against the continuation of slavery in the United States.

AFRICAN AMERICAN theology never exerted broad influence in antebellum society, but it did include several lines of rigorous antislavery biblical interpretation. As with theological efforts that enjoyed broader influence, the ability to act on messages purportedly from the Bible depended on the circumstances in which those messages were received as well as on the messages themselves. For African Americans, circumstances were as unpropitious as at least some of their arguments were strong.

The Shape of a Crisis

Despite what African American readers of the Bible concluded, the belief that the Scriptures sanctioned slavery in its black-only American form held sway among many white Northerners into the early months of the war — and among many white Southerners long thereafter. Several reasons, which were deeply rooted in broad American circumstances, made proslavery biblical interpretations seem more persuasive than antislavery readings. The first was abolitionist overstatement. When abolitionists maintained that the Bible condemned slavery per se, they contradicted conclusions that the vast majority of white Americans drew from Scripture by using the same interpretive principles almost everyone had employed in drawing on the Bible for evangelizing the nation and constructing American civilization.

As a consequence, abolitionist efforts left the impression in many minds that to employ Scripture for opposing slavery had to undercut the authority of Scripture itself. In particular, arguments that contrasted the principles or the "spirit" of the Bible with the clear message of individual texts (its "letter") were gravely suspect in a culture of democratic common sense that urged people to read and decide for themselves.

Capable arguments, which drew on interpretive methods endorsed by a vast majority of Americans (of all colors, regions, and religions), also demonstrated that the Bible allowed – and perhaps even sanctioned – slavery as an economic system.

Nonetheless, polemicists against slavery did succeed in gaining substantial agreement, even in large parts of the South, that the American slave system was beset with sinful practices (or, to slavery defenders, "abuses"), such as the breakup of families, sexual predations, the withholding of education, and what the Bible called "mansteading" (whether by original slave traders or later slave sellers). Antislavery polemicists did not succeed, however, in convincing many Caucasian Americans that sinful practices, or abuses, deligitimated the institution itself. The weight tipping the scales against that conclusion was whites' inability to regard African Americans as fully human, whether defined by classical Christian theologies or defined by American republican ideology.

It was the same with arguments pointing out that slavery in the Bible was colorblind. Proslavery forces never mounted even the beginnings of a successful counterargument against this conclusion. No matter. So seriously fixed in the minds of white Americans, including most abolitionists, was the certainty of black racial inferiority that it overwhelmed biblical testimony about race, even though most Protestant Americans claimed that Scripture was in fact their supreme authority in adjudicating such matters.

Finally, testimony from African American Bible readers, which was surprisingly rich under the circumstances, was never taken seriously. With the same skill as their white confreres, but with even more passion, African Americans deployed biblical arguments against slavery. Lemuel Haynes and Daniel Coker demonstrated that African American biblical reasoning could match in theological acumen the most profound arguments that any white put forward in that period. Yet since most of white America simply could not accept persuasion from a black source, this African American testimony had little impact.

In order for American Bible believers as a whole to have acted on distinctions between slavery as such and slavery as practiced in the United States, or between colorblind biblical slavery and black-only American slavery, a revolution in the nation's racial attitudes would have been necessary, and that revolution would have demanded a greater alteration in accepted convictions than the American War of Independence itself. Even the Civil War that preserved the Union, that broadened out to the Emancipation Proclamation, and that led to the Thirteenth, Fourteenth, and Fifteenth Amendments did not persuade most Caucasian Americans that African Americans were on their level of humanity. To have carried the country in 1860, the argument that a racially discriminatory slavery was a different thing from slavery per se would have required the kind of commitment to racial antiprejudice that the nation only accepted, after immense struggle, late in the twentieth century – if in fact it has accepted it even now. Advocates of emancipationist biblical arguments who in 1860 still wanted to keep blacks out of the territories and still expected colonization to solve the United States's race problem – not to speak of those who felt that the whole of the Bible sanctioned the whole of the American slave system – were not prepared to let a bare reading of the Bible overcome centuries of inherited race prejudice.

In sum, the theological crisis involving the Bible and slavery had several components:

- ‣ a failure to examine biblically the Southern charge that individualistic consumer capitalism was an ethically dangerous economic system;
- ‣ a blow to Christian orthodoxy caused by the abolitionist flight to the "spirit" of Scripture;
- ‣ an inability to act on biblical teaching about the full humanity of all people, regardless of race; and
- ‣ a confusion about principles of interpretation between what was in the Bible and what was in the common sense of the culture.

Even more than the obvious fact of incompatible interpretations of a commonly honored Bible, this set of difficulties constituted the theological crisis of the Civil War.

Chapter 5

The Crisis over Providence

Standard Christian teaching about God's control of the world and all events taking place in the world sprang vigorously to life as the dramatic events of the war unfurled. Belief that God controlled events had always been foundational wherever biblical religion prevailed. Yet in nineteenth-century America confidence in the human ability to fathom God's providential actions rose to new heights. When the prevalence of religious conviction was added to widespread self-confidence in the powers of human perception, assessment, and interpretation, the result was a flourishing of providential reasoning. Americans thought they could see clearly what the world was like, what God was like, what factors drove the world, who was responsible for events, and how the moral balance sheet should be read. They were children of the Enlightenment as well as children of God.

In such a situation, clarity about the workings of divine providence posed a particular problem because God appeared to be acting so strikingly at odds with himself. As with clashes over the interpretation of Scripture, the conflict in understanding providence was disconcerting by itself. Even more, the assumptions on which the interpretation of providence was based seemed to be flawed, thus pointing to a profound theological crisis.

The Workings of Providence

Immediately as war approached, theologians turned instinctively to God as the one who would decide the outcome. In January 1861 James Henley Thornwell of South Carolina carefully laid out the constitutional case for secession in order to demonstrate that if armed struggle arose, it would be because of the North's wrongdoing, not the South's. His concluding word, however, was providential: "We prefer peace – but if war must come, we are prepared to meet it with unshaken confidence in the God of battles."[1]

At the end of the war, the same confidence remained. But when Horace Bushnell expressed it at the Yale College commencement in July 1865, he dramatically reversed Thornwell's assurance about who and what it was that God was fighting for:

> In these rivers of blood we have now bathed our institutions, and they are henceforth to be hallowed in our sight. Government is now become Providential, – no more a mere creature of our human will, but a grandly moral affair. . . . We have not fought this dreadful war to a close, just to put our government upon a par with these oppressive dynasties [of old Europe]! We . . . owe it even to them to say, that a government which is friendly, and free, and right, protecting all alike, and doing the most for all, is one of God's sacred finalities, which no hand may touch, or conspiracy assail, without committing the most damning crime, such as can be matched by no possible severities of justice.[2]

In the North euphoria at the end of the war was everywhere expressed in similarly ardent providentialist language. John Williamson Nevin, the noted German Reformed theologian from Mercersburg, Pennsylvania, provided a typical performance with his Fourth of July address at Franklin and Marshall College in 1865. To Nevin the path of events could lead to only one conclusion: "The war, reaching out to the world-astounding issue in which it has now come to its close, stands revealed to our faith emphatically as God's work, just because it has been to so small an extent the result of any commensurate wisdom, or calculation, or plan on the part of men; and just because so large an amount of human corruption and error, to say nothing of Satanic wickedness, has entered into it all along, as to make it truly wonderful that the better powers still involved in it should ever have been able to triumph as they have done in the end." To Nevin, the North's lack of preparation for war, the many advantages enjoyed by Southerners fighting on their own terrain, the inexperience of Abraham Lincoln, and many other factors pointed toward Northern defeat. These were the very circumstances that now prepared his mind for "the great thought, namely, that our national deliverance has been wrought out for us, as a world-historical act, by God himself. . . . God has done great things for us, whereof we are glad; and this, itself, is our best reason for believing that he will do for us, still greater things hereafter. He will not forsake the work of his own hands."[3]

For more than a decade Nevin had been teamed with the Swiss expatriate Philip Schaff at the tiny German Reformed seminary in Mercersburg. During the summer of 1865, Schaff had returned to Europe, where before audiences in Germany and Switzerland he presented a view very similar to Nevin's. The recent history of the United States, with the great effusions of blood and the tremendous sacrifices demanded on all sides, was of a place "where the hand of God has visibly and wondrously led events to a happy end."[4] At the Yale commencement that summer, Bushnell used the same pattern of reasoning to foresee a great future for the United States: "The unity now to be developed, after this war-deluge is over, . . . will be no more thought of as a mere human compact, or composition, always to be debated by the letter, but it will be that bond of common life which God has touched with blood; a sacredly heroic, Providentially tragic unity, where God's cherubim stand guard over grudges and hates and remembered jealousies, and the sense of nationality becomes even a kind of religion."[5]

Of course, the hand of God did not look the same to an unrepentant Southerner. John Adger, editor of the *Southern Presbyterian Review* and, after the death of Thornwell, one of the main figures to whom Southern Christians looked for theological guidance, was also writing immediately after the war about the manifold course of God's providence. Adger went to great lengths to insist on "the justice of the Southern cause," but he also conceded that "there was one error . . . into which we acknowledge that some Southern ministers sometimes fell." The mistake was to believe "that God must surely bless the right." But what Southerners had forgotten was the lesson of history that God often let "the righteous . . . be overthrown." Despite the fact that the North was guilty of "a cruel, unjust, and wicked war of invasion upon free States . . . urged on, in great part, by an infidel fanaticism," and despite the fact that godly ministers "prayed fervently for the Success of the Confederacy," it still remained the case that "the result was with God alone." Because of this error, so Adger acknowledged, the faith of many in the South was shaken. But to Adger the explanation was clear: "We accept the failure of secession, as manifestly providential. The overthrow of that just cause made evident not so much the prowess of its foes, nor even their prodigiously superior resources, as it did the direct hand of the Almighty." And so to Adger the only possible conclusion was that God was chastening his people for their good. "Yes! the hand of God, gracious though heavy, is upon the South for her discipline."[6]

The idea that God used the destruction of war to discipline or chasten his people revived one of the standard themes of the Puritan jeremiad, which was often evoked in these years, but usually with less directly partisan purposes than in Adger's account. The Northern Episcopal church provided a notable instance of such jeremiad reasoning in the pastoral letter that its presiding bishop, Charles Pettit McIlvaine, sent out in the fall of 1862. McIlvaine began by quoting the Psalms to indicate how "unsearchable" were God's ways, but then he expounded at some length on how he understood them to be operating. The letter did address what McIlvaine called "*the agency of men*" in starting the war, by which he meant primarily the South's illegal rebellion. But mostly it explained why the Northern Episcopalians should understand that the war "*comes from the Providence of God.*" In particular, it was "His visitation and chastening for the sins of this nation." Those sins were primarily personal not political: profaneness, neglect of public worship, ungodliness, and, especially, rejection of Christ. In that desperate hour, McIlvaine's solution was spiritual. If repentance occurred—along with prayer, cultivation of holiness, and active support for the local parish—divine blessing would follow: "Search and try yourselves that you may duly humble yourselves under God's mighty hand, and He may, in due time, exalt us out of the present distress."[7]

The assumptions behind McIlvaine's reasoning stood behind many other pronouncements during the war. For instance, Daniel Alexander Payne told his African Methodist Episcopal congregation in Washington that even non-combatants could decisively influence the war's outcome by wielding "a power in behalf of the Government which neither rifled cannon, nor mortar, nor rocket-battery can assail, nor bomb-proof walls resist. *That power is the right arm of God*—of God, who lifts up and casts down nations according as they obey, or disregard the principles of truth, justice, liberty."[8] A circular letter from the Philadelphia Baptist Association expressed a similar, though even more strictly spiritual, confidence in God's ability to bring good out of the war's evil. The letter's author was uncertain about short-term prospects for the Kingdom of God, but not about what would happen ultimately: "We are sure that the cause of our Redeemer will in the end be advanced by these upheavings."[9]

As natural as it was for Christian believers to speak of providential rule over spiritual concerns, it was almost as instinctive for Americans in this era to see the divine rule over terrestrial matters as well. God was thought to be especially concerned about the fate of republican government. In March 1865, as desperate Southern leaders labored to sustain their fight, the editor of the *Army and Navy Messenger* from Shreveport, Louisiana, exhorted the troops with a view of divine power that was as distinctly republican as it was distinctly Christian: "The character of the war is, with us, essentially and necessarily religion. . . . In its simplest form, the war with us [is] for freedom of conscience – freedom to interpret the Bible and worship God according to the dictates of our own consciences."[10]

A similar ideology of republican providence spoke to very different ends in the North. On Sunday, April 23, just over a week after Abraham Lincoln's death, Henry Ward Beecher preached one of that day's most memorable memorial sermons. Not surprisingly, Beecher's understanding was quite different from the Shreveport editor's: "Republican institutions have been vindicated in this experience as they never were before; and the whole history of the last four years, rounded up by this cruel stroke, seems now in the providence of God to have been clothed with an illustration, with a sympathy, with an aptness, and with a significance, such as we never could have expected or imagined. God, I think, has said, by the voice of this event to all nations of the earth, 'Republican liberty, based upon true Christianity, is firm as the foundation of the globe.'"[11]

Secure, unequivocal readings of providence extended very broadly in those years. To indicate how broadly, it is instructive to look at the margins of American religious conviction. The *Christian Examiner*, a Unitarian journal from Boston, had long been accustomed to speak of God in immanent terms, as dwelling within human history, and it was equally well practiced at scorning the crude supernaturalism of the numerous evangelical sects and their unseemly lust for doctrinal orthodoxy. Yet the war worked atavistically on the Brahmin Unitarians who ran the *Examiner*. In May 1865 they affirmed that in the early days of Abraham Lincoln's presidency "it seemed almost as if a special miracle had been wrought to keep [him] from the hands of murderers";

they spoke of secession and states' rights as "that heresy"; and they ascribed the end of slavery ("one of the great social revolutions of all history") to the direct "appointment of Providence."[12]

A more famous outlier made even firmer references to providence at just about the same time. Ralph Waldo Emerson had been asked to provide the annual lecture in Concord, Massachusetts, to mark April 19 and the start of the American Revolution, when the assassination of the president offered him topical instead of historical material for his address. Emerson's deity was by no stretch of the imagination the traditional Christian God, but that deity was nonetheless the one who had given the United States a leader like Lincoln in its hour of need:

> There is a serene Providence which rules the fate of nations, which makes little account of time, little of one generation or race, makes no account of disasters, conquers alike by what is called defeat or by what is called victory, thrusts aside enemy and obstruction, crushes everything immoral as inhuman, and obtains the ultimate triumph of the best race by the sacrifice of everything which resists the moral laws of the world. It makes its own instruments, creates the man for the time, trains him in poverty, inspires his genius, and arms him for his task.[13]

Just as certain about the ways of God, but with an entirely different religious compass, was George Q. Cannon, a member of the Church of Jesus Christ of Latter-day Saints. Writing in early 1863, Cannon felt that the only thing that could account for the great destruction of the war was "that God has withdrawn his Spirit from [the Americans'] midst and turned their wisdom into folly, leaving them to the uncontrolled devices of their own hearts." Thus far, Cannon said no more than many others. But Cannon's explanation for why God had removed his Spirit was singular. In 1846, shortly before being killed by a mob in Alton, Illinois, Joseph Smith had stood for president of the United States. During his campaign, Smith had outlined how he would end slavery through compensated emancipation, drastically cut back the officers and budget of the national government, and in general bring peace and prosperity to the country. To Cannon, Smith's candidacy had been God's provision so "that the people might have the opportunity of accepting a servant of God, if they wished, to stand at the head of the nation, who possessed a sufficient knowledge of the Lord and his purposes to steer the ship of state out of the troubled sea in which she was then sailing, to a haven of peace." Instead of accepting this divine gift, however, the people did with Joseph Smith what Jesus predicted would always happen to his prophets. They rejected and then killed him. The result was that the people of the United States were left "without excuse." Now in the Civil War they were reaping what they had sown: "The Lord is proving to the inhabitants of the earth that he is God and that he cannot be trifled with. If they reject him and his messages of mercy, and are determined to take their own course, they must endure the awful consequences. . . . Dearly indeed have the enemies of the truth in the United States purchased their imaginary triumph over the Prophet Joseph and those associated him." In murdering Smith, "they did as Satan always prompts the rebellious children of earth to do – maltreat and kill those who would save them."[14]

So it was that a similar picture emerged from both the religious margins and the religious mainstream. American believers, with the sureties of their religion backed by the sureties of the Enlightenment, offered direct, simple answers to explain the war. Moreover, what was clearly seen could also be controlled; knowing what God was doing imparted confidence that Americans could align themselves with the course of events. They also felt that the war reconfirmed their singular destiny as a divinely chosen people. With these convictions, the chorus, though singing different notes, sang them all in the same way.

Slavery in Providential View

Like so many other dimensions of the war, the understanding of providence had slavery at its crux. As we saw in chapter 4, providence was the central motif in James Henley Thornwell's account, written in the opening months of the war, of why the slave system did not violate Christian principles of human rights. "Other men – . . . Englishmen . . . Frenchmen . . . his master, for example," are akin to the slave, he said, in one respect; God has "qualified him [the slave] to meet the responsibilities" that he has been assigned: the slave has been placed at a level fitted to his capacities. Thornwell was confident of this reasoning because he was confident in God: "The truth is, the education of the human race for liberty and virtue, is a vast providential scheme, and God assigns to every man, by a wise and holy decree, the precise place he is to occupy in the great moral school of humanity. The scholars are distributed into classes, according to their competency and progress. For God is in history."[15]

Opponents of slavery were just as convinced that "God is in history." Especially after the war they were not afraid to spell out how that divine superintendence had done its work. In the view of the Reverend G. I. Wood from Guilford, Connecticut, God had acted unilaterally to end the evil:

> Our position, just prior to the outbreak of the rebellion, was one of unexampled embarrassment. The Republic was nearly undermined and overthrown by the insidious influence of a social institution, in its very nature antagonistic to the distinctive principles of a free government. We were divided, enervated, corrupted, controlled, and distracted by slavery. . . . How was the nation to be exorcised of this evil spirit? What human wisdom could devise a way for the solution of this complicated problem? . . . Slavery had a kind of charmed existence. The nation could not touch it – the States would not. God only could, and He did.[16]

A very similar opinion, but this time backed by a full discussion of the Christian doctrine of providence, came from Charles Hodge of Princeton Theological Seminary as part of a major tribute to Abraham Lincoln that he published in the July 1865 number of the *Princeton Review*. As Hodge explained it, "the scriptural doctrine of Providence" contained four elements:

- First, the existence of the external world. Hodge was not a philosophical idealist in the style of Bishop Berkeley or Jonathan Edwards.
- Second, "the efficiency of secondary causes." Hodge believed that humans and also "material substances" had "properties or forces inhering in them" that allowed them to cause actions in the world.
- Third, the action of "proximate . . . causes" in all events, except miracles. Hodge was affirming that it was appropriate for Christians to describe all ordinary events as themselves resulting from an ordinary sequence of cause and effect.
- Fourth, over and surrounding all events, an omnipresent and active divine presence. "God, as an infinite and omnipresent spirit, is not a mere spectator of the world, looking on as a machinist upon the machine which he has constructed; nor is he the only efficient cause, so that all effects are to

be referred to his agency, and so that the laws of nature are only the uniform methods of his operation; but he is everywhere present, upholding all things by the word of his power, and controlling, guiding, and directing the action of second cause, so that all events occur according to the counsel of his will."

In Hodge's view, it was necessary to affirm both that humans acted with genuine freedom and that, under God, "nothing happens by necessity or by chance." In his summary, Hodge maintained that God "governs free agents with certainty, but without destroying their liberty, and material causes, without superseding their efficiency."[17]

Hodge was offering a sophisticated perspective that updated for the wrenching contingencies of 1865 the subtle providential theology found in the Presbyterians' Westminster Confession of Faith from the seventeenth century.[18] Yet, as Hodge expounded on current events, he was not able to escape the American longing for beneficent certainty. It was thus as clear to Hodge as it was to his theological confreres what God had done and why he had done it. The South's desire to perpetuate "a system so fraught with evil" in the end provoked "the Divine displeasure." The result of that provocation was the "universal overthrow of slavery within the limits of the United States. This is one of the most momentous events in the history of the world." And what brought it about? "That it was the design of God to bring about this event cannot be doubted." Hodge affirmed that despite foreign and domestic predictions of the Confederacy's success and the continuation of slavery, "God . . . ordered it otherwise." It was, therefore, the responsibility of faithful Christians to accept "the inevitable difficulties and sufferings consequent on such an abrupt change" since they resulted from "the design of God in these events."[19]

Hodge's reasoning recapitulated a common pattern. If natural causes (that is, God's mediated control over events) seemed to point in one direction and yet something different happened, commentators leapt to the conclusion that God's unmediated actions must be the explanation, rather than a previously overlooked set of mediated causes. Or, as the Kentucky Baptist J. M. Pendleton put it, since emancipation took place despite what President Lincoln had first desired, despite the general will of the nation, and despite the balance of American political power – "this being the case, it is evident that the overthrow of slavery was not man's work. There was a God in heaven, presiding over all, and causing 'the wrath of man to praise Him,' accomplishing His purpose by thwarting the designs of men, and even using them as instruments in His hands. The overthrow of American slavery was an epoch in the world's history, and it is the providence of God that creates epochs."[20]

Providence for the Nonelite

It would require a much fuller discussion than can be offered here to demonstrate that the reasoning of intellectual elites was shared broadly among the people at large. But ordinary folk also found it easy to reduce the complexities of the war to simple, if sharply contrasting, providential calculations. James Lynch, a minister and editor in the African Methodist Episcopal Church, saw clearly that "the hand of Providence was in the election of Mr. Lincoln to the Presidency" and then, four years later, that "Divine Providence" had ensured that "the deliverance of the slave from bondage [was] the *sine qua non* of the deliverance of the nation from the consuming fires of rebellion."[21] Mattie White Read, whose husband served with Stonewall Jackson, affirmed forthrightly in June 1862, "I believe that God leads Jackson and Jackson his men, just where it is best they should go." Her only worry was "that people are in danger of worshiping Gen. Jackson instead of God, who rules over all. If we idolize him, he will be taken from us."[22] Lydia Maria Child, a widely read New England author who moved in very different circles from Mattie Read White, nonetheless took comfort at the war's development because of the same kind of confidence. In the North's dark days of December 1862, she asserted that "human hands blunder shockingly; but the Divine Hand is overruling all in infinite wisdom." Her response was the same when she heard the fateful news of mid-April 1865:

> The assassination of our good President, shocked and distressed me. Yet I have been so deeply impressed by the wonderful guidance of Providence during this war, that five minutes after I heard the sad news, I said, "Dreadful as this is perhaps it is only another of the wonderful manifestations of Providence. The kind-hearted Abraham, was certainly in danger of making too easy terms with the rebels. Perhaps he has been removed, that he might not defeat his own work, and that

another, better calculated to carry it to a safe and *sure end*, might come into his place."[23]

William Taylor, a Unionist from East Tennessee, worked from the same cast of mind when in 1867 he resigned from his Primitive Baptist Church in Enon because of the church's persecution of him during the war. His brief against his former congregation was its failure to see the hand of God: "I will now give it to you as my honest opinion that when rebellion took place against the government of the United States, that the great god of the world was not pleased with it. If he had[,] his arm was sufficient to have carried them [Confederates] through, as he did Moses through the [Red] sea."[24] At just about the same time that William Taylor penned these words, Fanny Dowling wrote a poem, "The Land We Love," that became very popular among the very sort of Confederates whom Taylor was lecturing about the workings of God. As Dowling put it in her composition titled "The Land We Love":

> Man did not conquer her, but God
> For some wise purpose of his own
> Withdrew his arm; she, left alone,
> Sank down resistless 'neath his rod.
>
> God chastens most who he loves best,
> And scourges whom he will receive.[25]

The life of Thomas "Stonewall" Jackson together with religious opinion surrounding his life and death illustrate the depth of such providentialist thinking among ordinary Americans. Jackson, who was anything but ordinary in his military capacities, was also probably not ordinary in his profound trust in providence, which he expressed with astonishing frequency and fervency. Early in his adulthood, he started peppering his speech and correspondence with phrases like "an all-wise Providence" and "the hand of an all-wise God."[26] When in 1851, Jackson was incapacitated by illness at the same time he was appointed to the faculty of the Virginia Military Institute, a friend asked him if his illness did not indicate he should turn the post down. Jackson's reply was untypical only in spelling out at length what was his constant habit of mind: "The appointment came unsought, and was therefore providential; and I knew that if Providence set me a task, He would give me the power to perform it. So I resolved to get well, and you see I have. As to the rest, I knew that what I willed to do, I could do."[27] As James Robertson's fine biography shows, Jackson was almost incapable of accounting for any event or outcome during the war itself without referring it to God's sovereign direction. After the dreadful fighting of the battle of Second Manassas, an aide observed to Jackson that the Confederates "have won this battle by the hardest kind of fighting." Jackson, who had worked during the battle like a whirlwind, would not hear of it: "No, no, we have won it by the blessing of Almighty God."[28]

Not surprisingly, when Jackson died from wounds suffered at the battle of Chancellorsville in the spring of 1863, common people throughout the nation (as well as elites) instinctively sought the divine meaning in the passing of someone who had so consistently ascribed to God the rule over daily life. Yet what would that message be? As the historian Daniel Stowell shrewdly observes, "For a people committed to the belief that an omnipotent God controlled the destiny of men and of nations, Jackson's death was a spiritual crisis."[29] Some thought that Jackson's death was a result of sin, usually ascribed to the South and only rarely to Jackson. Some held the death was intended as a lesson to teach submission to God's will. The pious Northern general O. O. Howard thought God was intending to bless the Union cause with victory. In contradiction, some Southern ministers proclaimed that removing Jackson was a providential means of stripping away human props so that the glory for the South's forthcoming victory would be given to God alone. Only a few confessed that it was entirely a mystery. After the war, and indeed after the assassination of Abraham Lincoln had evoked a comparable flurry of assured but incompatible interpretations of God's purposes, a few attempts were made to add nuance to earlier certainties. But as both Jackson himself and reaction to Jackson's death demonstrated, ordinary ministers and the laity were as convinced as the elite theologians that God was in control and that they could understand clearly why God was acting the way he did.

Holdouts

Against this chorus of certainty, there were very few holdouts. Working directly against the grain, these observers modified the usual pattern. Most thought provoking among this small minority were those who, while not abandoning a firm belief in God, began to question their own ability to read the divine determinations.

So it was with General Edward Porter Alexander, chief of the South's artillery, who campaigned with Stonewall Jackson in 1862 and 1863. Writing long after the fact, Alexander complained about the willingness of several key Southern leaders to believe "that there *was* this mysterious Providence always hovering over the field & ready to interfere on one side or the other, & that prayers & piety might win its favor from day to day." Alexander was not so much impious as practical: "It was a weakness to imagine that victory could ever come in even the slightest degree from anything except our own exertions." Specifically, Alexander held that Stonewall Jackson's reliance on providence, combined with his rigorous Sabbatarianism, had led to neglectful passivity during the Seven Days' Battles of late June 1862: "I think that the one defect in General Jackson's character was his religious beliefs. He believed with absolute faith, in a personal God, watching over all human events with a jealous eye to His own glory—ready to reward those people who made it their chief care, & to punish those who forgot about it. And he specifically believed that a particular day had been set aside every week for the praise of this God, & that a personal account was strictly kept with every man as to how he kept this day." With such reasoning Alexander was not in sympathy. His conclusion was as forthright as it was untypical: "It is customary to say that 'Providence did not intend that we should win.' But Providence did not care a row of pins about it. If it did, it was a very unintelligent Providence not to bring the business to a close—the close it wanted—in less than four years of most terrible and bloody war." [30]

Alexander's disdain for Jackson's providentialism was very much a minority viewpoint during the war. Perhaps even less common was the occasional admission that an observer simply could not make out what God was doing in and through the war. But we do know more about this viewpoint since it was the one that Abraham Lincoln gradually came to express as the war went on. I have written elsewhere about the contrast between Lincoln's view of providence and the view of providence accepted by most of the era's formally recognized religious thinkers. [31] But it is worth noting again that Lincoln, a layman with no standing in a church and no formal training as a theologian, nonetheless offered a complex picture of God's rule over the world and a morally nuanced picture of America's destiny. By contrast, most of the country's recognized religious leaders offered a thin, simple view of God's providence and a morally juvenile view of the nation and its fate.

To be sure, early in his presidency Lincoln sounded much like his contemporaries. At his first inaugural in 1861, for instance, he invoked the divine purpose as if it were an easy matter to grasp its intentions: "If the Almighty Ruler of nations, with his eternal truth and justice, be on your side of the North, or on yours of the South, that truth, and that justice, will surely prevail, by the judgment of this great tribunal, the American people."[32] Yet there was also in Lincoln's personal development a more complicated view of how God directed the world. In an autograph fragment that Lincoln's secretaries and later editors, John Nicolay and John Hay, dated to October 1858, the future president meditated on God's will with respect to slavery. This fragment included a sharp critique of Frederick A. Ross, whose *Slavery Ordained of God* (1857) had made the conventional biblical defense of slavery. Lincoln's response pointed to the power of personal interest in determining biblical conclusions: "If he [Ross] decides that God Wills Sambo to continue a slave, he thereby retains his own comfortable position; but if he decides that God will's Sambo to be free, he thereby has to walk out of the shade, throw off his gloves, and delve for his own bread. Will Dr. Ross be actuated by that perfect impartiality, which has ever been considered most favorable to correct decisions?" But before he delivered himself of this judgment, Lincoln paused to confess a difficulty that few of his pious contemporaries could recognize: "Certainly there is no contending against the Will of God; but still there is some difficulty in ascertaining, and applying it, to particular cases."[33]

Once the war actually began, this deeper sense of providential mystery developed even further. As early as 1862, the idea was rising that perhaps the will of God could not simply be identified with American efforts to preserve the Union. Such thoughts Lincoln committed to paper in September 1862, at one of the darkest moments of the conflict. As Union armies suffered another series of defeats, he began seriously to ponder the radical step of proclaiming the emancipation of slaves in the Confederacy. At that time he penned a "Meditation on the Divine Will," which his secretaries later recalled was meant for Lincoln's eyes alone:

> The will of God prevails. In great contests each party claims to act in accordance with the will of God. Both *may* be, and one *must* be wrong.

God can not be *for*, and *against* the same thing at the same time. In the present civil war it is quite possible that God's purpose is something different from the purpose of either party – and yet the human instrumentalities, working just as they do, are of the best adaptation to effect His purpose. I am almost ready to say this is probably true – that God wills this contest, and wills that it shall not end yet. By his mere quiet power, on the minds of the now contestants, He could have either *saved* or *destroyed* the Union without a human contest. Yet the contest began. And having begun He could give the final victory to either side any day. Yet the contest proceeds.[34]

Significantly, at about the same time that Lincoln wrote this meditation, he offered a specific reading of providence to guide a course of action, evidently something he had not done before and would not do again. In September 1862, after the battle of Antietam provided just enough good news for Lincoln to move against slavery in the Confederate states, he explained to his cabinet how he was confirmed in this decision. Here are the notes that Secretary of the Navy Gideon Welles recorded at that time: "He had made a vow, a covenant, that if God gave us the victory in the approaching battle, he would consider it an indication of divine will and that it was his duty to move forward in the cause of emancipation. It might be thought strange that he had in this way submitted the disposal of matters when the way was not clear to his mind what he should do. God had decided this question in favor of the slaves. He was satisfied that it was right, was confirmed and strengthened in this action by the vow and the results."[35]

More typical of Lincoln's presidential years was the reasoning in his "Meditation on the Divine Will." In March 1865 that form of reasoning, which was focused on the mysteries of providence, provided the most compelling theme of his Second Inaugural Address. In particular, that reasoning was responsible for transforming the central section of this speech into a theological statement of rare depth. Lincoln's statement began with a startling thesis, at least for an American speaker: "The Almighty has His own purposes." He concluded with an acknowledgment that the United States was as nothing compared to the mysterious purposes of God: "Yet, if God wills that [the war] continue, until all the wealth piled by the bond-man's two hundred and fifty years of unrequited toil shall be sunk, and until every drop of blood drawn with the lash, shall be paid by another drawn with the sword, as was said three thousand years ago, so still it must be said 'the judgments of the Lord, are true and righteous altogether' [Psalm 19:9]."[36] Yet, despite the forcefulness of Lincoln's vision, there were few Americans who, in the end, could actually agree both that God was in control and that human observers might not know what he was doing.

Theological Agendas: Europe versus the United States

During the war years, while American theologians wrote voluminously about the conflict, they continued to comment at considerable length about other religious issues, including several matters of great moment brewing in Europe.[37] Most of their best writing appeared in the seminary journals, which as a group constituted the nation's most substantial periodicals of serious intellectual culture. That writing came from the Presbyterians Adger, Hodge, Thornwell, and Henry Boynton Smith, romantic innovators like Bushnell, the Roman Catholic Orestes Brownson, a small army of learned Congregationalists, a feisty troop of transcendentalists, and a full corps of Methodists, Lutherans, and Baptists. Especially for religious thinkers so at home with traditional Christianity, but also with Enlightenment conceptions of the world, the ideas coming from Europe opened unsettling possibilities. Thus during the war several journal articles explored the cosmological implications of scientific proposals from Charles Darwin's *Origin of Species* (1859) and Charles Lyell's *The Geological Evidence of the Antiquity of Man* (1863).[38] American theologians also canvassed the knotty issues of faith and history raised by Church of England progressives in *Essays and Reviews* (1860) and by Ernest Renan's radical *La Vie de Jésus* (1863).[39] They discoursed learnedly on the implications for philosophy, ethics, and Christian civilization of Henry Mansel's Bampton Lectures (1858), with Mansel's innovative effort to enlist Kant on behalf of Protestant orthodoxy.[40] In their discussion of other European developments, they also noticed Pope Pius IX's *Syllabus of Errors* (1864) and the questions of religious authority raised by that important document.[41]

Yet despite some cogent writing on these subjects, it is doubtful if the American theologians were taking European challenges to conventional thought seriously enough, since in the aggregate they represented a massive rebuke to the reigning American synthesis of Protestant and Enlightenment values. Against traditional Protestant views of an authoritative and self-authenticating Bible, *Essays and Reviews* questioned decorously whether it was wise to treat Scripture as uniquely transcendent or unusually perspicuous. Renan pressed home the same questions about Jesus, but with far less decorum. Against a well-honed natural theology that used science to demonstrate the power, goodness, and majesty of God, Charles Lyell opened up the troubling possibility that humans may have descended from animals, and Charles Darwin extended that challenge with his strong statement about the random character of natural selection. Against commonsensical assurance about the ability of humans to grasp things as they really were, Mansel's interpretation of Kant rested content with humans' apprehending only phenomena. And against the assumption that traditional supernatural theology could be sustained by the voluntary organizations of a liberal society, Pope Pius IX offered his reactionary, but also perceptive, account of why it was wrong to accommodate traditional Christianity with the liberal project of modern individualism.

The Europeans, in very different ways, were leaving the certainties of Enlightenment, or Christian-Enlightenment, thinking behind. They were posing for Americans questions about the adequacy of the dominant forms of religious thought in the United States, especially the hard-earned synthesis of Christianity, republicanism, common sense, the Enlightenment, and American covenantal exceptionalism. But this was exactly the framework in which both elites and nonelites described the workings of providence during the war.

To be sure, the evangelical-Enlightenment synthesis forged in the period 1776 to 1815 had come under fire before the Civil War itself.[42] Various Christian romantics had taken exception to the standard theistic mental science propounded by so many Presbyterian, Congregationalist, Baptist, Methodist, and Disciples theologians. Those challenges from Christian romantics ranged from the conservative use of European theology by John Williamson Nevin and the New York City Presbyterian Henry Boynton Smith to the literary theology of Harriet Beecher Stowe and the creative anti-Enlightenment musings of Horace Bushnell. Transcendentalism, with Ralph Waldo Emerson far in the lead, had posed a romantic challenge to theistic common sense from beyond the boundaries of Christianity. Yet none of the antebellum attempts to contest the reigning alliance of Enlightenment and Protestant convictions were as foundational as the efforts by Darwin, Lyell, Renan, Mansel (in his use of Kant), and the other Europeans whose work was being noticed in the American quarterlies during the war.

These Europeans were blazing a trail, as it turned out, that many elite American intellectuals would follow in the 1870s and thereafter. Such figures as Oliver Wendell Holmes Jr., Andrew Dickson White, John Dewey, and other progressive savants wanted science liberated from theology. They sought moral judgments based on pragmatic considerations rather than on the Bible. They looked on academic work as promoting the progress of modern civilization, not as paying homage to received theological tradition. Above all, they had no use for the confident trust in divine providence that was everywhere on display in the war years.

Considered as an episode in the history of theology, the Civil War occurred during a critical transition from theological certainties that had prevailed since the early sixteenth century and toward new paths characteristic of the recent past. Some of the new paths would still be seriously Christian – though in contradictory liberal, modernist, fundamentalist, pietist, primitivist, and traditionalist varieties. But more and more intellectual leaders would be secular, agnostic, or simply uninterested in religion. And by 1890 those more secular positions – rather than revived Protestant, or Lutheran, or Catholic, or Eastern Orthodox, or traditional Jewish positions – were the ones that dominated American elite intellectual life in the way that the Protestant-Enlightenment synthesis had dominated it in 1830. One of the most important reasons for this change of convictions over time was the hollowness of providential reasoning that was everywhere on display in the War between the States.

Taking Stock

It remains to speculate on what the theologians' bold confidence in their own understanding of providence during the antebellum era and the war had to do with the major transition in general intellectual authority that occurred after the war.

From a perspective early in the twenty-first century, it is obvious that, no matter how clear the theologians of the Civil War were in their own minds about the workings of providence, they were in almost all cases powerless to convince others that they were correct, unless the others already shared their partisan perspective on events. Religious beliefs about the course of affairs were strongly held but weak in affecting what transpired. By contrast, other forces were emerging that had, so the war convincingly demonstrated, tremendous effective power, especially the mobilization of arms and the organization of money, men, and material for industrial production. When set alongside such practical power, religious reasoning about the course of history seemed confused, simplistic, and ineffective.

On the level of personal religion, such a faltering did not occur. The war stimulated revivals in the camps both North and South, and it seems also to have increased the fervor of many on the home fronts as well. Perhaps as a result, it became easier for the great majority of Americans who retained traditional beliefs to view religion as a personal matter rather than claim its effectiveness in either the economic marketplace or the marketplace of ideas.

Some of the theologians were, in fact, developing nuanced accounts of why assured convictions varied so greatly within a population that shared basic convictions about Christianity, commonsense morality, republican values, and the special destiny of the United States. For instance, in the summer of 1865 Charles Hodge chided his fellow Northern Presbyterians for their harsh judgments of Southern counterparts. His reasoning was unusually frank and self-aware: "It is easy to say that we are right and they are wrong. This in the present case is, no doubt, in a great measure, true." But to Hodge the fact of being right or wrong was not a very good explanation of why the Northern Presbyterians upheld the Union and eventually condemned slavery, while the Southern Presbyterians took opposite positions. Rather, Hodge said, "it is largely in both cases, because every man, and every body of men, are more or less subject to the controlling influence of public opinion, and of the life of the community to which they belong."[43]

Despite this nuanced awareness, Hodge himself could not maintain a complex account of causation when he turned to explaining great events like the termination of slavery. As he used providential categories, even Hodge, who ranked among the most perceptive American theologians, substituted a simple belief in God's immediate action for a complex belief in God's mediated control through secondary causes. But by so doing, Hodge let himself off the hook. With a simplistic trust in immediate divine causation, it was no longer necessary to sweat over what one should do, and one was no longer required to think hard about what was happening and why it happened.

As explained in the illuminating books by George Fredrickson and Anne Rose on Americans whom the war pushed in secular directions, we know that there were other American intellectuals, contemporaries of Charles Hodge, who were, in fact, inspired by the war to sweat over what they should do and to think hard about what caused events. But perhaps because these individuals were repelled by the simplistic way in which traditional believers invoked providence during the war, they appealed less and less to providence themselves.

The result in American intellectual life can be keyed to the stance of Abraham Lincoln. Lincoln joined together trust in providence and much agnosticism about the work of God in the world. After Lincoln, American thinkers were increasingly divided between those who, on the one side, continued to trust in providence and who knew very well what God was doing in the world, and those, on the other, who gave up on providence and embraced agnosticism about the ultimate meaning of the world.

Regarded in traditional religious terms, it was certainly not unwise for American theologians (and ordinary believers as well) to trust in providence. Without such trust, it is hard to imagine that traditional Christianity could exist, or for that matter traditional Islam or most varieties of traditional Judaism. The difficulty was not trust in providence as such but trust in providence so narrowly defined by the republican, covenantal, commonsensical, Enlightenment, and – above all – nationalistic categories that Protestant evangelicals had so boldly appropriated with such galvanizing effects in the early decades of the nineteenth century. For that kind of providence, the war – with its clash of armies and ideologies, with its unprecedented moral, legal, governmental, and social complications, with its avalanche of death and destruction – should have posed insuperable difficulties. That kind of providence very much needed to be seen in light of what Abraham Lincoln finally concluded – in the apt summary of Phillip Paludan: "The war had become too complex, too astounding, for him to believe that mere argument made complete sense."[44]

Chapter 6

Opinions of Protestants Abroad

The opinions of non-Americans on religious aspects of the War between the States represent a minor theme in the more general question of how the Civil War was viewed from outside the country.[1] Yet even preliminary attention to the subject can aid us in understanding why the Civil War amounted to a theological crisis in the United States. Views from abroad were naturally shaped in their moral and religious evaluation of the American conflict by national, class, and denominational perspectives. In addition, up-to-date information about unfolding events and opinions in North America was harder to come by abroad in that era before successful deployment of the transatlantic cable, not to speak of air travel, radio, the Internet, and CNN. Yet, with those limitations duly recognized, it is still the case that foreign observers often saw what Americans could not see or, to put it more precisely, often saw certain things about singularities in the structure of American thought that were hard for Americans within that structure to comprehend.

In particular, concerned outside observers perceived with unusual clarity that American disputes over the Bible and slavery grew as much from broad interpretive assumptions brought to the text as from detailed exegesis of the Book. Some grasped a biblical distinction between slavery and race that only a few Americans were able to understand. Moreover, foreigners tended to be sharply conscious of how American economic practice and American political ideology influenced the shape of religious argument. Foreign Catholics were also alert to how traditions of Dissenting Protestantism bestowed a distinct coloration on American political developments. Outside observers, in short, testified to the deficiencies and advantages of viewing American developments from afar. Even if their opinions lacked the nuance afforded by extensive close observation, they illuminated the distinctive strengths and

the internal contradictions of American developments – religious as well as
political, intellectual as well as social.

My own efforts at charting foreign reactions to religious dimensions of
the Civil War are still only fragmentary. While I have been able to read in
books and articles from Scottish Presbyterians, Irish evangelicals, Anglicans
and other English Protestants, Upper Canadian Presbyterians and Methodists, Lower Canadian Catholics, Union Protestants and Roman Catholics from
Germany, Catholics and Protestants from France, and Jesuits from Rome itself,[2] and while I have been able to canvass some of the secondary literature
touching on this subject,[3] there is still much additional pertinent material to
be examined. Nonetheless, my preliminary inquiry has revealed fascinating,
if scattered, insights from abroad for this war at home.

In this chapter I describe salient opinions expressed by Protestants from
France as well as from Britain and its dependencies (England, Scotland, Ireland, Canada). These opinions are noteworthy not only for the seriousness
with which they examined the moral issues of the American conflict and the
ease with which they linked evaluations of slavery to evaluations of other
American circumstances, but also for the relative superficiality of their attention to the question of the Bible and slavery. Canvassing these examples of
Protestant opinion from abroad underscores what was distinctive in American Protestant debate and what was shared with overseas Protestant com-
munions. It also opens a path to initial consideration of larger questions
concerning the state of American religious thinking in the mid-nineteenth
century.

In the next chapter foreign commentary on the Civil War from Roman
Catholics is the central concern. Since Catholic opinion in America often
reflected European Catholic convictions, I pause in that chapter for a brief
review of domestic Catholic opinions. Even more than those of foreign Protestants, the views of foreign Roman Catholics, especially of conservative Catholics, are instructive precisely because they inverted so many American Protestant assumptions. To examine those inversions is to see more clearly the
distinctive character of American Protestant thought and also to understand
the major problems of theological reasoning occasioned by the war. Significantly, attention to the Bible – both the interpretation of the individual passages and reflection on broader hermeneutical issues – was almost as extensive among foreign Catholics as it was scarce among foreign Protestants.

Much of the foreign Protestant commentary that I have been able to survey shared the moral sentiments of Northern abolitionists on slavery, although with much less political support for the Union. Those opinions came from British, Canadian, and French sources. By contrast, commentary in the London *Times* offered a perspective closer to American proslavery biblical opinion. Viewpoints from Germany moved further away from the standard lines of American debate and were, therefore, more provocative in what they concluded about the broader religious situation in America. After a survey of the relevant writings, it will be possible to say more exactly what foreign Protestant opinion revealed about the distinctively American character of religious debate on the Civil War.

Trent and Beyond

To catch the flavor of Protestant commentary found abroad, it is useful to begin with foreign reactions to a diplomatic tangle early in the Civil War. In late 1861 and early 1862, tensions were high between the United States and Britain. Union seizure of two Confederate diplomats from the British mail steamer *Trent* on November 8, 1861, was the occasion for a crisis, but long-standing British apprehension about the tendencies of American politics (both North and South) and long-standing American suspicion of Britain's imperial aims fueled the inflammatory rhetoric heard on both sides of the Atlantic in late December and early January. Soon, however, cooler heads prevailed; the diplomats were released into British custody; and preparations for war between the United States and Britain (with its Canadian provinces) were called off. Yet for English, Scottish, Irish, and Canadian public opinion – religious as well as political – the *Trent* affair was a galvanizing moment. In Scotland, the monthly magazine of the United Presbyterian Church was appalled at the thought of war between the United States and Britain: "For two countries professedly Christian (and, if they are not so, Christianity has scarcely a home upon earth) to proclaim war upon each other, because some barbarous law is susceptible of a double interpretation, is enough to fill one with an agony of grief, and to lead us almost to despair of the advance of our race."[4] In Ireland, the *Evangelical Witness*, though maintaining a pro-North and antislavery stance, nonetheless opined that the Civil War with all its horrors was proving to be the "fiery baptism" that America needed to purge "the corruption" lingering on her shores as an inheritance from European despotism. In this Irish Protestant view, the distinctive American sins were clear: "vain-glorious devotion offered to the idol of the Constitution in every page of the nation's literature . . . the scandalous corruption and cupidity by which the whole body politic has been contaminated and defiled . . . [and] the atrocious virulence of party warfare."[5] In May 1862, after Britain and the U.S. had pulled back from the brink of war, a poem titled "A Voice from Canada" summed up the emotions that the crisis had evoked from one Presbyterian there:

> We thank our God for peace within our land,
>   But had the *time of trial* come indeed,
> We had been ready at our post to stand
>   For *Queen and Country*, in the hour of need.
>
> . . . .
>
> In all that realm on which no sun may set
> No land more loyal is than ours to *thee!*[6]

More than two years later, another Canadian posted a lengthy letter to the *Home and Foreign Record of the Canada Presbyterian Church* in which, once again, religious sensibility filtered commentary on the politics of the United States. The correspondent was a resident of British Columbia who had found himself in San Francisco on the Fourth of July. It proved to be a day "such as one is not likely soon to forget. . . . 'Our government' – 'Our nation' – 'Our principles' – 'Our flag' – 'the excelsior of the western continent,' and consequently of the eastern and every other, were the sentiments read, spoken, and published in a thousand ways throughout the rejoicing on that great historic anniversary." Such a display struck the Canadian as distinctly unseemly: "The Apostle's prudent and practical admonition, 'Let your moderation be known to all men,' seemed to be taken with some exception when applied to love of country." The political lesson to this Canadian was just as plain from observing "the institutions of our American neighbours": "They who are really sound and sincere in their profession of loyalty to king and country, must not fear when occasion requires boldly to avow it."[7] Such scattered opinions take on larger significance when it is realized that other, more comprehensive foreign views were also being published, and with unusual frequency.

Liberal Protestants: Count Gasparin and Goldwin Smith

Major works by a French Protestant statesman, writing from Geneva, and an English journalist-historian, who later emigrated to Canada, illustrate the nature of liberal Protestant opinion on the War between the States. Count Agénor Étienne de Gasparin (1810–71) was trained as a lawyer in Paris; during the European revolutions of 1848, he played an active part in French political affairs.[8] In 1849 Gasparin moved permanently to Geneva, where he continued the prolific advocacy for progressive Protestant causes he had begun in France. Gasparin's causes were the defense of Protestantism against Catholic and secular opponents, abolition of slavery and the slave trade, and freedom of religion in the face of oppressive regimes of all kinds. For Gasparin, following Alexis de Tocqueville's famous *Democracy in America* (1835, 1840), the United States was the place where both religion and statecraft had become most gratifyingly liberal in the nineteenth-century European meaning of the term (stressing the development of free individuals over the prerogatives of inherited traditional authority). His earlier interests in America, the anti-slavery cause, and religious freedom lay behind his publication in the early 1860s of two substantial books in which moral and theological assessment of the American situation featured prominently.[9]

Goldwin Smith (1823–1910) enjoyed a precocious career as a classicist and historian at Oxford before he entered into a broader life of journalism and public advocacy.[10] In 1869 he would emigrate to North America, eventually settling in Toronto, where he continued to support the progressive politics and liberal Protestantism that he had also advocated in England. Smith was a great opponent of traditional Anglican prerogatives in English religion and education and also a great promoter of political self-sufficiency for Britain's many colonies (except Ireland and India). Although his convictions on such issues would be expressed many times in many ways throughout his life, they were already well in place by 1863, when he published a small monograph in answer to the question, "Does the Bible sanction American slavery?"[11] Like Gasparin's books, Smith's work dealt seriously, but not necessarily thoroughly, with the theological debates stimulated by the American war.

In his volumes, Gasparin took pains to discuss both "the churches and slavery" and "the gospel and slavery" and to make a direct appeal "to Christians."[12] His first book, which was prepared for the press in its original edition before the outbreak of hostilities, was not without criticism of American excesses – the United States, "it is said, is the country of the dollar." But mostly it praised Americans for "bringing individual energies into action," for "religious liberty," and for "the voluntary system" that shaped public life.[13] Gasparin admitted that, since "the power of surroundings is incalculable," he could understand how someone whose "monetary interests" were "menaced by Abolitionism" and whose whole life was defined by the Southern context could defend slavery. But to Gasparin it was equally clear that, once having noted the power of environment over religious convictions, it was a relatively simple matter to demonstrate the incompatibility between true Christianity and slavery: "Take away the South, and no one in America, any more than in Europe, will dream of discovering in the Gospel the divine approbation of the atrocities of slavery."[14]

Gasparin was, in fact, mistaken in suggesting that biblical theories in favor of slavery "proceed" essentially from the South.[15] But that opinion probably explains why his refutation of proslavery biblical arguments remained relatively superficial. In both of his books, he did address particular scriptural passages used in the proslavery biblical defense: for example, by contending that Jesus "drew the line of demarcation between the law and the Gospel" and so eviscerated the Old Testament sanctions for slavery, by denying that Philemon's enslavement of Onesimus was relevant to contemporary debate, and by labeling as "gross literalism" the defense of slavery based on a failure of New Testament writers to condemn the system.[16] But for the most part he relied on a general sense of incompatibility between slavery and Christianity to carry his case. Thus the major thrust of his argument was to show that "there exist, thank God, between liberty and the Gospel, close, eternal, and indestructible relations": that there is "an implied abolition of slavery (implied but positive) at the bottom of that close fraternity created by the faith in the Saviour"; that it is "easy" to refute "such monstrous doctrines" as the biblical defense of slavery; and that, despite all appearances to the contrary, "the Christians of the United States have been unable to suppress even for a single day the fundamental antagonism which will always exist, thank God! between the Gospel and slavery."[17]

In short, Gasparin represented a rhetorically powerful European Protestant variation of the American abolitionist claim that slavery was simply incompatible with the essence of Christianity. Although his books failed to comprehend the broad American influence that biblical defenses of slavery enjoyed both North and South, they testified eloquently to the high hope that European Protestants of Gasparin's liberal convictions sustained for the course of American affairs.

Goldwin Smith's monograph, *Does the Bible Sanction American Slavery?*, offered much more particular attention to biblical proslavery arguments, but not quite as much as its title announced. It was, however, one of the most thorough European attempts of any sort to demonstrate how a reading of Scripture inspired by progressive Protestant convictions ruled out slavery in its American form. A great deal of Smith's book was given over to broad historical considerations of slavery in the ancient world, and much of his attention to Scripture developed arguments that proslavery advocates had long since answered to their own satisfaction. Smith, for example, claimed that if Americans defended slavery on the basis of the Old Testament, they should also defend practices like polygamy and the complete annihilation of defeated armies that are also prescribed in the Old Testament.[18] But biblical proslavery advocates had frequently pointed out that, while Christ and the apostles had specifically condemned the latter practices, they had not brought up slavery for similar denunciation.

In the course of his arguments, Smith did deal with almost all of the relevant scriptural passages, from regulation of slavery in the Pentateuch to the New Testament guidelines for the behavior of masters and servants. For his interpretation of these passages he cited a number of authorities, from the German mediating theologian August Neander and the American emancipationist Francis Wayland to the American Unitarian William Ellery Channing. Smith's argumentation was often telling, especially in contrasting American racial slavery with the nonracial slavery of the ancient world, as we shall discuss in more detail below.

With regard to one particular, Smith saw clearly what most Americans, including the learned Moses Stuart, did not grasp. As he discussed the details of Old Testament slavery, Smith stressed the many provisions for incorporating non-Jewish slaves into the Hebrew community. To Smith it was "the most important point of all" that the Jews of the Old Testament shared their religion with their slaves. With such provision, "the right of circumcision administered to all alike, and the participation of the whole household in the family rite of the Passover, . . . effectually incorporated even the foreign slave into the community."[19] With such incorporation, foreign slaves had to be treated as if they were Hebrew slaves, which meant that they would be liberated at the end of, at most, seven years of service. It was an effective demonstration.

Most prominently, however, Smith relied on what he considered the progressive moral character of the Christian religion to make his case. For example, right at the start of the essay, he admitted that the Old Testament recognized slavery and the New Testament did not condemn it. But he then went on with a brief statement about the overarching purpose of the Bible: it was "to implant in man's heart a principle, viz. the love of God and Man, which should move him to work (God also working in him) for the improvement of his own state and that of his fellows, and for the transforming of his and their life into the image of their maker."[20] Toward the end he returned to the general spiritual direction of Scripture, this time by contrasting New Testament norms with what he understood to be common practice in the South. Smith stressed that Christian celebration of the Lord's Supper exhibited a great "equalizing and reconciling power," but that this power was contradicted when blacks and whites worshipped separately and did not participate together in the service of communion.[21] This too was a strong argument, but it was one that relied more on what Smith understood as the general spirit of the New Testament than on careful exegesis of its letter.

Smith's opinions were representative of views held by most English Nonconformists as well as by many evangelical and broad church Anglicans. Although his conclusions about what the Bible taught concerning slavery were not widely shared by traditionalist Anglicans, for the rest of the English Protestant world they spoke clearly, and they were laid out at greater length than one could find in the work of almost any of his peers.

Voices from Scotland, Ireland, and Canada

Within a broadly abolitionist framework, there were significant variations of opinion among other English-language Protestants as one moved westward from Scotland to Ireland and then into Canada. The United Presbyterians of Scotland were one of the British denominations best prepared by their history for taking up the cause of antislavery. The denomination had resulted from a merger in 1847 of the United Secession and Relief churches, both of which had originated as eighteenth-century protests against the arbitrary authority of Church of Scotland patrons in appointing the ministers of local parishes, and both of which also sustained an elective affinity with Scotland's strong liberal and free-trade movements. The United Presbyterians were distinguished by their frank defense of traditional Calvinist theology and by their admiration for the doctrinally conservative theologians of American Presbyterianism. Coverage of the war by the United Presbyterians' monthly magazine was particularly alert to spiritual intelligence – for example, signs of revival in the Federal army or promises of the British Bible Society to support the distribution of Scripture in the States.[22] At least as witnessed by their periodical, these Scottish Presbyterians were also never uniformly pleased with the actions of the Union, which it accused of helping to pitch "the war-spirit" to "a most deplorable ardour" and of relying on its "blustering boosters" instead of hard calculation before the first battle of Bull Run.[23] Yet the main interest of the Scottish United Presbyterians in the American war was the elimination of slavery and what they hoped would become "the final struggle between slavery and freedom for the Blacks."[24] Without any of the compunction that held back their theologically conservative counterparts in the States, these Scottish Presbyterians were eager, even at the height of tension over the *Trent*, to hail "the heroic band of Abolitionists who held aloft the flag of freedom through bad report" and then, somewhat later, to affirm "that whatever may come out of the war, nothing good can come out of bondage, and that in any case, and on every supposition, it is a upas-tree to be utterly eradicated."[25]

In Ireland, similar opinions came from the *Evangelical Witness*, which spoke for Presbyterians who had taken part in the great Irish revivals of 1858-59, which many at the time linked to the well-publicized Business Men's Revival in the United States. The magazine's opinions on the American war were consistent throughout: it was pro-Union but even more ardently antislavery. To these Irish evangelicals, the founding of the American colonies had represented a great boon for "civil and religious freedom," but it was a boon threatened by slavery, which was "an accursed inheritance . . . transmitted from the old country to the new." Slavery, in turn, had encouraged in the South the "ebullition of . . . deadly hate against the New England and North-Western States . . . that restless spirit of aggression . . . [and] the

border-ruffianism and other kindred atrocities in Kansas." Months before
Lincoln published plans for freeing Confederate slaves, the *Evangelical Witness* indicated the way it thought he should go. Statesmen may say what they
wish, but "the war is essentially an anti-slavery one."[26] After Lincoln had
made his plans for emancipation public, the *Evangelical Witness* still focused
on the destruction that "the slave power . . . – a power, fierce, insolent, determined, outraging all law and principle, scowling defiance in the seat of government" – had caused in the United States with its "moral hurricane" and,
in so doing, "rendered their [that of the South? the U.S.?] boasted liberty the
opprobrium of the world." The Irish showed they were reasonably familiar
with American opinion by quoting James Henley Thornwell to the effect that
"the people whom we hold in bondage are the occasion of all our troubles,"
but then reversed Thornwell's own conviction by contending that all who
had helped perpetuate slavery, including the British, incurred a dreadful
price to pay for their wrong.[27] The magazine also showed that its knowledge of American affairs was limited, for it lavished high praise on both the
conservative Presbyterian Charles Hodge and the romantic Congregationalist Henry Ward Beecher, whom no one in the United States would have positioned together.[28]

   Through a regular series of sprightly reports, the Irish *Evangelical Witness* offered its readers a positive view of the course of events in the war. It
rebuked other Britons who left the impression that in the United States it
was all "silly braggadocio and senseless impertinence."[29] It hailed the triumph of the North as signaling "the irrevocable doom of the detested system
that gave [the war] birth" and averred that, with slavery removed, the United
States was poised "to take its place among the nations as the champion of
universal freedom."[30] With an emphasis not typically found in the States, its
eulogy for Abraham Lincoln in mid-1865 praised the "Calvinistic theology of
the last inaugural of the lamented" president.[31] In the *Evangelical Witness*, the
Union had a foreign friend whose thorough abolitionism was matched by
strong doctrinal orthodoxy and whose attention to the faults of the United
States did not make it waver in its support of antislavery Americans.

   Because Canadian Presbyterians were still divided into several parallel
strands at the time of the Civil War, it is not surprising that their journals
reflected differing attitudes toward the American conflict. The Presbyterian
Church of Canada was the group in central Canada that remained in fellow-

ship with the Scottish Kirk after the spin-off of the Scottish Free Church in 1843 had led to a corresponding spin-off of a Canadian Free Church from the main Scottish body in Canada. If evidence from its journal can be credited, the Canadian branch of the established Scottish church showed no particular interest in the American conflict except when war with Britain loomed in the wake of the Trent affair.[32]

Other Canadian Presbyterians, however, displayed more obvious concern for what was happening south of the border. The Canada Presbyterian Church, which was a North American union of Scotland's more pietistic Free and Secession denominations, featured devotional material and missionary reports in its publications, but it also made room for fairly regular commentary on the war. Most of that commentary urged prayer for a speedy peace or treated the war's effects on missionary efforts. On several occasions, however, the editors published more general assessments of political and religious conditions, such as the Fourth of July report from 1864 cited above. It also paused on one occasion to make the point that African Americans were also stressing: the missionary propagation of the Gospel was being hurt by the American toleration of slavery. After the cessation of hostilities, it expressed agreement with the "moderate and good men" of the North that full political rights were a necessity for the freed slaves.[33]

Broader and more frequent reports on the American conflict came from the Kirk Presbyterians in Nova Scotia, whose monthly journal kept up a fairly dyspeptic barrage of commentary on both the North and the South. Early on, the editor claimed that it would be "madness" for the North to try to force the South back into the nation, but he also argued that the earnestness of the South had gone "to the verge of madness."[34] Although the journal maintained a strong stance against slavery – "that moral nightmare" – it highly praised Stonewall Jackson after his death as "by far the most remarkable man that this sad contest has brought to the surface."[35] Its wartime commentary, though sporadic, was the most aggressive and opinionated that I have found in any English-language journal.

Compared to the Presbyterians, Canadian Methodists were more consistently engaged with the American conflict and less hesitant about defining the issue strictly in terms of slavery. Within the various Canadian Methodist churches, there existed a range of opinions as to whether slavery should be excised quickly through immediate abolition or whether it should be undermined through gradual emancipation. But few if any Methodist voices in Canada supported the institution or the confederacy that arose to protect it.

The *Christian Guardian* of the Wesleyan Methodist Church in Canada reflected the characteristic pietism of this denomination by tiptoeing around the politics of the war. Its desire to promote amity among Christian believers extended to a willingness to print lengthy correspondence from Methodists in the South who defended both slavery and secession. But the journal's own writers just as regularly rebutted those arguments.[36] The editors did urge ministers to be cautious in meddling with public issues that could compromise their religious calling and their role in moderating worldly passions. At the same time they also concluded that "the North seems to have right on its side" while predicting that the South would lose sympathy around the world, "for they are going to fight for a bad institution."[37] By the end of the first year of hostilities, the editors were becoming bolder: "We believe that in speaking favourably of the Northern cause, we express the feeling of the entire Methodist church of Canada."[38]

Even more assertive was the official organ of the Methodist Episcopal Church in Canada, the *Canada Christian Advocate*, which was published in Hamilton, Ontario. Well before fighting broke out, it defended resistance to fugitive slave laws, especially any effort to recover escaped slaves from Canada. Once the conflict started, it featured hard-hitting articles with titles like "The Barbarism of Slavery."[39] The abolitionism of the *Canada Christian Advocate* was almost as determined as that of the *United Presbyterian Magazine*.

The foreign Protestants who most closely resembled American Protestants were, in sum, exercised primarily about the evil of slavery, although they did not ignore political issues contested between the North and the South. In expressing their opinions, they showed little of the hesitation that held back so many of their American contemporaries.

The London *Times* as Exception

One prominent exception to the general judgments rendered by British and Protestant sources was the editorial voice of the London *Times*. This paper, with Tory and high-church leanings, commented regularly and at length on the American War between the States. Occasionally religious themes intruded into that commentary.

In January 1863, for instance, the *Times* took off by name after Henry Ward Beecher, the evangelical Episcopalian Stephen Tyng Sr., and the abolitionist Congregationalist George Cheever for preaching "the emancipation of every slave in the Union . . . as an absolute dogma . . . to be carried into immediate effect."[40] This particular article went on to offer a rare instance from Britain where the Bible was used against abolitionism (which is examined in more detail below). It closed its negative assessment of Northern moral pretensions by wondering why supporters of abolition did not go on to condemn Northern involvement in the economic products of slavery: "But will the North ever declare that slave-grown cotton, sugar, and tobacco are an unclean thing, and must not be touched or carried in Yankee ships, or bought and sold with Yankee money?"[41]

Ten weeks later the *Times* returned with an even sharper, more comprehensive critique of American abolitionism. As Philip Schaff had done at the start of the war, the *Times* insisted that "there are two distinct questions in America which the English people ought not to mix up with each other. . . . The one is the question of slavery; the other is the question of the Negro." It then went on to blame radical abolitionists for turning a political question into a sacred cause: "The Northern fanatic, who declared slavery to be humanly wrong, produced the Southern fanatic, who declared it to be divinely right."[42] Abraham Lincoln's particular evil with the Emancipation Proclamation was to threaten the South with a race war at the hands of liberated slaves; his greatest crime was "treason to his race." The *Times* had nothing but scorn for a Northerner who would wage war to eliminate slavery but who then would "refuse him [the freed slave] the right of citizenship."[43] It spotlighted Northern racism by pointing out how few, even among abolitionists, approved of interracial marriage, how the Northern population of free blacks was diminishing because of its ill treatment, and how the champions of abolition did nothing for the economic betterment of free blacks. As an instance of that last hypocrisy, it blasted Horace Greeley's New York *Tribune*, "the champion of the [black] race," for not being able to "employ a Negro compositor or machinist, under the penalty of a general and indignant strike of all its white workpeople." This particular indictment of the North's failure to deal with race ended with an unfavorable comparison between the fate of Northern workers and that of Southern slaves: "If the condition of the Southern Negro be slavery, it is slavery with health and life; and . . . if the condition of the Northern Negro be liberty, it is liberty with disease and death, as well as with social degradation."[44]

With regard to the Civil War, the *Times* was far from typical of British opinion; it was even more of an exception when it came to the general abolitionist views of British Protestants. But the newspaper was a significant voice precisely because it challenged prevailing opinions, especially in its willingness to raise embarrassing questions about Northern moral consistency.

Protestant Opinion from Germany

The opinions of continental European churches on the war differed from those of English-language denominations in their propensity to explain the conflict against a broader background of general Protestant history. To the modern researcher, they are intriguing because their assessments often reflected reports from fellow religionists who had emigrated to America. But in order to put that commentary in perspective, it is important to sketch first the course of German ecclesiastical contributions to the New World.

Owing to increased emigration, the Lutheran, Reformed, and Union churches in the German estates had by midcentury an ample flow of direct information from the United States. Increased contact made it possible for the Europeans to assess the sectional conflict with theological standards that for the immigrants had already begun to accommodate to American ways. On the continent, Lutherans especially had developed a set of theological principles that differed significantly from the characteristic Reformed or Calvinist principles infusing American public life. Thus Protestants of German heritage were in the same position as Roman Catholics, whose most interesting religious commentary on the war came from outside the United States instead of from within. In the Old World, Lutherans followed Martin Luther in stressing the principles of Law and Gospel, typically asking how any individual scriptural passage illuminated the standing of the reader before God in sin or in grace, rather than seeking immediately to discover the passage's ethical implications for the believer, as was more common with Reformed Protestants. Lutherans had also developed a strong Two Swords theology, in which a sharp divide was drawn between the proper business of the church in announcing sin and grace and the proper business of the state in maintaining public order.[45] Early polemics with Calvinists over the meaning of the Lord's Supper and later skirmishing with Anabaptists and Baptists on the question of who should be baptized and at what stage of life had given the Lutherans a habit of defending their distinctive views of the real presence of Christ in the Lord's Supper and baptismal regeneration for infants as much from the general meaning of the whole Bible as from the dictate of any one text.

Early Lutherans in America had sustained these perspectives. Henry Melchior Mühlenberg (1711–87), patriarch of Lutheranism in North America, eventually became skilled in the use of English, but he did not Americanize his approach to Scripture or Lutheran traditions.[46] Mühlenberg's successor as the leading American Lutheran, J. H. C. Helmuth, spoke out even more sharply than his predecessor about the need to retain Lutheran traditions in the American sea of democratic individualism. In 1793, for example, Helmuth registered a Lutheran protest to what, even at that early date, was becoming the characteristic American approach to the Bible: "It is altogether harmful when someone reads his whims and fantasies into this holy book. . . . This is to make a weather vane out of Scripture and so turn it in every direction of the imagination, for one person pointing to the East and for someone else who knows where."[47] After Helmuth's passing, however, Lutherans in the United States rapidly began to take on at least some standard American instincts.

The process of Americanization encouraged later Lutheran leaders like Samuel Schmucker of Gettysburg and John Bachman of South Carolina to soften Lutheran distinctiveness in order to assist the broader Protestant purposes of evangelization and Christianization, as defined by American Calvinists.[48] Schmucker, for example, came to resemble other Northern Protestants as a strong backer of the Evangelical Alliance, a strong defender of temperance, and a strong promoter of Sabbath observance. By the time of the Civil War, Schmucker's pronounced antislavery stance was of a piece with what Lutherans called "American" positions.[49] On the other hand, Bachman's defense of slavery was "American" in a Southern form rather than discernibly Lutheran.[50]

In the Old World, by contrast, more traditional assessments were still possible. One such assessment came from the *Protestantische Kirchenzeitung für das evangelische Deutschland* (Protestant Church Newspaper for Evangelical Germany), a journal out of Berlin that promoted the principle of "Evangelical

Union" as a way of joining the historical Lutheran and historical Reformed streams from the German Reformation into a single vigorous church. Its coverage of the American Civil War, which was drawn mostly from the reports of German or Swiss immigrants in the United States, was sympathetic to yet also clearly skeptical about certain "American" practices. In that coverage, persistent reference was made to the need for immigrants to maintain their original language, religion, and culture in the New World.[51] But more attention was devoted to the plight of American slaves, even to the point of floating the impractical scheme of raising money for the purpose of bringing black children to Germany for education and acculturation to German ways. Along the way, the *Protestantische Kirchenzeitung* also paused to commend armies both North and South for the leadership assumed by "Jünger des Evangeliums" (disciples of the Gospel).[52]

But far and away the most interesting commentary came early in the war when the journal reprinted and then discussed a lengthy dispatch from the editor of a German Reformed periodical in Ohio. The Berlin editors quoted this correspondent with approval when he claimed that Americans, including American Christians, lacked proper "respect for existing powers and authorities." A particular difficulty, according to the correspondent, was that Americans often claimed to be following a higher law even when that higher law turned out to be only "a personal persuasion." In the editors' view, that kind of individualism violated the principles of the first Protestants and even of the founders of Methodist and Baptist churches. Because of practices in America, "the truth and the honor of Christ suffer harm from such proceedings." The South's action in leaving the Union illustrated this characteristic American problem in the fullest measure, which was why the editor from Ohio held that God would ensure a Union victory, "so that through it all Americans might be shown anew that God takes no pleasure in schisms, separatism, or a special confederacy [*Sonderbund*], but rather that he wants us to defend and nurture the truth under the civil and ecclesiastical power and authority under which he has set us."[53]

With this assessment by the Ohio editor, the Berlin Protestants could not have been more in sympathy. But then they went on to point out that this same editor had left the Swiss church in which he had been born and thus had violated the very principles he articulated so well. Moreover, the Ohio editor's supposed loyalty to the objectivity of historical confessions was self-defeating, since even earnestly held confessions could not obliterate the fact that there were now multitudes of earnestly held confessions. So who could find among them the one true church? Why should the Ohio editor wonder, given the huge number of different churches in the United States, that there had been this "break up of the civil union"?

The solution offered by the Berliners to the dilemma of ever more fragmentation within the Protestant world was the movement toward ecumenical Union that their journal championed: "The splintering into ever smaller pieces is, however, nothing but the consequence of confessionalism, and it will continue in Germany, as everywhere else, as it has in England and America, where free right of association reigns independent of citizens rights, unless the spirit of evangelical union deprives separatistic tendencies of their sustenance." [54]

In short, the Berlin Protestants were pointing to the combination of religious seriousness and the absence of overarching religious authority as a prime source of American civil strife. It was a point to ponder.

Prominent Themes in Foreign Protestant Commentary

To examine the prominent themes in foreign commentary is to see where American religious analysis of the Civil War was distinctly American and where it was a more general function of religious opinions widely shared in the Western world. With regard to the latter category, it is interesting that United Presbyterians in Scotland, German Protestants in Berlin, and Count Gasparin from Geneva all linked success in battle to the observance of the Sabbath, which was also a regular feature of American religious commentary. [55]

More important was the idea of divine providence as the key to the American struggle because it was as pervasive outside the United States as it was domestically. Irish evangelicals, Scottish United Presbyterians, Canadian Methodists, Canadian Presbyterians, French Protestants, and German Protestants all raised the same chorus that was so widespread in the United States. To the Irish, "a higher hand has been apparent in the tremendous crisis, and amid the surging sea of treason and of blood that now surrounds her, America can look confidently to Him who, from the beginning, has directed her destinies." [56] To Count Gasparin, it was simply evident that "the influence of the Gospel is immense in America." He also felt that the Business Men's Revival of 1857–58, "which, save at a point in Baltimore, stopped short at the frontiers of the South," had amounted to a "great providential means against slavery."[57] The same clarity about God's purposes was reflected in a letter published by the Scottish United Presbyterians in 1863. It was from a missionary "standing upon the shores of Africa, and contemplating this accumulation of guilt in reference to Africa and her children," someone who knew "that a fearful day of retribution was coming"; indeed, he wrote, "It has come."[58] Similar references to "God in His Providence" and "an all-wise and over-ruling Providence" appeared with great regularity.[59] Also common was the reasoning similar to what appeared in scores of American jeremiads: "The calamities of this war [are] . . . a punishment of the American people for the sin of human oppression."[60] In these expressions the foreign observers were using a vocabulary that was second nature to the Americans.

It was similar, yet with a difference, with respect to the prominent strain of anti-Catholicism in commentary from abroad. The United States had by no means put aside the stiff anti-Romanism that had been so prominent in its history, but compared to the nativism that rose steadily from the early 1830s and then exploded into the Know-Nothingism of the early 1850s, anti-Catholicism during the Civil War itself was relatively restrained. But if American Protestants were relaxing their vigilance against Rome, Protestants outside the United States were not. At the time of the Trent affair, Irish evangelicals and Scottish United Presbyterians both urged moderation, at least in part because of what they anticipated would be the Catholic schadenfreude if Britain and the North went to war.[61] The editors of the *Protestantische Kirchenzeitung* got it wrong when they described the "overwhelmingly Catholic" character of the Southern slave states that seceded,[62] but the connection between slavery and Catholicism was a consistent Protestant assertion. One of the exchanges that the Canadian Methodist *Christian Guardian* published with Southern Methodists turned on this perception. The New Orleans *Christian Advocate* had complained that its Canadian counterpart had praised "John Brown, the horse-thief, robber, murderer, and traitor," even as it carried on its long-term campaign against "Romanism." But, according to the New Orleans Methodists, what John Brown stood for was far worse than Romanism. The Canadians shot right back: "We are not surprised that the *Advocate* [in New Orleans] prefers *Romanism* to our Methodism, for the simple reason, that as Romanism is a system of slavery, the adherents of Rome, and especially its agents in the United States, are generally found amongst the abettors of slavery."[63]

A more provocative evocation of anti-Catholicism came from the London *Times*. Its attack on the North included recognition of the abolitionist claim "that Slavery is at variance with the spirit of the Gospel." Yet to the *Times* this appeal to the spirit of Christianity was precisely what Catholics did in defending many of their practices that were not specifically mandated in Scripture: "The Roman Catholics have just as much to say for any one of their peculiar doctrines as the Abolitionists have for their one article of a standing or falling community."[64]

In the ongoing Protestant attacks on Rome that seem to have marked foreign commentary more strongly than American commentary, there is a hint of broader concerns. Outside the United States, Protestants continued to view Rome as the paradigm of religious despotism; within the United States, the great debate had become, at least temporarily, whether slavery was inherently despotic or, as the South's most skillful advocates claimed, the strongest republican bulwark against despotism. By temporarily displacing historical anti-Catholicism, American Protestants may have worked a subtle theological alteration in which Christian sanction or censure of a currently vexing American problem took precedence over a traditional theological agenda where anti-Romanism was the key to religious self-identity. If so, the war was modernizing American Protestantism by shaking it loose from history and substituting contemporary interests as stronger reference points for theological alignment.

More obviously telling in the foreign commentary was a prominent strand of vigorous antirepublicanism. Irish evangelicals, for instance, mocked the Confederacy for not following through on its vaunted ideological foundations when it came to slavery: "However much the Southern States might prize Republicanism, there was a 'peculiar institution' which they prized still more."[65] The United Presbyterians of Scotland thought they could see "an ambition in the North to have a big republic" in order "to create a power which shall humble Europe or 'whip creation'."[66] Even sharper was criticism from the Canadian Maritimes, where, early in the war, a Presbyterian editor rebuked the North for the "combined imbecility and bluster" that were responsible for restrictions on freedom of speech – "a most disgraceful thing in a republic." Later the editor went further. Quoting reports from the States, he concluded that "republican institutions were not so unmistakably good as had often been pretended" since it had become obvious that "the Northern republican" meant only "the representative man of the large trading class, believing in human equality, American greatness, and the almighty power of the dollar."[67]

Even more common in foreign observations than harsh treatment of republican traditions were general doubts about the North joined with stiff antislavery convictions. Into 1862, the Scottish United Presbyterians regularly chastised the North in just about the same terms as it did the South because the Union did not act against slavery. These sentiments were expressed forcefully in September 1862, in a report written shortly before word of Lincoln's intention to issue an Emancipation Proclamation reached Scotland: "One glorious issue will, to all appearance, under Providence, result, namely, the abolition of slavery throughout a region where liberty has always been paraded and insulted. In almost every other respect the war is an unmixed and atrocious evil."[68]

Canadians were capable of the same searing criticism of the North expressed alongside regular attacks on slavery. One of English Canada's leading theologians of the period, Robert Burns of the Presbyterian Knox College in Toronto, expounded on this combination at the end of the war. To Burns, God's providential action was responsible for the fact that candidates favoring the elimination of slavery had been winners in recent American elections. But Burns did not think that beneficent providence extended any further. Rather, the United States, this "boasted land of the brave and the free," had "clung convulsively to the gilded bait, and is now paying the penalty of her madness. In the meantime, God has been working great marvels" on his own in bringing the slave system to a close.[69] Canadian Methodists chimed in on the same issue early in the war when they argued against treating North and South as moral equals. To be sure, there had been little difference between the two at the start of the conflict; but once emancipation had been proclaimed, the North was being cleansed by its decision to eliminate slavery.[70]

An awareness that many foreign Protestant observers were less *for* the North than simply *against* slavery bears quite directly on the question of American theology during the conflict. In September 1865, the Irish evangelicals explained why, although they had maintained a consistent defense of

the North, so many in Britain had kept "a general disposition . . . to stig-
matize the Northerners as mean and tyrannical." The reasons were the pro-
Southern views of the London *Times*, a lack of sufficient information about
the American situation, a long-standing animus against the United States,
false views about the respectability of the South, and admiration for the brav-
ery of Southern armies.[71] Significantly absent in this list of British reasons
for favoring the South, which appeared in a periodical of strict theological
orthodoxy, was any mention of the scriptural defense of slavery.

The Bible and Slavery

Irish evangelicals and many other foreign Protestants simply took for granted
that the Bible ruled out slavery, although a few Protestants located abroad
did address this issue directly. In general, however, the most striking feature
of foreign Protestant commentary on the American Civil War is its weak engagement with the Bible.

As we shall see in the next chapter, foreign Roman Catholics, whom all
Protestants denounced as antiscriptural, did in fact examine the Bible at
length in connection with its teachings on slavery. Yet while American Protestants were tying themselves into knots over whether the Bible supported
slavery, foreign Protestants simply did not. For over thirty years Americans
battled each other exegetically on this issue, with the more orthodox and the
ones who took most seriously the authority of Scripture being also the ones
most likely to conclude that the Bible sanctioned slavery. Outside the United
States, one rarely encountered the conviction that to trust the Bible meant to
approve, however reluctantly, the slave system in its American form.

The key historical issue with respect to Scripture is best stated as two questions. First, why in the United States did simply quoting passages like Leviticus 25:45 or 1 Corinthians 7:20-21, which indicated approval or tolerance for
slavery per se, carry such weight for virtually all Americans, whether in the
North or the South, whether for abolitionists like Garrison (who was ready to
give up such a Bible), conservative emancipationists like Hodge (who rejected
the idea that slaveholding was sinful as such), or proslavery advocates like
Thornwell (who felt that such passages demonstrated absolutely the legitimacy of Southern slave society)? But, second, why outside the United States,
even among groups that were at least as theologically orthodox as conser-

vatives in America, did quoting the same biblical passages carry almost no weight at all? An answer to the first query is found in looking at the foreign observations. An answer to the second requires a broader comparison of cultural values.

To be sure, foreign Protestants were not quite unanimous in denying that the Bible supported slavery. In one of the very few contrary instances, the London *Times* set out an anti-abolitionist position that, with its words of concession, moved closer to moderate American opinion. Abolitionists, according to the *Times*, "preach with the Bible in their hands." But "in that book there is not one single text that can be presented to prove Slavery unlawful, though there is much which naturally tends to its mitigation, its elevation, and its final extermination." The *Times* was not the venue for extensive exegesis, but it did refer to the standard biblical proslavery arguments. The Apostle Paul, it asserted, was "the man who represents the last revealed phase and development of the Gospel," and yet he sent the slave Onesimus back to his master Philemon. Without directly citing the text, the *Times* claimed that legitimate debate over 1 Corinthians 7:21 concerned only whether slaves who were offered manumission should accept or reject it. And in attacking the abolitionists' use of the "spirit of Scripture," which we have already noted, it wondered why that spirit was not evoked against "ecclesiastical titles, . . . good clerical income, and many other things that are contrary to the spirit of the Gospel, or, at least can be proved so as easily as slavery."[72] Although the *Times* was a general interest newspaper, its parroting of prominent proslavery biblical arguments was no measure of their popular appeal in Britain, where the religious press and the learned theological journals hardly gave them attention.

In the vast majority of cases, foreign Protestants took note of biblical arguments in support of slavery only to dismiss them. Among the fullest treatments were those included in Count Gasparin's two books and the substantial pamphlet by Goldwin Smith. Yet even here, where biblical texts were quoted at some length and detailed contra-exegesis was provided, the quality of argumentation fell well below the high standard set by American advocates of the various positions. Goldwin Smith had his finger on a key element of the American situation when he claimed that "the philosophic theory as to ineradicable differences of race, on which Slavery is now founded by its defenders, is directly contradicted by the New Testament."[73] But the direct contradiction he offered was only to quote Acts 17:26 and then move on. Gasparin had even less patience when examining individual passages. After a rapid survey of New Testament teaching, his primary conclusion was to wonder at "that prodigious paradox according to which the Gospel is the patron of slavery."[74]

As a rule, foreign Protestants dispatched biblical proslavery arguments even more quickly. Some of the foreign commentators took the path followed by conservative American abolitionists, who wanted to retain an authoritative Scripture even as they opposed slavery. Thus Canadian Wesleyan Methodists gave a great deal of space in the *Christian Guardian* to reprinting an essay from the New England author and philanthropist Lydia Maria Child; in quoting many biblical texts, she underscored differences between how the mistreatment of slaves was mitigated in the Hebrew Bible and how it was exacerbated by legal statutes of the Southern states.[75] In 1864 the *Protestantische Kirchenzeitung* responded to a book published by Stephen Hopkins, the Episcopal bishop of Vermont, who defended slavery as a biblical institution; the editors offered what they considered an effective *reductio ad absurdum* by merely referring readers to another American publication that used Hopkins's type of arguments to justify the practice of polygamy.[76] For German Protestants, it was that simple.

Most foreign Protestants ignored the details of proslavery biblical exegesis and followed Goldwin Smith and Count Gasparin by appealing to Christian consciousness. The Methodist *Canada Christian Advocate* wrote scathingly about "the sin of worshiping the American God" that manifested itself in "the priests of the slave power [who] . . . extort from a tortured Bible, the justification of their deeds"; it was enough to contend to the contrary that "Jehovah has written the equality and inalienable rights of man on the conscience of intelligent men, as well as along the pages of Revelation."[77] Other Canadians were just as dismissive of efforts to "defend slavery, pronounce it scriptural, [or] describe it as an unspeakable blessing." Methodists could only wonder "what would Wesley and Asbury say to all that?" Or in responding to the London *Times'* biblical defense of slavery, they simply dismissed it as proving that "nothing is more tyrannical or exacting, than an evil cause."[78] The same note came from Ireland, where Benjamin Morgan Palmer's claim that the South was formed to preserve slavery was met with the prediction that "the cause of universal liberty and Christian civilization" would deal the

Confederacy "a fatal blow."[79] In Scotland a letter from Southern Presbyterians justifying secession brought the charge that "in these days of Christian light and liberty" religious defenses of slavery deserve not God's blessing "but His righteous wrath."[80]

Weighty as counter-exegesis or an appeal to the moral consciousness of enlightened Christians might appear outside the United States, American advocates of biblical proslavery confidently felt they could handle such arguments with ease. The most skillful use of the Bible in defending slavery came from Americans like Richard Fuller, Thomas Stringfellow, or even Moses Stuart who were careful exegetes of individual passages but who also knew how to pose the question of orthodox fidelity: will you follow God's faithful word in the Bible or the deliverances of your own finite and easily swayed conscience? That dilemma, which carried great weight in the United States, almost never exerted any force on Protestants abroad.

Two other arguments put forward by foreign Protestants were more perceptive and more fundamental. They repeatedly attacked American slavery in terms of racial oppression rather than of economic organization. They also condemned it for violating numerous ethical norms about which the Bible spoke unambiguously. As an illustration of the first, James Gibson in Ireland challenged those "Economists and Theologians" who proclaimed "it as a great physical, moral, and philosophical truth, that one race of the common brotherhood of mankind has been created to be eternal bond slave of another."[81] The missionary to Africa who wrote to the *United Presbyterian Magazine* in September 1863 offered a detailed defense of the spiritual and moral capacities of the Africans with whom he was personally acquainted. In his experience he had "nowhere seen evidence of that native inferiority which many good and learned men suppose to exist." Moreover, while speaking frankly about African civilizations as "deplorably ignorant and desperately depraved," he also suggested that much of the degradation he witnessed in African societies "exists generally where the foreign slave-trade has or does prevail."[82] At about the same time, the Free Church of Scotland's magazine described the legislation of the slave states as resting wholly upon the infidel science of George Gliddon and Josiah Nott (spelled here "Knolt"), which divided humanity up into different species, with Africans occupying "a place intermediate between man and the monkey"; to the Free Presbyterians, this was a "doctrine of devils."[83] As it happens, at least some biblical proslavery advocates like J. H. Thornwell also repudiated Gliddon and Nott's polygenetic conclusion that blacks constituted a lower species of humanity. But much foreign commentary stressed that for the American slave system racism rather than the protection of property was the deepest issue – and that the Bible flatly condemned racism.

In the lengthy treatises of both Goldwin Smith and Count Gasparin, attention to race played a prominent role. Smith put succinctly what only a few critics of American slavery were willing to argue: "Those who found slavery on a doom pronounced against the negro race must say no more about the recognition of their institution by the law of Moses or by the New Testament, for the slavery recognized by the law of Moses and the New Testament was not that of negroes, but of other races."[84] Gasparin was just as blunt: "American slavery, which its friends so strangely claim to place under the protection of the Apostles, has nothing in common with that of which the Apostles had cognizance. . . . Slavery, in the United States, is founded on color, it is *negro* slavery." Yet such a slavery was much more difficult to uproot than the type countenanced by biblical writers. To Gasparin the contrast was clear: "A normal servitude of right, based upon a native and indestructible inferiority was not then in question, but an accidental servitude among equals, to which the chances of war had given birth, and which emancipation suppressed entire. Quite different is the slavery that depends on race."[85]

The weakest proslavery argument was that a form of slavery limited to one race only was the form present in the New and Old Testaments. To foreign Protestants, the failure of this claim amounted to a failure of the proslavery biblical argument as a whole.

The second strong argument made repeatedly by foreign Protestants was their insistence on a distinction between slavery considered in the abstract, or as a very specific form of social organization in the ancient world, and slavery understood as the type of chattel bondage protected by law in the United States. The Germans registered this distinction in 1860 when they reported on the traumas of Northern Methodists concerning "the regrettable question of slavery," and particularly whether to condemn slavery entirely or just the buying and selling of human beings required to make the Southern slave system work.[86] The *Christian Guardian* in Canada went further in October 1861 by attacking the fugitive slave laws of the United States as a "direct violation and opposition to the Word of God, which says [in Deuteronomy

23:15], 'Thou shalt not deliver unto his master the servant which is escaped from his master unto thee.' " To these Canadian Methodists, a system that allowed such violations of biblical injunctions amounted to pure social poison: "Slavery has sapped the foundation of moral and religious principle in the North as well as in the South."[87] Even more direct was the *Canada Christian Advocate*, which in early 1861 published a substantial article under the title "Hebrew and Negro Slavery Unlike." This essay combined the criticism of American slavery as racially grounded with a lengthy recital of the differences between the slavery practiced in ancient Israel, which was guarded by many humane ameliorations, and the slavery practiced in the Southern states, which abounded in direct violations of the biblical commands prohibiting man-stealing, protecting families, providing for education, offering the possibility of manumission, and encouraging the development of citizenship. The *Advocate's* conclusion was unequivocal: "No two things on earth can be more unlike, both in principle and in practice, than Hebrew and Negro slavery."[88] Count Gasparin made the same point succinctly: "Does any one fancy Philemon treating Onesimus, after this epistle, as fugitive slaves are treated in America?"[89] It also loomed large in Goldwin Smith's assault. As Smith saw the situation, "In America . . . there appears to be no religious communion between the master and slave. . . . It is only by putting [i.e., substituting] names for things that the American master and slave can be said to be of the same religion."[90] This fact was for him proof positive that American slavery was very different from the slavery described in either the Old Testament or the New, where in both cases divine commands insisted on the integration of slave and master in a common worship.

Significantly, as we have seen, antislavery Americans also pushed the same objection upon biblical defenders of slavery – that is, because the American system entailed so many antibiblical practices, regardless of what one might want to say about slavery in the abstract, the American style of slavery was in biblical perspective a crime. Yet in the United States this objection was usually not linked to an attack on American slavery as racially grounded. Thus when attacks were mounted against abuses of the slave system, they were much easier to rebut by reference to general statements about slavery in Scripture than was the case abroad. By contrast, when foreign Protestants looked at America, they saw a racial slavery whose practices violated cardinal biblical norms. They did not see slavery per se, nor did they recognize what they saw in the United States as the slavery mentioned in the Bible. Anti-slavery arguments that did not seem to work in the United States exerted crushing force outside the country.

Taking Stock

Once it has been observed that the same arguments carried different weight inside and outside the United States, the pressing question is why this was so. One explanation is materialist. It emphasizes the economic interests of those who defended slavery. Goldwin Smith began his monograph with two examples of the many "strange things" that were found in America: "By the side of the Great Salt Lake is a community basing itself upon Polygamy. In the Southern States is a community basing itself upon Slavery." After noting that both Mormon polygamists and Southern slaveholders claimed the sanction of Scripture, Smith wondered, "Perhaps if the Mormonite were equally an object of political interest to a large party, his plea might be accepted also."[91] Count Gasparin reasoned similarly in responding to the biblical proslavery sentiments he had himself heard in New York City churches and from the Old School Presbyterian *New York Observer*. His explanation was that "these revolting excesses seldom appear except in seaports, and especially in New York," where "the interests of this great city are bound up to such a degree with those of the cotton States."[92] In modern parlance, Gasparin was saying that, for resolving the issue of Scripture and slavery, it was sufficient to follow the money. What better rationalization for defending material interests could be found in a Bible-besotted culture than use of the Bible itself?

Certainly, there is merit to this materialist explanation. Yet, just as certainly, it cannot comprehend the whole American situation. At least some Southern advocates of slavery did try to bring the system into line with other biblical norms. Many Northern defenders of slavery as biblical had virtually no stake in the system. Most important, many earnest Christians (both North and South) who would gladly have welcomed a sure biblical word against slavery concluded reluctantly that allegiance to Scripture simply had to override murmurs of conscience against the peculiar institution.

Explaining how a common trust in the one Bible led to such different conclusions gets further by referring to the broader social, cultural, and religious circumstances that shaped interpretations of Scripture. Four observations may be helpful. First, outside the United States, traditional orthodox Christianity was much more likely to be a- or antirepublican than Christianity in the United States; it was also more likely to be governed by inherited communities of interpretation and to be wary of claims for autonomous and freshly proposed understandings of the Gospel.[93] Consequently, biblical interpretation outside the United States was more often a corporate exercise, which respected the developmental traditions of Christian communities more than the individual's own grasp of Scripture. If that corporate consciousness condemned slavery, it could easily overrule what looked like individualistic or eccentric appeals to the Bible. A measure of this difference is the contrasting shape of revivalism during the nineteenth century. In the United States, revival worked mostly through voluntaristic, self-created structures. By contrast, in the vigorous British revivals of the era, renewal movements tended to energize tightly organized local communities (the Methodists), to draw on the long-standing traditions of state churches (the Presbyterian communion seasons in Scotland and the Protestant union movement in Germany), or to be guided by leaders of the dominant institutional churches (as in Ireland by Church of Ireland and Presbyterian ministers).[94]

Second, outside the United States, traditional orthodox Christianity was not particularly democratic. Thus it did not matter as much how self-selected individuals, whether populist or learned, interpreted the Scriptures compared to how the traditional churches interpreted the Bible. As in the United States, the Bible in Canada and Europe was foundational for Protestants. The contrast was that while prime contexts for interpreting Scripture were provided for these foreigners by history, tradition, and respect for formal learning, the prime American context was the interpretive will of the people.

Third, outside the United States, antislavery was not linked to heterodox theology or to the rejection of Christianity. Whereas in America a noticeable connection existed between ardent abolitionism and a willingness to abandon the Bible, in Britain and on the European continent the strongest opponents of slavery usually came from the more evangelical or more orthodox segments of the religious community. So it was that the biblical attack on slavery from the theologically liberal Goldwin Smith represented an exception for Europe.

Fourth, in Britain, both traditionalist and evangelical varieties of Christianity leaned against the literalist exegesis of Scripture that provided the greatest strength for biblical proslavery. In particular, British High Church and evangelical believers distrusted the principle that each and every Bible verse had a simple meaning to be extracted only by attending to just the words in that verse. Unfortunate recent experiences with the followers of Edward Irving and the early Plymouth Brethren, who developed novel eschatologies from this kind of literalistic biblical exegesis, confirmed many British Protestants in their resistance to overtly literal interpretations of Scripture.[95]

In sum, viewed from outside the United States, the issue of the Bible and slavery did not pose the difficulties that it did within. Trust in the Bible was virtually the same. But because trust in the people at large to interpret any part of the Bible by relying on republican and democratic common sense was much weaker abroad, foreign Protestant Bible believers easily turned aside the proslavery arguments that seemed so much stronger in the United States.

In the case of Roman Catholics outside the United States, whose views were echoed by American Catholics, there was much overlap with foreign Protestant commentary – and considerable difference. That Catholic-Protestant difference, to which we now turn, also illuminates much about the American theological situation as revealed by the crisis of the Civil War.

Chapter 7

Catholic Viewpoints

Opinions of Roman Catholics are unusually important for understanding the Civil War as a theological event. By the time of the war, Catholics in the United States were just beginning to emerge as a public force. Large-scale immigration from the 1830s onward was combining with a robust flourishing of new Catholic periodicals to create not only numerous self-conscious Catholic communities but also a distinct religious presence in a national life that had hitherto been almost exclusively Protestant. The assessment by American Roman Catholics of the war and related issues like slavery was not, however, as fully developed as Catholic commentary from abroad. Thus, although the neglected contribution by American Catholics to the midcentury theological debate deserves much fuller attention, this chapter focuses on how foreign Catholics probed the moral situation in the United States.

Catholic engagement with issues like the Bible and slavery is particularly instructive for the more general state of theology because Catholics were able to raise possibilities beyond the imagination of American Protestants. For example, they questioned the link taken for granted by many Americans (and described memorably by Alexis de Tocqueville) between expanding liberal democracy and flourishing orthodox Christianity. They suggested that the Protestant embrace of unfettered economic freedom actually damaged Christianity. They asked whether American definitions of liberty were the only, or the best, formulations for modern societies. And as a special contribution to debates over Scripture and slavery, they dared to wonder whether Protestant American individualism might not account for the sad fact of confusion in the interpretation of sacred writings. On this last sensitive matter, some Catholics even expressed the bold opinion that the vaunted Protestant attachment to Scripture as final religious authority may have undercut the power of the Bible rather than unleashed it. Because such Catholic commentary on slavery, the war, and American ideology more generally was unusually far reaching, it amounted to a fundamental assessment of prevailing beliefs and practices that American Protestants, whose main principles were so closely entwined with the nation's dominant ideologies, could not deliver. Whether or not Catholic solutions for dilemmas caused by conflicting interpretations of the Bible and providence were the right ones, they did offer a searching critique of the Protestant principles that during the early 1860s still worked so powerfully in every phase of the nation's life.

This chapter first summarizes the contribution of American Catholics to debates generated by the war. It then outlines at greater length the arguments of several progressive and conservative Catholics from outside the United States before examining what this Catholic commentary reveals about the general state of theology in Civil War America.

American Catholic Opinions

A number of important historical works have recently underscored the distinctive contribution of American Catholics to the contentious national issues surrounding the Civil War.[1] Several factors made that contribution distinctive. It is noteworthy, first, that until 1862 not a single well-known American Catholic came out unambiguously for abolition. In that year, both Orestes Brownson, the publishing cyclone who had passed through Protestant and transcendentalist phases before converting to Rome in 1844, and Archbishop John Purcell of Cincinnati, who had earlier taken part in memorable public debates with leading Protestants, became the first Catholics to demand immediate freedom for American slaves.[2] Significantly, Brownson and Purcell were prompted to take this step by the example of French progressive Catholics, some of whose works are examined below.

Catholic experience was also distinctive because Louisiana, where a French and Spanish Catholic past long predated incorporation into the United States, experienced a singular racial history. Into Louisiana's American period, some priests, brothers, and nuns (mostly from France) promoted a degree of interracial acceptance rare in other parts of the country, North as well as South.[3]

A few American Catholics also exploited the war to deliver blasts of prejudice that returned the widespread anti-Catholicism that was then so common among the era's Protestants. This counter-prejudice could take an academic form, as when early in the war Bishop Martin Spalding of Louisville dispatched a report on American developments to church authorities in Rome. According to Spalding, nations dominated by Protestants regularly made it difficult "to decide how slaves can be emancipated to their spiritual and also temporal profit." As a loyal Kentuckian, Spalding did not question the justice of slavery as such, and he was also an advocate for the Confederacy in that border state. But in his assessment of why it was so hard for blacks to make progress in America, he blamed "the proud Protestant English race" because it "does not wish to ever associate itself on a footing of social equality in its public relations with any race whatever considered inferior, whether Indian or Negro."[4]

Reverse prejudice against Protestants could also be inflammatory. So it was in April 1865 when the New York Tablet charged that "Protestantism is essentially rebellious; . . . its origin is the spirit of secession and revolt, . . . its history is but a chronicle of insurrection." This paper thought it could find an explanation for the American national trauma deep in Protestant history: "In short, sedition and mutiny are but fruits of the Lutheran leaven spreading under the special names of Liberty and Independence into all the ramifications of political, social and domestic life."[5]

Regarded from another angle, however, American Catholic thought on the war was neither particularly distinctive nor rich. The main public voices often merely reflected the dominant tenor of the particular regions from which they spoke, or they simply sidestepped contentious issues. Thus John England, the first Catholic bishop of Charleston, South Carolina, wrote in the early 1840s a learned defense of slavery as compatible with Christian principles in an effort to contain the antislavery effects of a papal condemnation of the slave trade that is discussed below.[6] Francis Patrick Kenrick, who before becoming archbishop of Baltimore in 1851 had lived in both slave Kentucky and free Philadelphia, published two editions of a major textbook in moral philosophy (1840–43, 1860–61) that dealt with slavery at some length. This text did cite historical Catholic teaching to affirm the essential humanity of slaves and to complain against mistreatment of slaves, but it also accepted the status quo by urging masters to treat slaves kindly and slaves to obey their masters.[7] Similarly, Archbishop John Hughes of New York succinctly articulated a twofold position that many other Catholics held, one that left them close to the stance of moderate American Protestants: "The Catholic Church condemns it [slavery] and has so taught that *naturally* all men are free and that it is a crime for one man to reduce another, both being equal and free, into bondage and slavery. Hence, she has ever set her face against what has in modern terms been called the 'slave trade.' But where slaves have been introduced into a country, she does not require of her members that [slaves] should be destined to their primitive condition when it would be often times worse than the one in which they are placed."[8] Bishop Augustin Verot of St. Augustine, Florida, used the Fast Day of January 4, 1861, which produced so many other definite (if contradictory) statements, to deliver a message even more favorable to slavery than what Hughes had said. Verot's text resembled the sermons of Protestant conservatives by concluding that "there is not a word in the New Testament to prohibit slavery, but . . . on the contrary, plain and evident approbations of it." It also critiqued abolitionism as having "no foundation whatever in nature or morality or the word of God, either in the Old or New Testament, or in the enactments of law-givers of the religious or political order." And while insisting that slavery in the South had "wrongs" that needed to be corrected and that "a man, by being a slave, does not cease to be a man," Bishop Verot approved the "public sentiment [that] repudiates amalgamation" between the races.[9]

Orestes Brownson wrote much more than most of his Catholic or Protestant contemporaries about slavery, abolition, the bearing of republican politics on religion, and the outbreak of hostilities between the regions.[10] On several related subjects Brownson's views did shift dramatically; for example, he moved in 1857 from the strong states' rights position of the Democrats to a more national approach concerning sectional conflict that drew him closer to the new Republican party. But his opinions in general, though colored by distinctly Catholic concerns, closely resembled those of other moderate emancipationists like Charles Hodge in that he refused to condemn slavery outright as a sin, strongly supported the Union, and gravitated rapidly to a more vigorous stance against slavery once the war started. As an example of his position, Brownson in 1857 expounded a standard Catholic conclusion, shared by many Northern Protestants, when he appealed for better treatment of slaves and called for the eventual extinction of slavery but also was frank about rejecting abolitionism: "Our leaders know that we are no abolitionists, and no one can suspect us of any sympathy with them. We say distinctly that we are strongly opposed to all efforts made in the non-slave-holding states to abolish slavery where it legally exists."[11] Brownson, like many of his Protestant peers, was constrained by what his biographer calls "the racism that undergirded his entire approach to emancipation and the so-called 'Negro question.' "[12] Even after he embraced Lincoln's emancipation plan, Brownson refused to consider blacks as potential equals in society or politics. He was, in other words, typically American.

On slavery and the war, American Catholics spoke with a muted voice.[13] They did so for several reasons, including the pressure of American circumstances. Although Catholics had established a presence by the 1640s in what would become the United States, the American Catholic community long remained small and relatively isolated. This situation changed rapidly with the onset of large-scale immigration. In 1842, the first year that immigration topped 100,000 people, almost half of the new arrivals were from Ireland, and they were overwhelmingly Catholic. Yet adjusting to America meant having to rethink settled European patterns. As a German priest put it in 1855 when writing from Wisconsin to his Austrian sponsors: "All the resolutions made in Europe as soon as one feels the breezes of the American coastline, every tie, including the one with God, must be retied here and it must undergo the American '*Probatum est*' before it can be said to be secure."[14]

Most of all, adjusting to America meant adjusting to public opinion that associated Catholicism with religious error, church-state collusion, the binding of conscience, moral slavery, and worse. The surge of immigration that created strong Catholic communities also created a cultural backlash. The backlash was general, but it took concentrated shape in the mid-1850s with the formation of the American (or Know-Nothing) Party. The principal doctrine of this short-lived but influential movement—which elected several members of Congress, took control of the Massachusetts legislature, and gained over 20 percent of the vote in the presidential election of 1856—was its opposition to Roman Catholic immigration. Creative political thinking on issues like slavery and sectional conflict was not going to be easy against such a background.

Yet more than the diffidence of newcomers lay behind Catholic reserve in the public arena. With regard to both specific situations and general principles, Catholics had good reason to be wary of dominant American opinions. The most specific issue concerned events in Rome that were taking place at the same time that American sectional antagonisms were drifting toward war.[15] The issue itself was loyalty to Pope Pius IX (r. 1846–78), whose standing as a major sovereign on the Italian peninsula was being threatened by politically liberal forces maneuvering for the creation of a modern Italian nation-state. From time immemorial the Catholic Church had taught that the pope's spiritual independence depended on his political autonomy as ruler of the Papal States. But since the European revolutions of 1848 Italian liberals had striven to deprive the papacy of its temporal domain, and among the world's most enthusiastic cheerleaders for the Italian antipapal forces were American Protestants, the loudest of whom were the United States' best-known liberals, the party of abolitionism. For American Catholics to show loyalty to the pope in his contemporary political turmoil was to invite the suspicion of those Americans who were most vocal in supporting the pope's opponents.

This specific situation spoke also of more general Catholic concerns. The abolitionists' willingness to upset society in pursuit of their goals, even to break the law if necessary (as in the case of John Brown), deeply troubled Catholics, most of whom believed that the church was charged by God to uphold stability in social as well as ecclesiastical domains. The concern that inherent Protestant tendencies fomented social disorder led to broader uneasiness about the American situation.

It certainly did not win over Catholics to the liberal schemes of their fellow Americans when they were constantly charged by Protestants with practicing a religion hardly distinguishable from slavery itself. In the course of one of the public debates involving Bishop John Purcell, which took place in 1837 in Cincinnati, Alexander Campbell, the leader of the Restorationist movement, expressed his suspicion bluntly: "The Roman Catholic religion, if infallible and unsusceptible of reformation, as alleged, is essentially anti-American, being opposed to the genius of all free institutions, and positively subversive of them, opposing the general reading of the scriptures, and the diffusion of useful knowledge among the whole community, so essential to liberty and the permanence of good government." Campbell went even further to charge that Catholics were "abject slaves to their priests, bishops, and popes" and that "the benumbing and paralyzing influence of Romanism is such, as to disqualify the person for the relish and enjoyment of political liberty."[16]

In the years immediately before the war, other Protestants published entire books that extended Campbell's denunciation – for example, N. L. Rice's *Romanism Not Christianity: A Series of Lectures in Which Popery and Protestantism Are Contrasted, Showing the Incompatibility of the Former with Freedom and Free Institutions* (Cincinnati, 1847) and Thomas Bayne's *Popery Subversive of American Institutions* (Pittsburgh, 1856). The Know-Nothings of the American Party were extreme, but they nonetheless represented a great swath of American opinion in their views, as illustrated by a broadside from the mid-1850s that called slavery the "natural co-worker" with Catholicism "in opposition to freedom and republican institutions."[17]

Yet another predisposition of Catholics, which set them apart even more clearly from their Protestant fellow Americans, had an indirect bearing on how they evaluated slavery. It had long been habitual for American Protestants to approach Christian life in the world with an activist mentality. Especially the broad Reformed, or Calvinist, tradition – which shaped Congregationalists, Presbyterians, Baptists, Restorationists, and even Episcopalians and Methodists – looked upon problems as challenges to be solved. The tremendous proliferation of nineteenth-century voluntary associations, each independently tailored to fix some moral or spiritual problem, was the fullest expression of this attitude. Obstacles impeding the advance of God's Kingdom should and could be identified, assessed, and eliminated. This spirit, which energized both abolitionist attacks on slavery and biblical defenses of the institution, helps explain why the clash of moral force and moral resistance was so severe in fueling the Civil War.

Catholics too could organize against specific ills, as witnessed by the profusion of religious orders founded and deployed to address particular problems in particular places. But by the mid-nineteenth century Catholics also shared another general attitude that worked against a reformist mentality. It was an attitude nourished by the great nineteenth-century revival in devotional piety that looked upon human suffering not just as a problem to be fixed but also as a condition to be embraced for spiritual good.[18] John McGreevy has well summarized how this attitude comported with the main events of midcentury European Catholic history: "The usefulness of suffering, the conviction that it served as part of human redemption, sustained a range of devotions associated with the Catholic revival; it was one reason for the devotions' enormous popularity in Ireland and Germany immedi-

ately after the famine and economic distress of the 1840s."[19] The harsh treatment received by Pius IX at the hands of Italian liberals offered a graphic
instance of bearing up under what Peter D'Agostino calls "the sense of re-
demptive suffering so central to ultramontane devotionalism."[20] When poor
immigrants were oppressed, directly or indirectly, by the Protestant power
structures of Boston, Philadelphia, and New York, they could follow the pope
in embracing their suffering with faith.

The link to sectional debates was that Catholic awareness of unjust slave
suffering did not lead naturally to mobilization against that suffering.
Rather, slave suffering might well be considered one of those intractable human conditions to be borne patiently for the sake of eternal reward.

With a devotional disposition so at odds with usual Protestant expecta-
tions and with American attitudes so suspicious of Catholicism as inherently
despotic, it is little wonder that Catholics remained mostly on the sidelines
as other Americans — preachers, pundits, statesmen, and religious thinkers —
vigorously debated the Bible's bearing on slavery, the morality of republican
rights, and the other contentious moral issues that led to war.

A Richer Commentary from Abroad

Outside the United States, especially in strongly Catholic parts of the world,
it was different. Diffidence was neither necessary nor expected. And so it is
possible to discover, with only a little effort, a remarkably broad as well as remarkably challenging quantity of foreign Catholic opinion on the theological
disputes of the American Civil War. The subtlety of those judgments can be
suggested by the pronouncements of Gregory XVI, who served as pope from
1831 to 1846 amid a gathering European storm of political and religious un-
rest. The difficulty for Americans in assessing this pope was that he was not
aligned neatly with the standard ideological categories of New World opinion. In 1832 Gregory issued an encyclical, *Mirari Vos*, that anticipated some of
his successor Pius IX's harshest criticisms of modern liberal society. Gregory's
prescriptions for what he considered the ills of Europe were conservative,
even reactionary. He defended the sovereignty of papal Catholicism in European Christianity; he attacked the claim "that *liberty of conscience* must be
maintained for everyone"; he defined the "license of free speech" as one of
the great threats to modern societies; and he asserted that ruin would come

from following "those who desire vehemently to separate the Church from the state, and to break the mutual accord between temporal authority and the priesthood."[21] This was the papacy that Alexander Campbell had in mind when he described Catholicism as fundamentally opposed to American freedom.

But then in 1839 Gregory issued an apostolic letter, *In Supremo*, that condemned the slave trade in very strong terms. In fact, as historian John Quinn has suggested, "the letter had enough antislavery language in it that it could easily be seen as an attack on the institution of slavery as well."[22] In the wake of this letter, American opinion was tied in knots. The abolitionist Wendell Phillips cheered Gregory and arranged for part of the pope's letter to be read in Boston's Faneuil Hall, a notable first in that city of the Puritans. Irish Catholics associated with the home-rule advocate Daniel O'Connell urged their fellow religionists in America to come out foursquare for abolition, but the allegiance of most American Catholics to the Democratic Party made it impossible for them to follow this advice. In addition, as we have noted, Bishop John England of South Carolina rushed to deny that the pope was an abolitionist. Somewhat later, the staunchly Protestant editors of the *New York Independent* printed the apostolic letter to convince American Catholics that they should be more active in opposing slavery.

The apparently contradictory messages conveyed by these two papal pronouncements— by American standards, a striking instance of retrograde antirepublicanism and a striking instance of almost radical near abolitionism — suggest that Gregory's reasoning was not following well-worn American paths. Instead, it was approaching general political issues and the morally charged special problem of slavery from its own theological perspective. Exploring this conservative Catholic vantage point, along with the views maintained by progressive Catholics that did align more easily with standard American patterns, opens a door to the broader Catholic assessment of American conditions, and so to insight into the broader challenges faced by American theologians at the time of the Civil War.

Progressive Catholics

Like American Protestants, foreign Catholics were not unanimous on the question of slavery. To be sure, most progressive Catholics agreed with most

European Protestants in condemning the institution. Such progressive Catholics were especially vocal in Quebec, France, Switzerland, and Ireland, where they often constituted a distinct party trying to speed up Catholic accommodation to political, social, and economic change. With only a few exceptions, progressive Catholics usually disposed of proslavery biblical arguments as casually as their European Protestant contemporaries did. They spoke out forthrightly for emancipation, though they differed about the details concerning the means and the timing used to implement it. Usually they were more impressive rhetorically than theologically.

Representative of this progressive stance were works published during the war by Louis-Antoine Dessaulles (1818–95), a Quebec seigneur, journalist, and politician who repeatedly fell afoul of the province's conservative bishops, and Félix Dupanloup (1802–78), a scholar who became the bishop of Orleans in France in 1849.

As a young man, Dessaulles had upset the Quebec authorities by supporting Louis-Joseph Papineau's short-lived attempt in 1837 to unleash a Canadian version of the American Revolution. Although Dessaulles remained active on the liberal side of many Quebec struggles, he failed in those efforts at the same time that he was failing in his financial affairs. He ended his life as an exile, first in the United States and then in France.[23] When in 1864 Dessaulles delivered a series of substantial lectures, published the next year as *La guerre americaine: Son origine et ses vraies causes* (The American War: Its Origin and Its True Causes), he deviated from the common foreign pattern that condemned slavery but also expressed doubts about the North. Such ambiguity was absent from his lectures, which hymned Northern virtue and excoriated Southern perfidy. Although Dessaulles rummaged among the long centuries of Catholic history to support his cause, most of what he said was categorical rather than argumentative. Not only did slavery represent a practical negation of "the Christian ideal," but it was also "at bottom the practical negation of republican institutions." For the clergy of the United States to hesitate in attacking slavery was little more than "putting themselves in palpable contradiction to Christian doctrine as a whole." To Dessaulles it was clear that by violating the Golden Rule and the Great Commandment (which he paraphrased from Matthew 19:19 and Matthew 22:37–39), American slavery stood condemned without equivocation: "If there is in my view anything incontestable, it is that slavery is from all points of view the direct negation of two great principles that Christianity has brought to the world: first, equality before God for all members of the human family; second, charity, or the love of others taking the place of love of self. Slavery is the most absolute violation of these two fundamental principles of all religion and all morality."[24]

Félix Dupanloup, a French bishop with much more influence than Dessaulles, anticipated the Canadian's approach when on Passion Sunday in April 1862 he preached a sermon denouncing slavery in the United States and elsewhere in the world.[25] Dupanloup knew there were "theoretic questions" concerning slavery that church authorities had labored over through the centuries in great detail. But in this sermon he was not interested in "abstractions and hypotheses." Instead, he was keen to explain slavery in terms of basic Christian doctrine: "How did man reduce man to slavery? I defy its explanation to me unless by Original Sin. How did the slave again become equal to his master? I defy its explanation except through Redemption." The bishop did take note of the many papal pronouncements that had condemned the trade in African slaves, which began with Pius II's declaration ten years before Columbus's first voyage, but he was far less interested in what he called "doctrinal subtleties" than in "the truths of experience" expressed in sweeping theological judgments. To Bishop Dupanloup, the most pressing matter could be simply stated: "There are, then, on the same earth with myself, children of God and children of men like myself, saved by the same blood that I am, destined to the same heaven that I am, five or six millions of my fellow beings . . . who are slaves." His response was blunt: "Just Heaven! Is it not yet time, after eighteen centuries of Christianity, for us all to begin to practice the ever enduring law, 'Do not to another that which you would not he should do to you.'" While Dupanloup thought it was only fair to provide indemnification for masters who freed their slaves, his greatest concern was to follow "Jesus Christ, St. Paul, and the Apostles, [who] laid down the principles of universal emancipation."[26]

Progressive Catholics like Dessaulles and Dupanloup usually followed European Protestants in moving rapidly to the moral high ground. One exception, who was determined to remain on the plains of biblical and theological argument as long as it took to make his case, was Augustin Cochin (1823-72), a French politician who enjoyed a central place among the liberal Catholics of his generation.[27] In 1861 Cochin published a substantial tome in Paris with the straightforward title L'abolition de l'esclavage. Two years later, in a superb translation by Mary Booth, who had also rendered Count Gasparin's works into English, part of Cochin's study was published in a very substantial volume as *The Results of Slavery.*[28] This translation included book 7 of the original, "Christianity and Slavery," which mounted one of the most thorough biblical, theological, and historical attacks on slavery of the entire era.

Cochin began dramatically with an argument keyed to the spirit of biblical teaching:

> Christianity has destroyed slavery.
>
> Yes, He who is pre-eminently the Redeemer, he who has ransomed woman from degradation, children from abandonment, subjects from tyranny, the poor from contempt, reason from error, the will from evil, the human race from punishment, Jesus Christ has restored fraternity to mankind and liberty to man. Jesus Christ has destroyed slavery.[29]

Yet after that opening flourish, Cochin engaged in a detailed exegetical examination of almost all the passages from both Testaments that defenders of slavery employed to make their case. This work rose to at least the high level of Francis Wayland's careful responses to Richard Fuller. Even more than Wayland, Cochin insisted that the slavery that actually existed in the American South was something entirely different from the slavery that might be defended from Scripture. Cochin was most cutting at the end of his extensive scrutiny of Old Testament texts: "Such," he concluded, "is Hebrew slavery." True, it was far from "Christian liberty," but it was also very far from other forms of slavery practiced in the ancient world. Most important, Hebrew slavery bore no resemblance to American slavery: "No slave-trade, no fugitive slave law, no slavery among natives; a year of jubilee; the purity of woman, the weakness of childhood, the rights of manhood, placed under the provident protection of the law; equality professed, fraternity professed." Having spelled out these differences, Cochin challenged defenders of modern slavery to stop taking "arguments" from the Bible: "Let them rather take examples." His conclusion resounded: "On the day that the law of the Jews shall become the law of one of the self-styled Christian Southern States of the American Union, immense progress will be accomplished, and the unhappy slaves may await and catch a glimpse of full liberty."[30]

Cochin's combination of arguments debating the letter of the Bible and

evoking its spirit resembled the best abolitionist or emancipationist theology
in America. He was particularly effective in urging defenders of slavery to
be as literal with texts like James 5:4 ("Behold, the hire of the laborers who
have reaped down your fields, which is of you kept back by fraud, crieth: and
the cries of them which have reaped are entered into the ears of the Lord of
Sabaoth") as with those mentioning slavery.[31]

But Cochin also went beyond that argumentation, as no American Protestant did, to a lengthy defense of the Catholic record on slavery.[32] Cochin
conceded that the Catholic Church did teach subordination to lawful authority, including that of slaves to masters. He also admitted that in the late
fifteenth and the sixteenth centuries, all nations had "sinned" by following
Islamic example in sanctioning the European enslavement of Africans – both
Catholics, who "had destroyed ancient slavery," and Protestants, who "it has
been sought to make the parent of modern liberty."[33] Cochin's main concern,
however, was to present a detailed defense of the Catholic Church as working throughout the centuries to apply "absolute principles" of Scripture that
defined "the equality of men before God, the lawfulness of wages, the unity
and brotherhood of the human race," the duties of mutual love to neighbors,
and the Golden Rule. Cochin put into the present tense what he claimed the
leaders of the Catholic Church had always done: "Occupied, moreover, before
everything with the enfranchisement of souls, they seek to make of the master and the slave two brethren on earth, and of these brethren two saints in
heaven. To those who suffer, they say, 'Wait!' to those who inflict suffering,
'Tremble!' "[34]

This robust defense of Catholicism as the friend of liberty extended also to
praising the church for how it interpreted the Bible. In a challenge to American habits of exegesis of the sort that never appeared from Protestants, he set
out succinctly a contrast that his conservative Catholic contemporaries developed at greater length: "The manner in which men find in the Bible all that
their interest desires fills me with astonishment, and I thank God once more
for having caused me to be born in the bosom of a Church which does not
abandon the Holy Books to the interpretations of caprice and selfishness."[35]

Given that so much of what Cochin had to say about slavery resembled
attacks from Protestants, it was fitting that his translator, Mary Booth, described Cochin's treatment of the relevant Scriptures as "an able exposition
of slavery in the evangelical point of view, which, designed for a Catholic, is

equally useful in a Protestant community."[36] Yet the elements that set his
work apart from Protestant parallels – especially the treatment of Catholicism as the long-term friend of liberty and his challenge to capricious biblical interpretation – constituted a distinctively Catholic contribution.

Conservative Catholics

For conservative Catholics those two considerations were central: Catholicism was the surest support of liberty, and it guaranteed a unified use of the
Bible.[37] Conservative Catholics in the mid-nineteenth century could be identified by their support for efforts by Gregory XVI and Pius IX to shore up papal
spiritual authority and defend papal temporal rule. Led by these pontiffs,
conservative Catholics were skeptical about the supposed virtues of modern
society – including democracy, unrestricted capitalism, free speech, liberty
of conscience, public schools, denominational pluralism, and the separation
of church and state. They were just as skeptical about the supposed inade-
quacy of what these modern phenomena were replacing – paternal authority,
corporate economic solidarity, disciplined public utterance, consciences bent
to the truth, religious education, Catholic supremacy, and a well-regulated
cooperation of church and state. Catholic conservatives also usually partici-
pated in the nineteenth century's broad devotional revival, which Pius IX
especially encouraged when in 1854 he defined the immaculate conception of
the Blessed Virgin Mary. As a consequence, conservatives were not convinced,
as many progressive Europeans seemed to be, that the United States should
be hailed as the wave of the future. When analyzing developments at midcentury, some conservative Catholics even specified the toleration of slavery,
along with a dreadful record of racism, as distinctly American problems that
demonstrated the evils of modernity.

Such views came from, among others, traditional Quebec Catholics, such
as the editors of *Courrier du Canada*, who ridiculed the affection of French
progressives for "this deceptive and dangerous fad which is indiscriminately
called the *modern spirit, human progress*." Only a few years after the Civil War,
an expatriate American in Quebec, Jules-Paul Tardivel (1851-1905), echoed this
judgment by calling American republicanism an "essentially anti-Christian"
extension of the godless French Revolution.[38]

Similar views came from conservative Catholics in Switzerland, who wanted to maintain an older, more communal notion of freedom against progressive liberal individualism. In opinions that received their full development elsewhere, conservative Swiss Catholics expressed considerable sympathy for the South, while still judging slavery to be evil. Swiss conservatives criticized the North for discriminatory treatment of free blacks, but even more for encouraging a mad scramble for money in which nothing meant more than stiff-necked, heedless selfishness. They also concluded that the political counterpoint to this atomization of the individual was an aggressive, all-encompassing, and overweening state. In the view of the Catholic *Schwyzer Zeitung*, the Civil War was caused primarily by "the rawest despotism of northern radicalism"; moreover, plans for emancipating slaves were only smokescreens for realizing the North's unprecedented "centralization and radical governing system."[39] Behind this critique lay a Swiss Catholic conservatism that distrusted the modern ideal of individual self-determination and prized older ideals of freedom, defined as the liberty of a fellowship or community (*Eidgenossenschaft*, *Gemeinschaft*) in which individuals worked together freely under respected authorities in the state and church for common purposes.

Such conservative voices may have resonated in Quebec and Switzerland, but they were even more forceful among Catholic circles in Germany and Rome that had mobilized to support the popes in their battles against the tides of modernity. These well-educated, well-funded, and articulate groups had surprisingly expansive opinions on the American Civil War. Their opinions highlighted many of the issues that religious thinkers in the United States were also examining, but they did so with very different presuppositions about what constituted true religion, political morality, and a healthy social order.

Historisch-politische Blätter für das katholische Deutschland

In Germany the most extensive Catholic critique of the American war, and of much else, came from the *Historisch-politische Blätter für das katholische Deutschland* (Historical and Political Newspaper for Catholic Germany, abbreviated hereafter as HPB).[40] This hefty biweekly had been founded in 1838 by colleagues of Joseph Görres (1776-1848), a key figure in the development of nineteenth-century German political Catholicism. Görres and his colleagues, such as the noted theologian and church historian Johannes Joseph Ignaz von Döllinger (1799–1890), wanted to promote Catholic devotion even as they enlisted traditional Catholic theology to influence the social and political development of modern German states. In these efforts the great enemies were political and social liberalism, state-dominated churches, and progressive Protestantism. By the 1860s, the HPB was being edited by Joseph Edmund Jörg (1819–1901), an archivist who would later become leader of the Bavarian Patriot Party and play a substantial role in Bismark's national Reichstag as well as in the Bavarian parliament. During and immediately after the Civil War, Jörg himself published six long articles on the American situation. He was joined in the pages of the HPB by a correspondent who in the wake of the conflict filed four reports from the United States and by a reviewer who in 1868 explored the question of "Christianity and slavery" in a lengthy essay.[41]

For Jörg and his journal, which featured extensive commentary on all manner of social and political events, the American Civil War amounted to a full-scale demonstration of the perils of modern liberalism. The overwhelming burden of the HPB's American articles was to point out the self-destructive principles and practices of the Protestant-influenced and politically liberal North. The journal's basic stance on moral and theological questions paralleled the views published in a prize-winning German book from 1865, which was later singled out in the HPB for highest praise. The work was titled *Kirche und Sklaverei seit der Entdeckung Amerika's* (Church and Slavery since the Discovery of America), and its author, J. Margraf, took pains to explain why Catholics were not enthusiastic about American abolitionism:

> A party whose chief organ in the daily press, the *New York Tribune*, is well known as a depository for all destructive tendencies in religion and society – a party that through the *New York Times* has let its intention be freely announced that as soon as the insurrection of the Southern states is settled it would like to immediately attack the Catholic Church – a party that in a most unjust manner equates Catholicism and slavery ("No slavery, no popery!") – such a party can sooner find a sincerely devoted ally anywhere in the world more easily than in the bosom of the Catholic Church.

Margraf also stated succinctly what in his view, and also in the view of the editors of the HPB, had been the proper attitude of the Catholic Church toward modern slavery, in contrast to the destructive practices that had prevailed in America: "The church's missionary spirit did not allow the slavery of Indians to take hold; it made Negro slavery more bearable; it condemned the slave trade; it preserved emancipation from one-sided excess; and it thankfully and joyfully greeted the breaking of physical chains as a step toward the rescue of the spirit from the bonds of slavery to sin."[42]

Indictment of the North was the central theme in J. E. Jörg's extensive writings on the war. At the outset of his first lengthy article he wanted to get on record "how wickedly the liberals have used a philosophy of state" to undercut the health of the Union. That same first article also employed inflammatory language, which evoked the terrors of the French Revolution, to decry the connection between liberal principles and the centralizing power of the Northern state: division among Democrats and the triumph of Lincoln were inevitable "with the growing terrorism of liberal or radical ideas and with the colossal growth of wealth in the North." In somewhat more reserved tones, Jörg summarized his complaint against the North aphoristically: "In the name of freedom, freedom is abrogated, and in the name of the Constitution, the Constitution is destroyed."[43]

Subsequent treatments fleshed out Jörg's negative assessment of the American situation. He repeatedly described the root cause of war as the North's deeply ingrained lust for wealth: "In Boston and New York, as in London and Liverpool, they turn away their eyes with Puritan holiness from the horrors of slavery; but they still reap a profit from slavery and leave the odium to someone else."[44] Along with seeking to gratify that cupidity, the North had also engaged in a headlong pursuit of consolidated power. Thus the South's struggle was "the battle of federalism against centralizing liberalism."[45] One of the HPB's on-site reports from immediately after the war sustained the charge of avarice by predicting further national disarray: "A nation in which among a great part of the population the crassest egoism and an all-absorbing greediness for money threaten to suffocate every honorable feeling cannot hold together for the long haul."[46] In general, when the HPB looked at the North, it saw only individualism, power, and greed.

On the specific question of slavery, the journal frequently insisted that it was a "Vorwand," a pretext or smokescreen hiding the real issues of money and state power.[47] In support of this contention, Jörg offered an idyllic picture of slavery in the South, criticized the North for its shoddy treatment of free blacks, and called sudden emancipation a disaster for both blacks and whites.[48] Postwar reports in the HPB soon noted that the Freedmen's Bureau was tyrannizing the former slaves it was supposed to help.[49] They also pictured governmental efforts to assist emancipated slaves as contributing to a great burgeoning of corruption, which was "reigning especially among the monied aristocracy."[50] The theme of greed was ever favored.

Although the HPB's jaundiced view of republican principles was hardly subtle, the journal did display some nuance when it discussed the morality of slavery. Early on, Jörg examined the Southern claim that Africans were innately inferior to Caucasians. To Jörg the claim represented a "lamentable" contradiction of "the principles of Christendom and all teachings that had developed over nearly two thousand years." It also heightened the contrast between the Catholic Church, in which "there is never any difference made between black and white skin," and Protestant churches, especially in the United States, which never extend equal rights even to a freed slave, who is rather treated "like a black . . . pest." Yet Jörg, more typically, held that it was the "radical distortion" of Northern abolitionists that had precipitated extreme proslavery positions in the South, and he was willing to speculate that some "discovery of free science" might one day force the Catholic Church to revise its teachings on the essential equality of all humans.[51]

In contrast to the HPB's extensive treatment of the war's social and economic meaning, its coverage of the specifically religious questions of the hour was relatively scant. Yet that coverage did advance a provocative interpretation that in some particulars resembled what Americans like Harriet Beecher Stowe and Orestes Brownson also said. Jörg recognized at the start that "from the perspective of the slave question," the War between the States was "a formal war of religion."[52] To explain how Americans could use a single Bible to support sharply antithetical positions, Jörg offered two specific possibilities as well as a more general interpretation.

The first possibility was materialist: "As the cotton produced by blacks created ever greater wealth, slavery began to look like a sacred institution and so was defended by the Bible."[53] Jörg's second possibility was hermeneutical: he quoted with approval a Lutheran journal from Berlin that was posing the question of "how people who read and preached the Word of God could justify an institution [slavery] which so directly contradicted its spirit." The answer was that an older Puritan approach to Scripture continued to prevail in the American South, where the Bible was regarded "as a code of definite positive laws."[54] Jörg and the Lutheran journal that he quoted were wrong in thinking that this approach had "largely vanished" in the North, but they were correct in sensing that the American debate about the Bible and slavery was a contest over *how* to interpret the Bible as much as it was over *what* the Bible said.

Jörg's more general interpretation of American theological debate came at the very end of the war when he compared the situation in the United States with what had occurred in other countries. His opinion was that "the slavery question" could never have reached such a boiling point in Catholic lands, where typically "a proper middle way" had been followed: slavery was treated as "a necessary evil" that could be gradually eliminated through the influence of religion. In the United States, by contrast, the prevalence of "arbitrary theology" made such a moderate course impossible: "One group with their subjective vision reads out of the Bible that the servitude of blacks was an abomination before the Lord that must be exterminated at once with force. . . . On the other side the 1863 Episcopal Synod of the South proved from the Bible that this opinion – that slavery must 'someday' be abolished – was not only malicious but impious. Against such biblical arguments [Offenbarungen] a popular orator beloved in the North slanderously rejoined: 'We need an antislavery Constitution, an antislavery Bible, and an antislavery God.'" Jörg wanted readers to understand clearly that "from such extremes of subjective Christianity there can of course be no salvation [Heil] for blacks at all."[55] To Jörg, Protestantism's vaunted trust in Scripture had failed to define a unifying public morality. Given the dominance of Protestantism in the United States, that failure amounted to a practical argument on behalf of Catholicism.

The HPB's one thorough theological and historical treatment of slavery appeared in 1868 when it published a long review of four German books, two that looked at slavery as it had developed in the New World and two on the subject in general. (One of these was the volume by J. Margraf cited above.) The author of the article, Paul Joseph Münz (1832-99), was a priest who reprised much of the journal's earlier commentary while also providing a systematic defense of the Catholic Church's relationship to slavery. As part of this defense, he blasted abolitionists as "fanatics" who were responsible for "liberal novelties and philanthropies."[56] But most of Münz's review focused on the Catholic Church as, in his opinion, the one institution in both ancient and modern times that had provided long-term protection of human freedom and a truly effective counterforce to slavery. Like Jörg and other foreign Catholics, Münz observed that the Bible in America was a flexible instrument put to use on both sides of the conflict: "Special virtuosity in presenting long citations from the Bible—in the North against slavery, in the South for—was a special skill of the Methodist preachers." [57] Of the books he had under review, Münz agreed with one by a German Lutheran that asserted "the incompatibility of slavery with the basic conceptions of Christianity," but he felt that the author and other Protestants had neglected the centuries-long efforts of official Catholicism to mitigate and destroy the system. [58] He argued specifically that while Catholics had never been unambiguously abolitionist, they had always defended the full humanity of slaves—for example, by maintaining a racially blind mass—and had worked in many times and places for gradual emancipation. In recent centuries these practices had left liberated black slaves much better off in Catholic territories than in any Protestant land. Münz closed with words that already in 1868 could have given Americans pause, if any had read this German journal: "The North can free the slaves with force, but it cannot civilize them and deliver them from contempt and mistreatment. Here no one can help except the Church, whose main task is precisely this concern." [59]

Such a forecast, along with J. E. Jörg's assessment of the subjective character of American biblical usage, comported well with the negative tone of an on-the-scene report that the HPB published early in 1867. The report offered an alarmist picture of the struggles between Congress and President Andrew Johnson over the course of Reconstruction. The general disillusionment with how Reconstruction was progressing led the conservative Catholic correspondent to declare that amid the postwar chaos "only the Catholic Church" stood "steady as a rock," which was why so many people were ostensibly flocking to it. By contrast, the ability of Protestants to play a stabilizing role was undercut by "the great mischief of revivals and camp meetings," the intemperate nature of which exceeded what "the insane fanatics of the Orient in their madness" did. Then in a throwaway line, the correspondent alluded to the Mormons, whom we shall shortly see became the focus of the Roman Jesuits of La Civiltà cattolica in their full-scale assessment of American religion and its role in fomenting a great civil war. According to the HPB's correspondent, only in America, "der Heimath des 'Humbugs'" (the home of humbug), was Mormonism possible, "this shameful scandal based on lies, deception, and immorality."[60]

Before turning to the Italian Jesuits' calmer and more thoroughgoing assessments, it is worth noting that if the German Catholics who contributed to the HPB often lacked nuance in their interpretation of the American war, they nonetheless offered a thought-provoking critique. From their angle of vision, political liberalism seemed to be working against both order (through the revolutions of 1848) and traditional religion (via attacks on the Papal States), and radical abolitionists seemed to be America's most advanced liberals. It made a certain sense, then, to read Northern actions as guided by greed as much as by principle. It also made sense to dismiss America's earnest theological debates as the pointless meanderings of an incoherently individualistic religious system. These fragmentary theological judgments, which lay at the edges of the HPB's political and economic concerns, came to the fore in what the Roman Jesuits wrote about the Civil War and about the meaning of the war for American religion more generally.

La Civiltà cattolica

The gold standard for Catholic commentary on the American Civil War, on the Bible and slavery, and on the religious character of the United States was La Civiltà cattolica (Catholic Civilization).[61] This journal, like the HPB a thick biweekly that published nearly 3,000 pages each year, was founded in 1850 by a group of Italian Jesuits at the request of Pope Pius IX. After the European revolutions of 1848, Pius had become increasingly disillusioned with modern notions of liberalism, democracy, and progress and sought a learned outlet for the defense of church traditions. While the Jesuits of La Civiltà cattolica shared the HPB's intense fear of the damage that could be done by an aggressive liberal government like that of the United States, they were even more content than their German contemporaries with ultramontane – or papally directed – solutions to modern problems.

In response to the pressing issues of the day, La Civiltà cattolica swiftly emerged as the Catholic Church's primary champion. It was particularly articulate in opposing the movement for Italian political unification, a stance that contributed materially to its perspective on developments in the United

States. Just as it was important to defend traditional church prerogatives against liberal Italian politicians, so it was useful to show how America's liberal political principles created serious difficulties for religion and society. The journal also urged that the theology of Thomas Aquinas be used constructively as an antidote to the diseases of secularism, liberalism, and progressive Protestantism. For its reports on America, the team of Jesuits who guided the magazine had the benefit of correspondence from American bishops like John Hughes of New York and Martin Spalding of Louisville.[62] Yet the journal's articles reflected much more its own European assessments of American affairs than judgments transmitted from the New World.

From 1860 through 1866, *La Civiltà cattolica* published at least six substantial articles on topics related to the United States or to slavery, along with many additional news reports. One of the articles dealt directly with the American war;[63] four treated slavery theologically and historically;[64] and one, in many ways the most germane for our consideration, provided a general interpretation of Protestant Christianity by focusing on the history of Mormonism.[65] Together these articles offered a magisterial defense of the Catholic Church in relationship to slavery and a sober assessment of American Protestant religion in relation to the Civil War.

La Civiltà cattolica's general position resembled in some respects the stance of American moderate emancipationists like Moses Stuart. Where it went further was in adding long historical accounts of papal actions against the excesses of ancient, medieval, and modern slavery. The basic argument maintained that, unlike radical liberals, the Catholic Church could never categorically condemn slavery, but that it had nonetheless worked consistently through its entire history to mitigate the wrongs of slavery, to move toward gradual and peaceful emancipation, and to act for the benefit of slaves and masters in harmony together.

La Civiltà cattolica's fullest attention to biblical material appeared in its February 1865 article on the moral idea of slavery. This essay was prompted by a complaint in a Montreal journal, *Débats*, that when the pope's secretary of state had written about the horrors of the American war, he did not mention slavery, which *Débats* held to be as terrible as the war itself. The accusation prompted an extensive review of slavery as mentioned in Scripture, but not before *La Civiltà cattolica* considered the institution in the light of natural law. On the basis of what could be known by relying on reason alone, its conclusion was twofold: "slavery in a restrained sense is not absolutely contrary to the law of nature," yet slavery should never be allowed to override the essential human rights of the slave.[66] The article put it this way: "The master has the authority of a head in his family. . . . But at the same time he has the obligation of providing the slave with appropriate religious education, of guarding his habits carefully, of correcting him, and of cautioning him against going astray. . . . The slave, yielding the use of his labors, retains intact that which is proper to his being a human."[67] Only after drawing these conclusions from natural law did the article take up scriptural teaching.

Not surprisingly, the Jesuits found the same thing in Scripture as they discovered from nature. Slavery as such could not be condemned absolutely, especially given the fact that the apostles Paul and Peter both counseled slaves on how they should act with respect to masters (Ephesians 6:7, Colossians 3:22, and 1 Peter 2:18).[68] At the same time, these very passages demonstrated that masters owed a lengthy set of obligations to their slaves. Against the claim that slavery was always sinful, La Civiltà cattolica offered the standard conclusion of biblical conservatives: "The abuse and not the appropriate use of slavery was condemned as culpable by the Apostle [Paul]."[69]

To this interpretation of the Bible, which would have been approved by many moderate American Protestants, La Civiltà cattolica added a final word that would not have been: "The Catholic, however, does not have to interpret the Scripture capriciously [a capriccio], but takes the holy fathers as a guide [a guida i santi Padri]."[70] There followed then several pages of citations from Jerome, Augustine, and John Chrysostom, whose precedents showed how to interpret the Bible's injunctions for slaves and masters. According to the article, by following these honored church fathers, Catholics possessed a continuity and sobriety in the interpretation of Scripture that Protestants did not.

Stability in biblical interpretation echoed a main theme that had earlier appeared in La Civiltà cattolica's direct examination of American religion. But for its other articles on slavery, the Bible faded into the background while vindication of Catholic history came to the fore. These articles were the ones that most clearly reflected the local Italian situation, where self-proclaimed champions of liberty and progress were maneuvering to deprive the Catholic Church of the Papal States. To defend the popes as the patrons of true liberty in their dealings with slavery throughout the Middle Ages and in the New

World was also to deliver a message about true liberty on the Italian peninsula in the 1860s.

A substantial article from March 1865, "The Church as Guardian of Liberty in America," responded to several charges that had been made concerning the actions of the Catholic Church during the period of colonization. These charges included the claim that papal pronouncements had destroyed the autonomy of native Americans and that the church's actions in general had compromised the integrity of Spanish and Portuguese settlements. In rebuttal, the author used Pope Alexander VI's *Inter Caetera*, a papal bull from 1493, and the precedents it established to argue that "papal actions had worked to confirm laws and preserve liberty."[71]

Less than six weeks later, *La Civiltà cattolica* published another weighty defense in an article titled "The Negro Slave in America." The article offered graphic accounts of the horrors of the slave trade and of iniquities perpetuated by the American slave system, but it also dwelt at length on the papal pronouncements and the Catholic initiatives that over the centuries had restrained the abuses of slavery. The polemical bite here was the claim that in Catholic countries and colonies the basic human rights of slaves, such as the preservation of Christian marriage, were defended much better than in other countries. With an eye to both American circumstances and charges by Italian liberals about papal despotism, *La Civiltà cattolica* asked an ironic question: "Which of the two systems [Catholic, liberal] has treated the slave as a man and which as a beast? That arising from the Catholic despot or that derived from the liberal anti-Catholic governor? The reality is so manifest that it is useless to belabor the point."[72] To its own question, "What has Catholicism done for the advantage of the negro slave?" it answered confidently: "Thanks to the work of legislators inspired by the church's principles, it proclaimed loudly the natural rights that were guaranteed to slaves and opened for them the door of liberty and of citizenship when the opposite was happening under other legislators."[73] More specifically, it hailed the work of dedicated priests, brothers, and nuns who had given themselves in service to the slaves of North and South America: "The minister of the Lord goes quickly to visit them, to instruct them, to recommend them to the master, to inculcate in them the duty of going to church; thus rendering to all what they need."[74]

La Civiltà cattolica's final defense of the church soon followed, this time with specific reference to the contemporary United States. In an article from October 1866, titled "The Abolition of the Slave Trade and of Slavery," the Jesuits defended the church for having taken the proper actions in the proper way. By contrast, they pointed to Abraham Lincoln as someone who acted for mainly utilitarian ends. Their evidence was Lincoln's early profession that if he could save the Union by guaranteeing the continuation of slavery where it already existed, he would do so. The article pointed out that only when it became useful as a war stratagem did Lincoln move against slavery. It then asked what had done more in the long run for the betterment of the slaves – this utilitarian approach in America, where "the philosophy of revolution" was so strong, or the steady practices of the church.[75] The answer was that "the church has rooted slavery out of paganism, has guided it out of barbarism without tumults, massacres, and slaughters, and has caused the master and the emancipated slave to live in peace and love under the shadow of true fraternity."[76] By comparison with "modern liberalism," which championed freedom precipitously and dangerously, the church had been active on behalf of slaves for centuries. To prove that point, the article then recited a long list of medieval councils, which in many European lands had mitigated slave oppressions. It also provided a long list of papal actions, which worked to the same end, stretching back for more than a millennium before the mid-nineteenth century. The article closed with a long statement of categorical assertions:

We have thus seen on the one side that politics and utility, founded on its own civil laws, began the slave trade from Africa, introduced Negroes into America, . . . and in giving free reign to this movement carried the slave trade and slavery to the summit of injustice and iniquity: while on the other side we have found that the Catholic Church, not without good effect, worked hard in Africa, did what was allowed by the heretical conquistadores and mercantile greed to mitigate [ispiatarvi] the slave trade and slavery by the conversion of the Negroes, that it exerted itself in America not only in alleviating the hard lot of slavery but also in liberating the subjected ones, that in every period it shone a blazing light on injustice and demanded the rights of the oppressed Negroes, and that at last pronounced abolition in the name of those principles that the Catholic Church has always professed and invoked with the pen of its writings and with the living voice of its popes [colla penna dei suoi scritti e colla voce de suoi Pontefici].[77]

If the Roman Jesuits were definite about the integrity of the Catholic Church in the long history of Western slavery, they were no less definite about the current problems of religion in the world's most Protestant and most republican nation. *La Civiltà cattolica* reported on the American Civil War with more nuance than the German Catholics of the HPB, but it was no less harsh in its censure. Two long articles took the measure of the contemporary United States and its Protestant character: first, in 1860, a general indictment and then, in 1861, a specific explanation of why the Civil War should be regarded as a dramatic example of the inherent problems of Protestantism.

The first article was authored by an aristocratic cardinal archbishop, Karl August von Reisach (1800–1869), who had earlier guided several delicate church-state negotiations in his native Bavaria and would later aid Pope Pius IX in preparing for the First Vatican Council.[78] Reisach's subject, "Mormonism in its connections with modern Protestantism," touched on politics only indirectly, but the cardinal did set out in great detail a picture of American Protestantism that would be applied by *La Civiltà cattolica* less than a year later for the specific purpose of interpreting the Civil War. Reisach's thesis was straightforward: by studying Mormonism in "its fundamental principles," one could find in "this most fantastic religious system" a backhanded testimony to "the truth of the principles of the Catholic Church" over against all Protestant faiths.[79]

Reisach began by contending that because the Protestant sects agreed in viewing the individual as standing "in a direct relationship with Jesus Christ, or with God" and because they excluded "any other objective and real mediation," they thereby "demolished the notion taught by Catholic doctrine concerning the nature and authority of the church as a divine institution established by God for the salvation of men." Although Mormonism responded to the inherent weaknesses of Protestantism by setting up "an authoritative and visible church as a mediator between God and the individual human being," it also represented a logical end product of American religious history, as Reisach would explain in considerable detail.[80]

The cardinal's history of American religion began with the Puritans, who tried to found "a new social and political life on the basis of their own religious doctrine." The result was a merger of church and state, as well as "an extensive despotism" over every detail of life. Reisach acknowledged the Puritan desire to base all existence on the Bible, but he held that such attempts were doomed to failure because of inbred hermeneutical confusion: "Such a state of total biblicism – since the Bible was their only code of law – was able neither to moderate nor to constrict the absolute liberty and independence of the individuals who were reading and explaining the same Bible; and thus the same foundational principle of the Reformation naturally and necessarily caused the collapse of such a theocratic system and caused new sects and religious societies to be born." [81]

In reaction to Puritan despotism, the United States then lurched to the other extreme by setting up an absolute separation of church and state. This effort again reflected "the fundamental principle of the Reformation," in particular its tendency to "religious individualism," which in itself was "a consequence of the doctrinal errors of the Reformation." [82] The principle, when fully realized in the American setting, did offer unprecedented liberty, but so great was this liberty that it undercut the Protestants' professed desire to order all of life by the Bible: "Although in these sects the Bible is acknowledged as the rule of faith and although some of them attend strictly to the letter of Scripture, revealed and dogmatic truths disappear more and more from the common beliefs of these sects; the sacred text is explained by each one according to his own will and under the influence of a rationalistic philosophy." [83] Moreover, when Protestants stressed "the principle of justification by faith" and defined the church as invisible, they lost all stability whatsoever. These circumstances explained why they were constantly founding new churches on the claim of "new effusions of the Holy Spirit." [84]

Reisach went on to opine that the current situation in America showed the evil influence of such beliefs. There was no capacity in Protestantism to restrain "moral corruption and spreading materialism." With so complete a separation of church and state, "the individual [was] independent and sovereign," but with fateful consequences. [85] Reisach then spelled out the theological reasons for what the HPB would later criticize as American materialistic greed: "The sectarian spirit, with its dualism [between the personal and the social] has given an immense boost to materialism in the new United States; this religious individualism also produces the general egotism that characterizes the society of that country and testifies clearly that these people lacked any social tradition and that they had not been educated in a religious community chosen and founded by God."[86] In short, the sectarian spirit produced not only bad religion but also a corrupt society.[87]

But precisely this sectarian spirit explained the rise of Mormonism. To prove his point, Reisach quoted a Mormon leader, Parley Pratt, who had argued that the mere presence of many American denominations made it impossible to receive a clear and authoritative word from Scripture: "Thus the usefulness of the Bible is made the most uncertain of all books. It would have been better for people if God had revealed nothing than to have revealed a book which leaves them uncertain and dubious and that forces them to dispute continually over the significance of what is contained in it."[88] For Cardinal Reisach, Parley Pratt was making exactly *his* point: "So the Mormon doctor, with consummate reason, refutes the Protestant system."[89] In other words, the rise of Mormonism underscored the disaster of Protestant fragmentation and pointed toward the abiding human need for religious authority, stability, and community.

Of course, to the Catholic cardinal Mormonism was not the answer but only an advanced sign of the problem. The absurdity of Mormonism was shown by its reliance on continuing fresh revelations: "the most impudent fables" spun out by Joseph Smith "totally destroy the foundations of Christ."[90] By contrast, the Catholic Church "conserves, unfolds, applies, and promulgates – under the continual assistance of the Holy Spirit promised to the church until the end of time – the revelation that God, 'speaking to our fathers through the prophets, now in these last days has spoken to us by his Son' [Hebrews 1:1-2 quoted from the Latin Vulgate]. He has given [this revelation] to the world as a precious deposit, completed and perfected, which by means of the church's priesthood [per mezzo dell'ecclesiastico ministero] still comes forth as a permanent deposit and is present at all times."[91]

Reisach interpreted the prophetic principle of Mormonism as a corrective intended to counter the fragmenting force of Protestant individualism, but also as creating "a perfect social theocracy" based on "a pure religion of materialism."[92] Mormonism, for this conservative Catholic, was thus a perfect case study to show how wrong the history of Protestantism in America had gone. As an outgrowth of Protestant principles, it represented a very late manifestation of Protestantism's fatal weakness; as an outgrowth of American political liberalism, it embraced a religion of materialism; as an outgrowth of Joseph Smith's heated fancy, it was a perverted reflection of the Catholic Church as guardian of divine revelation. In sum, by trying to correct American and Protestant problems, but by doing so the wrong way, Mormonism "produced the monstrous socialistic theocracy of the most shameful materialism [la mostruosa teocrazia socialistica del più vergognoso materialismo]."[93]

According to Reisach, the Mormon illustration of Protestant failings underscored the strength of the Catholic Church, which erred neither on the side of theocracy (as illustrated by the Puritans and the Mormons) nor on the side of unrestrained individualism (as illustrated by the chaotic culmination of sectarianism in the United States). Catholics taught, by contrast, that while church and state should be distinct, they should run along parallel lines so that societies could benefit from God's laws and thus flourish. To "distinguish" church and state but not "separate" them was the Catholic way.[94]

At the end of his examination of the American situation, Reisach brought to the surface the concerns for Europe that so obviously underlay everything he had written. Especially those who were behind the "movement waging war on the Catholic Church" should learn from the American example: "Religious individualism attacks the divine authority of Christ; religious indifference – [championed as] freedom of conscience and religion – is sought and proclaimed everywhere."[95] To anyone who doubted these conclusions, the story of Mormonism in Protestant America should demonstrate conclusively the merits of the Catholic system: "This unique sight, not viewed even in past ages, proves most convincingly that there really exists in the world an intimate society of common faith and of common love and divine authority that conserves in itself the principles and the energy for maintaining and restoring a truly Christian social and political order. 'The gates of hell will not prevail against it' [Matthew 16:18 quoted from the Latin Vulgate]."[96]

Reisach's general indictment of the course of American Protestantism provided the background for La Civiltà cattolica's major interpretation of the Civil War, which appeared in a substantial article in February 1861, "Disunion in the United States." The article asserted that American civil dissolution should give pause to the Europeans who had expressed such admiration for American political principles and for the great prosperity the young nation had come to enjoy so quickly. What makes this article so interesting as a religious analysis is its effort to tie the breakup of the United States as a political entity to its history as an experiment in Protestant public order. The Jesuits expressed mingled admiration and humor in finding that "suddenly both parties have become theologians, the one side quoting the Pentateuch to justify slavery, the other side quoting the gospel to condemn it: . . . the people of the thirty-three United States, who are eminently and essentially political, cannot discuss a political matter without quoting the Old and New Testaments!"[97]

While there was much to praise in American religion, the Jesuits nonetheless saw a "great mistake," a "missing principle . . . dissolving a great union." That missing element was "religious unity." Reconciliation, so the Jesuits thought, would elude the Americans "because they are divided on a moral question, and moral questions are fundamentally grounded in religious dogma." As they viewed the American conflict, it seemed to them that different American factions were using the Scriptures to mask their economic and political interests. But if Americans understood the true character of religious authority, then it would be possible to use the Bible with greater effect. If the Americans lived where their rights and their trust in Scripture "were assured by an *authority* respected by both parties, then the Bible could come into the conflict not as a plaything but as in a contest of truth over against falsehood." Such an authority, which obviously meant the Roman magisterium, could exercise "an almost invincible strength over the two parties, so that one would surrender or that both would be reconciled to each other." But "dogmas there are very free, as are also moral principles, and everything in these spheres is mere probability. Between two equal possibilities it is hardly a marvel that the two opposite factions come without scruple to opposite conclusions. Their independence makes it impossible to find a solution to their quarrel, both because they lack a central religious authority and because they lack moral honesty, which is itself a consequence of not having a central religious authority."[98]

"Disunion in the United States" reiterated this judgment when it offered a sympathetic, but still negative, interpretation of the choices facing Abraham Lincoln. La Civiltà cattolica did not demean the president, unlike the HPB, which called Lincoln "the little country lawyer" (der kleine Landadvokat Lincoln).[99] But it left no doubt about its preference for a papal solution: given the American situation, its president must act "without having at his disposal either the infallibility to define doctrine or the effectiveness of grace to assuage the contending parties or the force of authority to hold back anarchy. Without such means of uniting society, with such spacious territory, such active commerce, such free opinions, the only result can be an accelerating decline of the state."[100]

When considering the depths to which political liberalism and Protestant individualism had led the United States, La Civiltà cattolica expressed the wish that "the sharp minds and the practical genius of the Anglo-Americans would ponder seriously the necessity of the Catholic element for the continuation of social unity." But it also hoped that in Italy civil reformers would learn from the American scene the proper steps that could be taken for "regenerating" that country.[101]

TO THE AUTHORS who wrote in La Civiltà cattolica, the theological crisis of the American Civil War was grounded not just in differences of opinion over what the Bible taught concerning slavery. It was rooted even more clearly in a Protestant heritage that left Americans without a trusted arbitrator who could adjudicate such differences of opinion. The Bible was certainly the true and authoritative word of God, but without the magisterium of the Roman Catholic Church to guide interpretation of the Bible, Americans were doomed to suffer the ill effects of excess democracy, excess republicanism, and excess Protestant individualism. From this conservative Catholic perspective, the individualism of American Protestantism could offer no protection against the forces of materialism that defined the American spirit and that played such a decisive influence in debates over slavery. Hence it was not Americans' professed desire to follow the Bible alone that wrote the moral history of the war but rather their inability to escape individual caprice and unchecked materialism.

Chapter 8

Retrospect and Prospect

The commentary of European Protestants and Catholics on moral aspects of the Civil War added depth to the already substantial commentary from within the United States. Europeans did not see more than their American counterparts, but because they viewed the conflict against a backdrop of European conditions, they inevitably saw things differently. How what they saw related to what happened after 1865 is the theme of this brief last chapter.

A Catholic Contribution

The special contribution of Roman Catholic opinion, especially conservative Catholic opinion, was to assess American difficulties within a broader framework than most on the western side of the Atlantic could imagine. Besides pointing out how hard it was to disentangle race from slavery or to free the Bible from the certainties of "common sense," Catholics posed even more basic questions. Bluntly in the *Historisch-politische Blätter für das katholische Deutschland* and with more subtlety in *La Civiltà cattolica*, conservative Catholics argued that the history of American culture revealed a set of elective affinities: fundamental principles of the Protestant Reformation linked to a liberal economic order linked to unfettered access to the Bible linked to liberal democracy linked to practical materialism linked to a bloated and dangerous republican government linked to theological confusion. Progressive Catholics, who recognized only some of these links, held out greater hope for renewed stability and spiritual maturity in the New World. Conservative assessment was both more pessimistic and far-reaching.

Although the conservative Catholic analysis pushed deeper than most American assessments of the war's moral and religious consequences, it could never be persuasive for all audiences. Conservative Catholics were much too committed to traditions of church authority, habits of church-state cooperation, patterns of top-down institutional organization, and principles of monarchical religion ever to speak impartially about the problems of democracy, political liberalism, Protestant theology, or Protestant interpretations of Scripture. Besides, whatever their own problems, most American Protestants were still convinced – even during brutal disputes over Scripture – that their reasons for rejecting Catholicism were sound.

Yet by broadening the assessment of America's moral history to include economic organization, economic practice, Protestant hermeneutics, and Protestant ecclesiology, Catholic criticism made an unusually important contribution. The inability of evangelicals to agree on how slavery should be construed according to Scripture, which all treated as their ultimate religious norm, was in fact connected to the economic individualism of American society. The recourse to arms for civil war did reflect, at the very least, a glaring weakness in republican and democratic polity. From the outside, it was clear that American material interests exerted a strong influence on American theological conclusions. The success of the North's military machine in resolving the debate over slavery in combination with the failure of freewheeling theological discussion to handle that same problem did suggest the need for some overarching authority to pacify moral disputes before they turned violent. The callousness of a liberal society (the United States) about racial discrimination vis-à-vis a relatively broad concern (on the part of Roman Catholicism) for all races as near equals did highlight some moral limitations of democratic civil society. The conservative Catholic critique, in other words, examined the American situation with an unblinking realism of unusual depth, even though the solutions it proposed might not have been persuasive to most Americans. When as a new Catholic Orestes Brownson published in 1845 an essay titled "Catholicity Necessary to Sustain Popular Liberty," he was not necessarily a prophet, but he did intimate the criticism that foreign Catholics were to make with much greater force during the war: "The Roman Catholic religion . . . is necessary to sustain popular liberty, because popular liberty can be sustained only by a religion free from popular control above the people, speaking from above and able to command them – and such a religion is the Roman Catholic. . . . It was made not by the people, but for them; it is administered not by the people, but for them; is accountable not to the people, but to God."[1]

Recovering Catholic opinion on the religious meaning of the Civil War makes it possible to take Brownson's assessment more seriously. Like the secular rejection of the national-Protestant-Enlightenment synthesis, a rejection that grew in strength after the Civil War, the Catholic assessment posed basic questions about how Protestant religion had been joined to national purpose during the first half of the nineteenth century. But of course the Catholic assessment arose from within a Christian framework that the later secularists could not accept. To both Catholic outsiders and later secularists, it was obvious that the war revealed serious fault lines within America's main theological traditions. As much as these fault lines affected actions during the war, they may have meant even more for what came later.

Before and After 1865

Our attention to a wide range of religious comment – North and South, black and white, foreign and domestic, Protestant and Catholic – has demonstrated the depth of the theological crisis occasioned by the Civil War. That crisis was most obvious in what might be called practical theology, above all in the way it highlighted issues of religious authority.

Foreign commentary makes clear how tightly American religious convictions were bound to general patterns of American life. Only because religious belief and practice had grown so strong before the conflict, only because they had done so much to create the nation that went to war, did that conflict result in such a great challenge to religious belief and practice after the war. The theological crisis of the Civil War was that while voluntary reliance on the Bible had contributed greatly to the creation of American national culture, that same voluntary reliance on Scripture led only to deadlock over what should be done about slavery.

After the shooting stopped, two great problems in practical theology confronted the United States. One was the enduring reality of racism, which displayed its continuing force almost as virulently through the mob and the rope as it had in the chain and the lash. The other was the expansion of consumer capitalism, in which unprecedented opportunities to create wealth were matched by large-scale alienation and considerable poverty in both urban and rural America. For religion to have addressed these two problems constructively, America's believers would have needed the kind of intellectual vigor that evangelical Protestants had brought to bear on so many tasks between the Revolution and the Civil War. That vigor was embodied in culturally aggressive expressions of basically orthodox theology.

But the Civil War was won and slavery was abolished not by theological orthodoxy but by military might and a hitherto unimaginable degree of industrial mobilization. Although the war freed the slaves and gave African Americans a constitutional claim to citizenship, it did not provide the moral energy required for rooting equal rights in the subsoil of American society or for planting equal opportunity throughout the land. Although the war showed what could be accomplished through massive industrial mobilization, it did not offer clear moral guidance as to how that mobilization could be put to use for the good of all citizens. The evangelical Protestant traditions that had done so much to shape society before the war did possess theological resources to address both America's deeply ingrained racism and its burgeoning industrial revolution. But the Civil War took the steam out of Protestants' moral energy. Protestants remained divided North and South. They became even more divided along racial lines. The theology that had risen to preeminence in the early nineteenth century continued to work effectively for vast multitudes in private; but because of its public failure during the war, it had little to offer American society more generally in the decades that followed the war.

The question of interpretive authority was raised by the *Protestantische Kirchenzeitung* in Berlin, by the London *Times*, and with special force by German and Italian Catholics. It highlighted a particularly troubling issue having large historical and theological implications. Foreign observers could see more clearly than Americans a situation that had become intractable: regardless of how much voluntary reliance on scriptural authority had contributed to the construction of national culture, if no higher religious authority existed than the private interpretation of Scripture, then a major problem existed whenever there arose a public deadlock that was caused or strongly supported by conflicting interpretations of the Bible.

The issue for American history was that only two courses of action seemed open when confronting such a deadlock. The first was the course taken in the Civil War, which effectively handed the business of the theologians over to the generals to decide by ordeal what the Bible meant. As things worked out, military coercion determined that, at least for the purposes of American public policy, the Bible did not support slavery. The second course, though never self-consciously adopted by all Americans in all circumstances, has been followed *since* the Civil War. That course is an implicit national agreement not to base public policy of any consequence on interpretations of Scripture. The result of following that second course since the Civil War has been ambiguous. In helping to provoke the war and greatly increase its intensity, the serious commitment to Scripture rendered itself ineffective for shaping broad policy in the public arena. In other words, even before there existed a secularization in the United States brought on by new immigrants, scientific acceptance of evolution, the higher criticism of Scripture, and urban industrialism, Protestants during the Civil War had marginalized themselves as bearers of a religious perspective in the body politic.

The effects of that marginalization and consequent secularization have been mixed, but all observers should consider much of it positive. As a considerably more secular country than existed before the war, the United States became more genuinely hospitable to Protestants who were not from Britain, to Christians who were not Protestants, to theists who were not Christians, and to citizens of any sort who did not believe in God. In addition, the United States has been spared, at least to the present, further shooting wars caused by the kind of strong but religiously divided self-assurance that fueled the Civil War. The republican traditions of liberty and the strong commitments to procedural democracy that have continued in this more secular America have also done a great deal of good at home and abroad.

On the other side of the ledger, however, in the more secular America brought on by the Civil War, it has been much harder for deep, religiously rooted moral conviction to exert a decisive influence on the shaping of public life – be it, to take some examples, against unfettered capitalism, against violent ethnic discrimination, for environmental protection, for the unborn human fetus, for equal educational opportunity, or for universal medical protection. In other words, since the Civil War theological arguments have only rarely been able to overcome the inertia behind institutions and practices sanctioned by the evolving usages of a voluntaristic, democratic consumerist culture.

From a Christian perspective, the secularization occasioned by the Civil War has been in many ways a very good thing and in other ways not a good thing at all. Historically considered, it is certainly significant that the only time in the twentieth century when something like the Civil War's clash of moral principles came close to fomenting rebellion was the era of the civil rights movement, which actually succeeded in changing public policy. Race was by far the deepest moral problem involved in the War between the States. That it also remained the United States' deepest moral problem after the war perhaps explains why the the campaign for civil rights, which reprised many religious as well as social elements of the Civil War, was so significant a century later.

In their perceptions of the theological crisis of the Civil War, foreign observers clearly identified a significant issue. How, in fact, are Bible believers, especially Protestant Bible believers, supposed to act in harmony when interpretations of the Bible seem to fly nearly everywhere – when, as the Europeans put it in the 1860s, there is no "autorità riverita" (respected authority), no "Ehrfurcht vor den bestehenden Ordnungen und Obrigkeiten" (respect for the established orders and authorities)?

In fact, biblical interpretation in America, even biblical interpretation by individualistic Protestant evangelicals, has never been as chaotic in practice as democratic assertions about the right of private judgment would lead a neutral observer to expect. But American interpretive chaos has still been bad enough. The Reign of the Scholarly Expert, which lasted from the founding of the Society of Biblical Literature and Exegesis in 1880 for almost exactly one century – to the discovery of postmodernism in the early 1980s – brought, on balance, no noticeable improvement over the Reign of the Democratic Populace, which had prevailed from the 1780s to the Civil War.

Since at least the time of the fundamentalist-modernist battles early in the twentieth century, older strands of Protestantism, both liberal and conservative, have been enervated by repeated uncertainties about the interpretation of Scripture. Over the course of the twentieth century, they have been joined in similar interpretative dilemmas by Protestants of traditional European background, Roman Catholics, and Jews. What believers might do about those dilemmas is a question worthy of another set of lectures. From the historical record it is clear that the American Civil War generated a first-order theological crisis over how to interpret the Bible, how to understand the work of God in the world, and how to exercise the authority of theology in a democratic society.

Notes

CHAPTER ONE

1. Henry Ward Beecher, "Peace Be Still," in *Fast Day Sermons; or, The Pulpit on the State of the Country* (New York: Rudd and Carleton, 1861), 276, 289.

2. James Henley Thornwell, "Our National Sins," in *Fast Day Sermons*, 48, 44.

3. Henry Van Dyke, "The Character and Influence of Abolitionism," in *Fast Day Sermons*, 137.

4. M. J. Raphall, "Bible View of Slavery," in *Fast Day Sermons*, 230, 233, and 237-41, with discussion of the following texts: Exodus 20:10 and 17, 21:2, 22:3; Leviticus 25:39 and 44-46; and Deuteronomy 5:14, 22:3.

5. Ibid., 235-36.

6. Tayler Lewis, "Patriarchal and Jewish Servitude No Argument for American Slavery," in *Fast Day Sermons*, 180.

7. Ibid., 222.

8. John H. Rice, "The Princeton Review on the State of the Country," *Southern Presbyterian Review* 14 (Apr. 1861): 31-33, 40.

9. Daniel Alexander Payne, *Welcome to the Ransomed; or, Duties of the Colored Inhabitants of the District of Columbia* (Baltimore: Bull and Tuttle, 1861), 10-11, as collected in Payne, *Sermons and Addresses, 1853-1891*, ed. Charles Killian (New York: Arno, 1972).

10. Especially in Mark A. Noll, *America's God: From Jonathan Edwards to Abraham Lincoln* (New York: Oxford University Press, 2002), 365-438.

11. George M. Fredrickson, *The Inner Civil War: Modern Intellectuals and the Crisis of the Union* (New York: Harper and Row, 1965), 111, 172-76, 199-201.

12. Anne C. Rose, *Victorian America and the Civil War* (New York: Cambridge University Press, 1992), 13.

13. Alfred Kazin, *God and the American Writer* (New York: Knopf, 1997), 133.

14. Louis Menand, *The Metaphysical Club: A Story of Ideas in America* (New York: Farrar, Straus and Giroux, 2001), x.

15. Phillip Shaw Paludan, *"A People's Contest": The Union and Civil War, 1861-1865* (New York: Harper and Row, 1988), chap. 14, "The Coming of the Lord: Religion in the

Civil War Era"; and Allen C. Guelzo, *The Crisis of the American Republic: A History of the Civil War and Reconstruction Era* (New York: St. Martin's, 1995), esp. 322-27.

16. James M. McPherson, *Battle Cry of Freedom: The Civil War Era* (New York: Oxford University Press, 1988); quotation from the chapter titled "Religion Is What Makes Brave Soldiers" in McPherson, *For Cause and Comrades: Why Men Fought in the Civil War* (New York: Oxford University Press, 1997), 63.

17. James M. McPherson, "Afterword," in *Religion and the American Civil War*, ed. Randall M. Miller, Harry S. Stout, and Charles Reagan Wilson (New York: Oxford University Press, 1998), 412.

18. Examples include James I. Robertson, *Stonewall Jackson: The Man, the Soldier, the Legend* (New York: Macmillan, 1997), passim; William Garrett Piston, *Lee's Tarnished Lieutenant: James Longstreet and His Place in Southern History* (Athens: University of Georgia Press, 1987), 111-16; and Frederick J. Blue, *Salmon P. Chase: A Life in Politics* (Kent, Ohio: Kent State University Press, 1987), 7-17, 25. See, above all, the portrayal of Abraham Lincoln in books like Allen C. Guelzo, *Abraham Lincoln: Redeemer President* (Grand Rapids, Mich.: Eerdmans, 1999); Lucas E. Morel, *Lincoln's Sacred Effort: Defining Religion's Role in American Self-Government* (Boston: Lexington, 2000); William Lee Miller, *Lincoln's Virtues: An Ethical Biography* (New York: Knopf, 2002); Ronald C. White, *Lincoln's Greatest Speech: The Second Inaugural* (New York: Simon and Schuster, 2002); Richard Carwardine, *Lincoln* (Harlow, Eng.: Pearson Longman, 2003); Joseph R. Fornieri, *Abraham Lincoln's Political Faith* (DeKalb: Northern Illinois University Press, 2003); and Stewart Winger, *Lincoln, Religion, and Romantic Cultural Politics* (DeKalb: Northern Illinois University Press, 2003).

19. For example, James Oscar Farmer Jr., *The Metaphysical Confederacy: James Henley Thornwell and the Synthesis of Southern Values* (Macon, Ga.: Mercer University Press, 1986); A. James Fuller, *Chaplain to the Confederacy: Basil Manly and Baptist Life in the Old South* (Baton Rouge: Louisiana State University Press, 2000); Preston D. Graham, *A Kingdom Not of This World: Stuart Robinson's Struggle to Distinguish the Sacred from the Secular during the Civil War* (Macon, Ga.: Mercer University Press, 2002); and Sean Michael Lucas, *Robert Lewis Dabney: A Southern Presbyterian Life* (Phillipsburg, N.J.: P and R Publishing, 2005).

20. Lewis G. Vander Velde, *The Presbyterian Churches and the Federal Union, 1861-1869* (Cambridge, Mass.: Harvard University Press, 1932); James W. Silver, *Confederate Morale and Church Propaganda* (1957; repr., New York: Norton, 1967); James H. Moorhead, *American Apocalypse: Yankee Protestants and the Civil War, 1860-1869* (New Haven, Conn.: Yale University Press, 1978); and Gardiner H. Shattuck Jr., *A Shield and Hiding Place: The Religious Life of the Civil War Armies* (Macon, Ga.: Mercer University Press, 1987).

21. John R. McKivigan and Mitchell Snay, eds., *Religion and the Antebellum Debate*

over *Slavery* (Athens: University of Georgia Press, 1998); Miller, Stout, and Wilson, *Religion and the American Civil War*; Steven E. Woodworth, *While God Is Marching On: The Religious World of Civil War Soldiers* (Lawrence: University Press of Kansas, 2001); and Kent T. Dollar, *Soldiers of the Cross: Confederate Soldier-Christians and the Impact of the War on their Faith* (Macon, Ga.: Mercer University Press, 2005).

22. Richard J. Carwardine, *Evangelicals and Politics in Antebellum America* (New Haven, Conn.: Yale University Press, 1993); John R. McKivigan, *The War against Proslavery Religion* (Ithaca, N.Y.: Cornell University Press, 1984); Drew Gilpin Faust, *The Creation of Confederate Nationalism: Ideology and Identity in the Civil War South* (Baton Rouge: Louisiana State University Press, 1988); Elizabeth Fox-Genovese, *Within the Plantation Household: Black and White Women of the Old South* (Chapel Hill: University of North Carolina Press, 1988); Eugene D. Genovese, *The Slaveholders' Dilemma: Freedom and Progress in Southern Conservative Thought, 1820-1860* (Columbia: University of South Carolina Press, 1991); Mitchell Snay, *Gospel of Disunion: Religion and Separatism in the Antebellum South* (New York: Cambridge University Press, 1993); Kenneth Startup, *The Root of All Evil: The Protestant Clergy and the Economic Mind of the Old South* (Athens: University of Georgia Press, 1997); John Patrick Daly, *When Slavery Was Called Freedom: Evangelicalism, Proslavery, and the Causes of the Civil War* (Lexington: University Press of Kentucky, 2003); and Michael O'Brien, *Conjectures of Order: Intellectual Life and the Antebellum South, 1800-1860* (Chapel Hill: University of North Carolina Press, 2004).

23. David B. Chesebrough, ed., *God Ordained This War: Sermons on the Sectional Crisis, 1830-1865* (Columbia: University of South Carolina Press, 1991); and Chesebrough, *"No Sorrow like Our Sorrow": Northern Protestant Ministers and the Assassination of Lincoln* (Kent, Ohio: Kent State University Press, 1994).

24. For example, "The Untold Story of Christianity and the Civil War," *Christian History*, no. 33 (1992); and the cluster of eleven articles on the Civil War in *Books & Culture: A Christian Review*, July/Aug. 2003, pp. 16-37.

25. Harry S. Stout, *Upon the Altar of the Nation: A Moral History of the American Civil War* (New York: Viking, 2006); and Eugene D. Genovese and Elizabeth Fox-Genovese, *The Mind of the Master Class: History and Faith in the Southern Slaveholders' Worldview* (New York: Cambridge University Press, 2005).

26. For one review, see Mark A. Noll, "Getting It Half Right," *Books & Culture*, July/Aug. 2003, pp. 18-19.

27. I cite some of the rich scholarship on questions of Scripture and providence in chapters 3, 4, and 5. For ongoing treatment of general literature, including books dealing with religion, see the journal *Civil War History*.

28. See especially Roger Finke and Rodney Stark, "How the Upstart Sects Won America: 1776-1850," *Journal for the Scientific Study of Religion* 28 (Mar. 1989): 27-44.

29. For learned consideration of the possible ratios, see Carwardine, *Evangelicals and Politics*, 44.

30. Ibid.

31. For an expansion of these comparisons, along with documentation, see Noll, *America's God*, 197-202.

32. For postal comparisons, I am relying on Richard John, *Spreading the News: The American Postal System from Franklin to Morse* (Cambridge, Mass.: Harvard University Press, 1995), 4.

33. From Charles I. Foster, *An Errand of Mercy: The Evangelical United Front, 1790-1837* (Chapel Hill: University of North Carolina Press, 1960), 241.

34. For the complicated religion-market relationships of the day, see discussions in Mark A. Noll, ed., *God and Mammon: Protestants, Money, and the Market, 1790-1860* (New York: Oxford University Press, 2001).

35. These figures, and much other interesting material, is from *Statistical View of the United States . . . Being a Compendium of the Seventh Census* (Washington, D.C.: Bureau of the Census, 1854); and *Statistics of the United States . . . Being a Compendium from . . . the Eighth Census* (Washington, D.C.: Bureau of the Census, 1866).

36. A standard hymnbook of the Lutheran Church in Bavaria contains hymns by eighty-two authors from "Das Zeitalter des 30 Jährigen Krieges" (the period of the Thirty Years' War); for biographical sketches, see *Evangelisches Kirchengesangbuch* (Munich, ca. 1960), 742-99. Comparable hymnbooks for American Protestants include hymns from no more than ten to fifteen American writers from the period 1835-65.

37. The Presbyterian Robert Breckinridge's family divided, with two sons fighting for the North and two for the South (James C. Klotter, *The Breckinridges of Kentucky, 1760-1981* [Lexington: University Press of Kentucky, 1986], 141-42); two of J. W. Nevin's sons served in the Union army (Theodore Appel, *The Life and Work of John Williamson Nevin* [Philadelphia: Reformed Church, 1889], 634); the Lutheran Samuel Schmucker, a prominent defender of emancipation, was forced to flee his seminary at Gettysburg when Lee's troops moved in at the end of June 1863 (Peter Anstadt, *Life and Times of Rev. S. S. Schmucker* [New York: Anstadt and Sons, 1896], 294); Presbyterian Robert L. Dabney was devastated by the war that rolled over his Virginia property and that he witnessed as an aide to Gen. Stonewall Jackson (Thomas Cary Johnson, *The Life and Letters of Robert Lewis Dabney* [1903; repr., Edinburgh: Banner of Truth, 1977], 288-308); a son of Presbyterian James Henley Thornwell was killed in battle in 1863, one year after his own death (B. M. Palmer, *The Life and Letters of James Henley Thornwell* [Richmond: Whittet and Shepperson, 1875], 519-21); and two of Orestes Brownson's sons died while on military duty (John T. McGreevy, *Catholicism and American Freedom* [New York: Norton, 2003], 89; Patrick W. Carey, *Orestes Brownson: American Religious Weathervane* [Grand Rapids, Mich.: Eerdmans, 2004], 281).

38. Richard J. Wolf, introduction to William Clebsch, *Christian Interpretations of the Civil War* (Philadelphia: Fortress, 1969), vii; the booklet is a reprinting of Clebsch's article of the same title that appeared in *Church History* 30 (June 1961): 212–22.

CHAPTER TWO

1. For an expansion on the themes of this chapter, see Mark A. Noll, *America's God: From Jonathan Edwards to Abraham Lincoln* (New York: Oxford University Press, 2002), 53–252.

2. The best account of this "discipline" is provided in Daniel Walker Howe, "The Evangelical Movement and Political Culture in the North during the Second Party System," *Journal of American History* 77 (Mar. 1991): 1216–39.

3. From the viewpoint of American Protestants, it was natural to treat Catholics in America as a foreign presence; this is a perspective that I will take up in chapter 7.

4. For further reflections on this characteristic of the most numerous variety of American Protestants, see Mark A. Noll, "Revolution and the Rise of Evangelical Social Influence in North Atlantic Societies," in *Evangelicalism: Comparative Studies of Popular Protestantism in North America, the British Isles, and Beyond, 1700–1990*, ed. Mark A. Noll, David W. Bebbington, and George A. Rawlyk (New York: Oxford University Press, 1994), 129–30.

5. My thanks to Harry S. Stout for this information on Northern Democrats.

6. On the understanding of republicanism in the early United States, see the appendix, "Historiography of Republicanism and Religion," in Noll, *America's God*, 447–51.

7. The most important studies describing these attitudes are Henry F. May, *The Enlightenment in America* (New York: Oxford University Press, 1976); and Gordon S. Wood, "Conspiracy and the Paranoid Style: Causality and Deceit in the Eighteenth Century," *William and Mary Quarterly* 39 (1982): 401–41. I have expanded on this connection in "The Rise and Long Life of the Protestant Enlightenment in America," in *Knowledge and Belief in America: Enlightenment Traditions and Modern Religious Thought*, ed. William M. Shea and Peter A. Huff (New York: Cambridge University Press, 1995), 88–124.

8. Robert J. Breckinridge, *The Knowledge of God, Subjectively Considered* (New York: Robert Carter, 1860), 444–45.

9. Henry J. Van Dyke, "The Character and Influence of Abolitionism," in *Fast Day Sermons; or, The Pulpit on the State of the Country* (New York: Rudd and Carleton, 1861), 139.

10. Gerrit Smith, "The Religion of Reason," in his *Sermons and Speeches* (New York: Ross and Tousey, 1861), 4–5.

11. Drew Gilpin Faust, "Evangelicalism and the Meaning of the Proslavery Argument," *Virginia Magazine of History and Biography* 85 (Jan. 1977): 8.

12. *Independent*, Dec. 15, 1864, p. 4, as quoted in James H. Moorhead, *American Apocalypse: Yankee Protestants and the Civil War, 1860–1869* (New Haven, Conn.: Yale University Press, 1978), 118.

13. Phoebe Palmer, "Witness of the Spirit," *Guide to Holiness* 47 (June 1865): 137, as quoted in Nancy A. Hardesty, *Your Daughters Shall Prophesy: Revivalism and Feminism in the Age of Finney* (Brooklyn: Carlson, 1991), 65–66.

14. See Kenneth Startup, *The Root of All Evil: The Protestant Clergy and the Economic Mind of the South* (Athens: University of Georgia Press, 1997); and Stewart Allen Davenport, "Moral Man, Immoral Economy: Protestant Reflections on Market Capitalism, 1820–1860" (Ph.D. diss., Yale University, 2001).

15. Perry Miller, *The Life of the Mind in America from the Revolution to the Civil War* (New York: Harcourt, Brace and World, 1965), 46, 47.

16. Charles Taylor, "Religion in a Free Society," in *Articles of Faith, Articles of Peace: The Religious Liberty Clause and the American Public Philosophy*, ed. James Davison Hunter and Os Guinness (Washington, D.C.: Brookings Institution, 1990), 107.

17. For Thornwell's constitutional defense of secession, see "The State of the Country," *Southern Presbyterian Review* 13 (Jan. 1861): 860–89.

18. The phrase "power to choose and refuse" is from N. W. Taylor, *Regeneration the Beginning of Holiness in the Human Heart: A Sermon* (New Haven, Conn.: Nathan Whiting, 1816), 12. Charles G. Finney, *Lectures on Systematic Theology*, vol. 2 (Oberlin, Ohio: J. M. Fitch, 1847), 17.

19. Key works describing this move are Stephen Marini, *Radical Sects of Revolutionary New England* (Cambridge, Mass.: Harvard University Press, 1982); and Nathan O. Hatch, *The Democratization of American Christianity* (New Haven, Conn.: Yale University Press, 1989).

20. Earlier, it had been the more populous evangelical groups that opened such possibilities. See Catherine Brekus, *Strangers and Pilgrims: Female Preaching in America, 1740–1845* (Chapel Hill: University of North Carolina Press, 1998).

21. See the works referenced in n. 7 of this chapter. For the particular coalition of evangelical and Enlightenment reasoning, see D. W. Bebbington, *Evangelicalism in Modern Britain: A History from the 1730s to the 1980s* (London: Unwin and Hyman, 1989), 20–74.

22. John M. Murrin, "A Roof without Walls: The Dilemma of American National Identity," in *Beyond Confederation: Origins of the Constitution and American National Identity*, ed. Richard Beeman, Stephen Botein, and Edward C. Carter II (Chapel Hill: University of North Carolina Press, 1987), 344, 347.

23. Nathan Bangs, *A History of the Methodist Episcopal Church*, 4 vols. (New York: T. Mason and G. Lane, 1838–41), 1:46.

24. The phrase at the head of the paragraph is from C. C. Goen, *Broken Churches, Broken Nation: Denominational Schisms and the Coming of the Civil War* (Macon, Ga.: Mercer University Press, 1985).

25. Clay, quoted in ibid., 106.

26. Richard K. Crallé, ed., *The Works of John C. Calhoun*, vol. 4, *Speeches of John C. Calhoun, Delivered in the House of Representatives and the Senate of the United States* (New York: D. Appleton, 1854), 557–58.

27. Alexis de Tocqueville, *Democracy in America*, ed. and trans. Harvey Claflin Mansfield and Delba Winthrop (Chicago: University of Chicago Press, 2000), 278.

CHAPTER THREE

1. For Holmes, Howells, and Trescot, respectively, see Louis Menand, *The Metaphysical Club* (New York: Farrar, Straus and Giroux, 2001), 49–69; Anne C. Rose, *Victorian America and the Civil War* (New York: Cambridge University Press, 1992), 29–30; and Michael O'Brien, *Conjectures of Order: Intellectual Life and the Antebellum South, 1810–1860*, 2 vols. (Chapel Hill: University of North Carolina Press, 2004), 2:1176–85.

2. Garrison, *Liberator*, 15 (1845): 186, as quoted in *William Lloyd Garrison, 1805–1879: The Story of His Life Told By His Children* (New York: Century, 1889), 146–47.

3. Henry Van Dyke, "The Character and Influence of Abolitionism," in *Fast Day Sermons; or, The Pulpit on the State of the Country* (New York: Rudd and Carleton, 1861), 163–64.

4. On the biblical debate over slavery, there has grown up a substantial secondary literature. For outstanding examples, see David Brion Davis, *The Problem of Slavery in the Age of Revolution, 1770–1823* (New York: Oxford University Press, 1975), 523–56; Robert Bruce Mullin, "Biblical Critics and the Battle over Slavery," *Journal of Presbyterian History* 61 (Summer 1983): 210–26; John R. McKivigan, *The War against Proslavery Religion: Abolitionism and the Northern Churches, 1830–1865* (Ithaca, N.Y.: Cornell University Press, 1985); Eugene D. Genovese, *"Slavery Ordained of God": The Southern Slaveholders' View of Biblical History and Modern Politics* (Gettysburg, Pa.: Gettysburg College, 1985); Elizabeth Fox-Genovese and Eugene D. Genovese, "The Divine Sanction of Social Order: Religious Foundations of the Southern Slaveholders' World View," *Journal of the American Academy of Religion* 55 (Summer 1987): 211–33; Larry Tise, *Proslavery: A History of the Defense of Slavery in America, 1701–1840* (Athens: University of Georgia Press, 1987); Albert Harrill, "The Use of the New Testament in the American Slave Controversy: A Case History in the Hermeneutical Tension between Biblical Criticism

and Christian Moral Debate," *Religion and American Culture* 10 (Summer 2000): 149–86; Stephen R. Haynes, *Noah's Curse: The Biblical Justification of American Slavery* (New York: Oxford University Press, 2002); David Daniell, *The Bible in English* (New Haven, Conn.: Yale University Press, 2003), 705–22; and Eugene D. Genovese and Elizabeth Fox-Genovese, *The Mind of the Master Class: History and Faith in the Southern Slaveholders' Worldview* (New York: Cambridge University Press, 2005). Well-introduced samples of the arguments are found in Mason I. Lowance Jr., ed., *A House Divided: The Antebellum Slavery Debate in America, 1776–1865* (Princeton, N.J.: Princeton University Press, 2003), 51–87.

5. I am following here Davis, *Problem of Slavery*, 531–33.

6. See, for example, Tise, *Proslavery*, 10, 79.

7. See Richard Fuller and Francis Wayland, *Domestic Slavery Considered as a Scriptural Institution: In a Correspondence between the Rev. Richard Fuller . . . and the Rev. Francis Wayland* (New York: Lewis Colby, 1845); and, for helpful context, Deborah Bingham Van Broekhoven, "Suffering with Slaveholders: The Limits of Francis Wayland's Antislavery Witness," in *Religion and the Antebellum Debate over Slavery*, ed. John R. McKivigan and Mitchell Snay (Athens: University of Georgia Press, 1998), 196–220.

8. Fuller, *Domestic Slavery*, 4–5.

9. Ibid., 10. The sense is confused because of the way this sentence was printed. Probably the punctuation and the wording at the end should be "which may, and perhaps in the case of many Christians, does exist without them," with reference to "slavery" rather than "accidents" or "sins."

10. Moses Stuart, *Conscience and the Constitution; with Remarks on the Recent Speech of the Hon. Daniel Webster in the Senate of the United States on the Subject of Slavery* (Boston: Crocker and Brewster, 1850). On Stuart's reputation as the premier biblical scholar in the United States, see John H. Giltner, *Moses Stuart: The Father of Biblical Science in America* (Atlanta: Scholars Press, 1988). On the theological debates in 1850, see Laura L. Mitchell, " 'Matters of Justice between Man and Man': Northern Divines, the Bible, and the Fugitive Slave Act of 1850," in McKivigan and Snay, *Religion and the Antebellum Debate*, 134–65.

11. Stuart, *Conscience and the Constitution*, 55.

12. Ibid., 113.

13. See the discussion early in chapter 1 and n. 2 of that chapter.

14. I owe this quotation to Kurt O. Berends, "Confederate Sacrifice and the 'Redemption' of the South," in *Religion and the American South: Protestants and Others in History and Culture*, ed. Beth Barton Schweiger and Donald G. Mathews (Chapel Hill: University of North Carolina Press, 2004), 105.

15. Samuel Hopkins, *A Dialogue concerning the Slavery of the Africans; Shewing It to Be*

the Duty and Interest of the American States to Emancipate All Their African Slaves (1776; repr., New York: Robert Hodge, 1785), 26.

16. Samuel Hopkins, *A Discourse upon the Slave-Trade, and the Slavery of the Africans* (Providence: J. Carter, 1793), 8.

17. George Bourne, *The Book and Slavery Irreconcilable* (Philadelphia: J. M. Sanderson, 1816), 3, 67.

18. On this debate I have been guided by Laura Rominger, "The Bible, Common-sense, and Interpretive Context: A Case Study in the Antebellum Debate on Slavery" (seminar paper, Wheaton College, 2004), which was awarded the 2004 Phi Alpha Theta Nels Andrew Cleven Founder's Prize for undergraduate research.

19. *A Debate on Slavery, Held on the First, Second, Third, and Sixth Days of October, 1845, in the City of Cincinnati, between Rev. J. Blanchard, Pastor of the Sixth Presbyterian Church, and N. L. Rice, Pastor of the Central Presbyterian Church* (Cincinnati: W. H. Moore, 1846), 228, 328.

20. Ibid., 44.

21. See Daniel J. McInerney, "'A Faith for Freedom': The Political Gospel of Abolition," *Journal of the Early Republic* 11 (Fall 1991): 377: "Republican liberty, a cardinal principle of Christian belief for the abolitionists, structured the ways they discussed a wide range of religious subjects: the purposes of God, the message of Scripture, the qualities of faith and duty, the character of divine justice, and the course of redemption." The entire article by McInerney (371–93) is valuable.

22. Harriet Beecher Stowe, *Uncle Tom's Cabin* (New York: Library of America, 1982), 218.

23. Ibid., 114.

24. Ibid., 151, 152.

25. Ibid., 100–101.

26. See, for example, Cheever's commentary on 1 Timothy 1:9 ("Knowing this, that the law is not made for a righteous man, but for the lawless and disobedient, for the ungodly and profane, for the murderers of fathers and murderers of mothers, for man-slayers, for whore-mongers, for them that defile themselves with mankind, for men-stealers"), in George B. Cheever, *The Guilt of Slavery and the Crime of Slaveholding, Demonstrated from the Hebrew and Greek Scriptures* (Boston: John B. Jewett, 1860), 415–20.

27. Ibid., 58, 462.

28. Henry Ward Beecher, "Peace Be Still," in *Fast Day Sermons*, 288.

29. Leonard Bacon, *Slavery Discussed in Occasional Essays, from 1833 to 1846* (New York: Baker and Scribner, 1846), 180. For context, see Hugh Davis, "Leonard Bacon, the Congregational Church, and Slavery, 1845–1861," in McKivigan and Snay, *Religion and the Antebellum Debate*, 221–45.

30. From my viewpoint as a Christian believer at the start of the twenty-first cen-

tury, these antislavery arguments offered the most promising way of using the Bible during the interpretive battles of the mid-nineteenth century. But given the historical situations outlined in this book, it is also fairly easy to show why such arguments carried relatively little weight in the United States of that period.

31. See Davis, *Problem of Slavery*, 552–55.

32. Wayland, *Domestic Slavery*, 58 (with argumentation on following pages).

33. For essential background on Pendleton and his efforts, see Luke E. Harlow, "Antislavery Clergy in Antebellum Kentucky, 1830–1860" (M.A. thesis, Wheaton College, 2004).

34. J. M. Pendleton, *Letters to Rev. W. C. Buck, in Review of His Articles on Slavery* (Louisville: n.p., 1849), 3.

35. Ibid., 9–10.

36. M. J. Raphall, "Bible View of Slavery," in *Fast Day Sermons*, 244.

37. Tayler Lewis, "Patriarchal and Jewish Servitude No Argument for American Slavery," in *Fast Day Sermons*, 181, 204, 205, 210 (manumitting converted slaves), 217.

38. Mark A. Noll, "The Bible and Slavery," in *Religion and the Civil War*, ed. Randall M. Miller, Harry S. Stout, and Charles Reagan Wilson (New York: Oxford University Press, 1998), 66.

CHAPTER FOUR

1. See Philip Schaff, *America: A Sketch of Its Political, Social, and Religious Character* (1855), ed. Perry Miller (Cambridge, Mass.: Harvard University Press, 1961); and Schaff, *Der Bürgerkrieg und das christliche Leben in Nord-Amerika* [The Civil War and Christian Life in North America] (Berlin: Wiegandt und Grieben, 1866). On Schaff's role as mediator between Europe and America, see Stephen R. Graham, *Cosmos in the Chaos: Philip Schaff's Interpretation of Nineteenth-Century American Religion* (Grand Rapids, Mich.: Eerdmans, 1995); and Gary K. Pranger, *Philip Schaff (1819–1893): Portrait of an Immigrant Theologian* (New York: Peter Lang, 1997).

2. Philip Schaff, "Slavery and the Bible," *Mercersburg Review* 13 (Apr. 1861): 316–17.

3. David Brion Davis, "Reconsidering the Colonization Movement: Leonard Bacon and the Problem of Evil," *Intellectual History Newsletter* 14 (1992): 4.

4. Eugene D. Genovese, *A Consuming Fire: The Fall of the Confederacy in the Mind of the White Christian South* (Athens: University of Georgia Press, 1998), 102; and Kenneth Startup, " 'A Mere Calculation of Profit and Loss': The Southern Clergy and the Economic Culture of the Antebellum North," in *God and Mammon: Protestants, Money, and the Market, 1790–1860*, ed. Mark A. Noll (New York: Oxford University Press, 2002), 220. For development of this theme, see David H. Overy, "When the Wicked Beareth Rule:

A Southern Critique of Industrial America," *Journal of Presbyterian History* 48 (Summer 1970): 130–42; Kenneth Startup, *The Root of All Evil: The Protestant Clergy and the Economic Mind of the South* (Athens: University of Georgia Press, 1997); and especially Eugene D. Genovese and Elizabeth Fox-Genovese, *The Mind of the Master Class: History and Faith in the Southern Slaveholders' Worldview* (New York: Cambridge University Press, 2005).

5. See Stuart Davenport, "Moral Man, Immoral Economy: Protestant Reflections on Market Capitalism, 1820–1860" (Ph.D. diss., Yale University, 2001).

6. For orientation, see Henry F. May, *Protestant Churches and Industrial America* (New York: Harper and Row, 1949); Paul A. Carter, *The Spiritual Crisis of the Gilded Age* (DeKalb: Northern Illinois University Press, 1971); Douglas Frank, *Less than Conquerors: How Evangelicals Entered the Twentieth Century* (Grand Rapids, Mich.: Eerdmans, 1986); and Robert T. Handy, *Undermined Establishment: Church and State Relations in America, 1880–1920* (Princeton, N.J.: Princeton University Press, 1991).

7. On Hammond, see Drew Gilpin Faust, *James Henry Hammond and the Old South: A Design for Mastery* (Baton Rouge: Louisiana State University Press, 1982); and on Fitzhugh's conviction that "slavery was a proper social system for all labor, not merely for black labor," see Eugene D. Genovese, *The World the Slaveholders Made: Two Essays in Interpretation* (New York: Vintage, 1971), 115–244 (quotation on 130).

8. J. M. Pendleton, *Letters to Rev. W. C. Buck*, in *Review of His Articles on Slavery* (Louisville: n.p., 1849), 3. For Pendleton, again, and also for the material on John G. Fee and Robert Breckinridge below, I am indebted to Luke E. Harlow, "Antislavery Clergy in Antebellum Kentucky, 1830–1860" (M.A. thesis, Wheaton College, 2004).

9. On how Breckinridge's attacks on slavery fit into a lifetime of polemical activity, see Peter J. Wallace, "The Bond of Union: The Old School Presbyterian Church and the American Nation, 1837–1861" (Ph.D. Diss., University of Notre Dame, 2004).

10. John G. Fee, *The Sinfulness of Slaveholding Shown by Appeals to Reason and Scripture* (New York: John A. Gray, 1851), 36, 23, 5.

11. Ibid., 29, 28.

12. "Speech at Cincinnati, Ohio," Sept. 17, 1859, in *The Collected Works of Abraham Lincoln*, ed. Ray P. Basler, 9 vols. (New Brunswick, N.J.: Rutgers University Press, 1953), 3:445.

13. For ancient and American interpretations of this story, see, respectively, David M. Goldenberg, *The Curse of Ham: Race and Slavery in Early Judaism, Christianity, and Islam* (Princeton, N.J.: Princeton University Press, 2003); and Stephen R. Haynes, *Noah's Curse: The Biblical Justification of American Slavery* (New York: Oxford University Press, 2001).

14. Laura L. Mitchell, " 'Matters of Justice between Man and Man': Northern Divines, the Bible, and the Fugitive Slave Act of 1850," in *Religion and the Antebellum De-*

bate over Slavery, ed. John R. McKivigan and Mitchell Snay (Athens: University of Georgia Press, 1998), 149, 148.

15. Benjamin Rush, An Address to the Inhabitants of the British Settlements in America upon Slave-Keeping, 2nd ed. (Philadelphia: John Dunlap, 1773), 2. The same argument is expanded in Rush, A Vindication of the Address to the Inhabitants of the British Settlements, on the Slavery of the Negroes in America (Philadelphia: John Dunlap, 1773), 24–31.

16. Samuel Hopkins, A Dialogue concerning the Slavery of the Africans; Shewing It to Be the Duty and Interest of the American States to Emancipate All Their African Slaves (1776; repr., New York: Robert Hodge, 1785), 26 (Bible as a whole), 29–30 (blacks' enslaving whites).

17. David Brion Davis, The Problem of Slavery in an Age of Revolution, 1770–1823 (Ithaca, N.Y.: Cornell University Press, 1975), 537.

18. For treatment of this text with regard to its role in 1850, see Mitchell, "Matters of Justice," 147–49.

19. The quotations in the next several paragraphs are from Moses Stuart, Conscience and the Constitution; with Remarks on the Recent Speech of the Hon. Daniel Webster in the Senate of the United States on the Subject of Slavery (Boston: Crocker and Brewster, 1850), 30–32.

20. Ibid., 32.

21. Hopkins, Dialogue concerning the Slavery of Africans, 29.

22. Moses Stuart, A Commentary on the Epistle to the Romans, 2nd ed. (Andover: Warren F. Draper, 1859), 344, 359, 364.

23. Davis, Problem of Slavery, 207–10.

24. For his exposition, see Thornton Stringfellow, "The Bible Argument: or, Slavery in the Light of Divine Revelation," in Cotton Is King, and Pro-slavery Arguments, ed. E. N. Elliott (Augusta, Ga.: Pritchard, Abbott and Loomis, 1860), 459–91. For orientation, see Drew Gilpin Faust, "Evangelicalism and the Meaning of the Proslavery Argument: The Reverend Thornton Stringfellow of Virginia," Virginia Magazine of History and Biography 85 (Jan. 1977): 3–17.

25. Stringfellow is here cited from the lengthy extract from Slavery, Its Origin, Nature, and History found in A House Divided: The Antebellum Slavery Debate in America, 1776–1865, ed. Mason I. Lowance Jr. (Princeton, N.J.: Princeton University Press, 2003), 72.

26. Thornwell, "Address to All Churches of Christ" (1861), in The Collected Writings of James Henley Thornwell, vol. 4, Ecclesiastical, ed. John B. Adger and John L. Girardeau, (Richmond: Presbyterian Committee of Publication, 1873), 456. On Thornwell, see outstanding treatments in the strong, but contradictory, interpretations of Genovese and Fox-Genovese, Mind of the Master Class, 373, 494–95, 517, 530–32; and Michael

O'Brien, *Conjectures of Order: Intellectual Life and the Antebellum South, 1810–1860*, 2 vols. (Chapel Hill: University of North Carolina Press, 2004), 2:1114–57.

27. Thornwell, "Address to All Churches of Christ," 460, 461, 462 (italics mine).

28. See, for only some of the key works, James Weldon Johnson, *The Book of American Negro Poetry* (New York: Harcourt, Brace, 1922); Eugene D. Genovese, *Roll, Jordan, Roll: The World the Slaves Made* (1972; repr., New York: Vintage, 1976), 213–54; Dena J. Epstein, *Sinful Tunes and Spirituals: Black Folk Music to the Civil War* (Urbana: University of Illinois Press, 1977), 217–37; Theophus Smith, *Conjuring Culture: Biblical Formation of Black America* (New York: Oxford University press, 1994); Albert J. Raboteau, "Exodus, Ethiopia, and Racial Messianism: Texts and Contexts of African-American Consciousness," in *Many Are Chosen: Divine Election and Western Nationalism*, ed. William R. Hutchison and Hartmut Lehmann (Minneapolis: Fortress, 1994), 175–96; Vincent L. Wimbush, ed., *African Americans and the Bible: Sacred Texts and Social Textures* (New York: Continuum, 2000); and Eddie S. Glaude Jr., *Exodus! Religion, Race, and Nation in Early Nineteenth-Century Black America* (Chicago: University of Chicago Press, 2000).

29. "The Present Crisis" and "Doctrinal Basis of Christianity," *Christian Recorder*, April 13, 1861, p. 54.

30. A good introduction to much of this literature is provided by E. Brooks Holifield, *Theology in America* (New Haven, Conn.: Yale University Press, 2003), 313–17, 563–65.

31. Daniel Coker, *A Dialogue between a Virginian and an African Minister . . . Humbly Dedicated to the People of Colour in the United States of America* (Baltimore: Benjamin Edes, 1810), in *Negro Protest Pamphlets*, ed. Dorothy Porter (New York: Arno, 1969).

32. Lemuel Haynes, "Dissimulation Illustrated" (Rutland, Vt., 1814), in *Black Preacher to White America: The Collected Writings of Lemuel Haynes, 1774–1833*, ed. Richard Newman and Helen Maclam (Brooklyn: Carlson, 1990), 149–69; for orientation in regard to this important African American minister, see John Saillant, *Black Puritan, Black Republican: The Life and Thought of Lemuel Haynes, 1753–1833* (New York: Oxford University Press, 2003).

33. David Walker, *Appeal, in Four Articles; Together with a Preamble, to the Coloured Citizens of the World, but in Particular, and Very Expressly, to Those of the United States of America*, ed. Charles M. Wiltse (New York: Hill and Wang, 1965).

34. David Ruggles, *The Abrogation of the Seventh Commandment by the American Churches* (1835), in *Early Negro Writing, 1760–1837*, ed. Dorothy Porter (Boston: Beacon Press, 1971), 478–93.

35. Frederick Douglass, "The Pro-Slavery Mob and the Pro-Slavery Ministry," *Douglass' Monthly*, Mar. 1861, 417–18.

36. The series ran in each weekly issue of the *Christian Recorder* from Feb. 23, 1861, into the summer.

37. Coker, *Dialogue*, 25.

38. Douglass, "Pro-Slavery Mob," 418.

39. Ruggles, *Abrogation of the Seventh Commandment*, 479–80.

40. Ibid., 481.

41. Ibid., 487.

42. Coker, *Dialogue*, 34.

43. Walker, *Appeal*, 14, 66, 59.

44. Haynes, "Dissimulation Illustrated," 167.

45. Walker, *Appeal*, 43, 75.

46. Coker, *Dialogue*, 33.

47. See also, for example, Walker, *Appeal*, 37.

48. Ibid., 42.

49. Douglass, "Pro-Slavery Mob," 417–18.

50. "Chapters on Ethnology," *Christian Recorder*, Feb. 23, 1861, p. 26; March 2, 1861, p. 30.

51. The quotations that follow are from Coker, *Dialogue*, 19–21.

52. Ibid., 22.

53. See Jonathan Edwards, "The Nature of True Virtue," in *Two Dissertations* (Boston: S. Kneeland, 1765).

54. Haynes, "Dissimulation Illustrated," 151–52.

55. Ibid., 154–55.

56. Ibid., 157.

CHAPTER FIVE

1. James H. Thornwell, "The State of the Country," *Southern Presbyterian Review* 13 (Jan. 1861): 889.

2. Horace Bushnell, "Our Obligations to the Dead," in *Building Eras in Religion* (New York: Charles Scribner's Sons, 1881), 328–29.

3. J. W. Nevin, "The Nation's Second Birth," *German Reformed Messenger* 30, no. 47 (July 26, 1865): p. 1, cols. 2, 4, 6. An even more elaborate reading of providence, where the flourishing of the United States was understood as bringing on the Return of Christ, occurred in Nevin's commencement address at Franklin and Marshall College in 1867, as found in Theodore Appel, *The Life and Work of John Williamson Nevin* (Philadelphia: Reformed Church Publication House, 1889), 634–54.

4. Philip Schaff, *Der Bürgerkrieg und das christliche Leben in Nord-Amerika* (Berlin: Wiegandt und Grieben, 1866), 16–17.

5. Bushnell, "Obligations to the Dead," 328–29.

6. John Adger, "Northern and Southern Views of the Province of the Church," *Southern Presbyterian Review* 16 (Mar. 1866): 398–99, 410.

7. Charles Pettit McIlvaine, *Pastoral Letter of the Bishops of the Protestant Episcopal Church in the United States of America to the Clergy and Laity of the Same . . . October 17, 1862* (New York: Baker and Godwin, 1862), 3–7.

8. Daniel Alexander Payne, *Welcome to the Ransomed; or, Duties of the Colored Inhabitants of the District of Columbia* (Baltimore: Bull and Tuttle, 1861), 12, as collected in Payne, *Sermons and Addresses, 1853–1891*, ed. Charles Killian (New York: Arno, 1972).

9. John H. Castle, "Circular Letter: The Effect of Our National Troubles on the Kingdom of Christ" (Oct. 1861), in *Minutes of the Philadelphia Baptist Association* (Philadelphia: Philadelphia Baptist Association, 1861), 27.

10. "The Rev. C. C. Gillespie at Camp Chase," *Army and Navy Messenger for the Trans-Mississippi Department*, Mar. 2, 1865, p. 1, as quoted in Kurt Berends, " 'Thus Saith the Lord': The Use of the Bible by Southern Evangelicals in the Era of the American Civil War" (D.Phil. diss., Oxford University, 1997), 236.

11. Henry Ward Beecher, "Abraham Lincoln," in *Patriotic Addresses* (New York: Fords, Howard, and Hulburt, 1887), 711.

12. "The Nation's Triumph, and Its Sacrifice," *Christian Examiner* 58 (May 1865): 435, 441, 439.

13. Ralph Waldo Emerson, "Abraham Lincoln: Remarks at the Funeral Services Held in Concord, April 19, 1865," in *The Complete Works of Ralph Waldo Emerson*, 12 vols. bound in 6 (New York: W. H. Wise, 1926), 11:337–38.

14. George Q. Cannon, "Emancipation of the Slaves – The Prophet Joseph's Plan – Results of Its Rejection," *Latter-Day Saints' Millennial Star* (London) 25, no. 7 (Feb. 14, 1863): 99–101.

15. J. H. Thornwell, "Address to All Churches of Christ," in *The Collected Writings of James Henley Thornwell*, vol. 4, *Ecclesiastical*, ed. John B. Adger and John L. Girardeau (Richmond: Presbyterian Committee of Publication, 1873), 461.

16. G. I. Wood (Guilford, Conn.), "A Divine Actor on the State," *New Englander* 24 (Oct. 1865): 691–92.

17. Charles Hodge, "President Lincoln," *Biblical Repertory and Princeton Review* 37 (July 1865): 435.

18. Westminster Confession, chap. 5: Of Providence, pars. 1–3: "(1) God the great Creator of all things does uphold, direct, dispose, and govern all creatures, actions, and things, from the greatest even to the least, by His most wise and holy providence, according to His infallible foreknowledge, and the free and immutable counsel of His own will, to the praise of the glory of His wisdom, power, justice, goodness, and mercy. (2) Although, in relation to the foreknowledge and decree of God, the

first Cause, all things come to pass immutably, and infallibly; yet, by the same providence, He orders them to fall out, according to the nature of second causes, either
necessarily, freely, or contingently. (3) God, in His ordinary providence, makes use of
means, yet is free to work without, above, and against them, at His pleasure."

19. Hodge, "President Lincoln," 439–40.

20. J. M. Pendleton, *Reminiscences of a Long Life* (Louisville: Press Baptist Book Concern, 1891), 125. The biblical quotation is from Psalm 76:10.

21. Lynch as quoted in William B. Gravely, "James Lynch and the Black Christian
Mission during Reconstruction," in *Black Apostles at Home and Abroad*, ed. David W.
Wills and Richard Newman (Boston: G. K. Hall, 1982), 165, 170.

22. Read Family Correspondence, University of Notre Dame Library Special Collec-
tions (Notre Dame, Ind.), as quoted in Lydia Dole, "Letters from the Valley: The Loyalty of Women of the Confederate South" (seminar paper for Prof. George Marsden,
University of Notre Dame, 2004).

23. Correspondence from Dec. 1862 and Apr. 1865, *Letters of Lydia Maria Child*, ed.
John G. Whittier and Wendell Phillips (Boston: Houghton Mifflin, 1882), 171, 453. I
thank Patti Mangis for this material on Child.

24. Stephen V. Ash, ed., "Conscience and Christianity: A Middle Tennessee Unionist Renounces His Church, 1867," *East Tennessee Historical Society's Publications* 54–55
(1982–83): 114.

25. Quoted in William Garrett Piston, *Lee's Tarnished Lieutenant: James Longstreet and
His Place in Southern History* (Athens: University of Georgia Press, 1987), 114.

26. James I. Robertson Jr., *Stonewall Jackson: The Man, the Soldier, the Legend* (New
York: Macmillan, 1997), 19 ("Providence"), 55, 59, 118 ("all-wise God").

27. Ibid., 108.

28. Ibid., 569. For only some of the other instances of Jackson's use of such language, see ibid., 221, 234, 239, 250, 263, 270–71, 295, 311, 328, 363, 377, 412, 449, 518, 547,
569, 605, 617, 639.

29. Daniel W. Stowell, "Stonewall Jackson and the Providence of God," in *Religion
and the American Civil War*, ed. Randall M. Miller, Harry S. Stout, and Charles Reagan
Wilson (New York: Oxford University Press, 1998), 187. Stowell's fine article (187–207)
is the source of the information in this paragraph.

30. *Fighting for the Confederacy: The Personal Recollections of General Edward Porter Alexander*, ed. Gary W. Gallagher (Chapel Hill: University of North Carolina Press, 1989),
59 (first two quotations), 96–97, 58–59. For other Southerners who by the time of the
Civil War were also giving up old providential certainties, see Michael O'Brien, *Conjectures of Order: Intellectual Life and the American South, 1810–1860*, 2 vols. (Chapel Hill:
University of North Carolina Press, 2004), 2:1161–1202.

31. Mark A. Noll, *America's God: From Jonathan Edwards to Abraham Lincoln* (New York: Oxford University Press, 2002), 426–38.

32. Roy B. Basler, ed., *The Collected Works of Abraham Lincoln*, 9 vols. (New Brunswick: Rutgers University Press, 1953), 4:270–71.

33. Ibid., 3:204–5 (punctuation and capitalization as in original).

34. Ibid., 5:403–4 (emphasis in the original).

35. Don E. Fehrenbacher and Virginia Fehrenbacher, *Recollected Words of Abraham Lincoln* (Stanford: Stanford University Press, 1996), 474. For expert setting of this scene, see Allen C. Guelzo, *Lincoln's Emancipation Proclamation: The End of Slavery in America* (New York: Simon and Schuster, 2004), 149–54.

36. Basler, *Collected Works of Lincoln*, 8:333.

37. August Wenzel, "Theological Implications of the Civil War," mimeograph (Evanston, Ill.: Garrett Theological Seminary Library, 1971). Material in the next paragraphs is digested from Wenzel's very useful survey.

38. As examples, see Edward F. Williams, "On the Origin of Species by Means of Natural Selection — Darwin," *Evangelical Quarterly Review* 16 (Jan. 1865): 11–23; and, on Lyell, Daniel R. Goodwin, "The Antiquity of Man," *American Presbyterian and Theological Review*, ser. 2, 2 (Apr. 1864): 233–59.

39. "Renan, Strauss, and Schleiermacher," *Biblical Repertory and Princeton Review* 38 (Jan. 1866): 133–40.

40. For example, "Are Our Necessary Conceptions of God Reliable," *Christian Review* 25 (Oct. 1860): 539–57.

41. For example, C. M. Ellis, "The Encyclical Letter," *Christian Examiner* 78 (Jan.–May 1865): 399–409.

42. See comment on romantic theological influences in E. Brooks Holifield, *Theology in America: Christian Thought from the Age of the Puritans to the Civil War* (New Haven, Conn.: Yale University Press, 2003), 468–71.

43. Charles Hodge, "The General Assembly," *Biblical Repertory and Princeton Review* 37 (July 1865): 506.

44. Phillip S. Paludan, "Lincoln and the Rhetoric of Politics," in *A Crisis of Republicanism: American Politics in the Civil War*, ed. Lloyd C. Ambrosius (Lincoln: University of Nebraska Press, 1990), 88.

CHAPTER SIX

1. On the more general commentary, see Helen G. MacDonald, *Canadian Public Opinion on the American Civil War* (New York: Columbia University Press, 1926); George Müller, *Der amerikanische Sezessionskrieg in der schweizerischen öffentlichen Meinung* [The

American War of Secession in Swiss Public Opinion] (Basel: Helbing und Lichtenhahn, 1944); Belle Becker Sideman and Lillian Friedman, eds., *Europe Looks at the Civil War* (New York: Orion, 1960); D. P. Crook, *The North, the South, and the Powers, 1861–1865* (New York: John Wiley and Sons, 1974); Robin W. Winks, *Canada and the United States: The Civil War Years*, new ed. (Lanham, Md.: University Press of America, 1988); Greg Marquis, *In Armageddon's Shadow: The Civil War and Canada's Maritime Provinces* (Montreal: McGill-Queen's University Press, 1998); R. J. M. Blackett, *Divided Hearts: Britain and the American Civil War* (Baton Rouge: Louisiana State University Press, 2001); and Duncan Andrew Campbell, *English Public Opinion and the American Civil War* (Rochester, N.Y.: Royal Historical Society/Boydell, 2003).

2. I am pleased to offer special thanks to David Bebbington of the University of Stirling and his student assistants for securing some of the British periodical literature.

3. See, as examples, an important series of articles by W. Harrison Daniel, including "The Reaction of British Methodism to the Civil War and Reconstruction in America," *Methodist History* 16 (1977): 3–20; "The Response of the Church of England to the Civil War and Reconstruction in America," *Historical Magazine of the Protestant Episcopal Church* 47 (1978): 57–72; and "English Presbyterians, Slavery and the American Crisis of the 1860s," *Journal of Presbyterian History* 58 (Spring 1980): 50–62. Also helpful are Clare Taylor, *British and American Abolitionists: An Episode in Transatlantic Understanding* (Edinburgh: Edinburgh University Press, 1974); Barbara Karsky, "Les libéraux français et l'émancipation des esclaves aux États-Unis, 1852–1870," *Revue d'histoire moderne et contemporaine* 21 (1974): 575–90; C. Duncan Rice, *The Scots Abolitionists, 1833–1861* (Baton Rouge: Louisiana State University Press, 1981); Craig I. Stevenson, " 'Those Now at War Are Our Friends and Neighbors': The Views of Evangelical Editors in British North America toward the American Civil War, 1861–1865" (M.A. thesis, Queen's University, 1997); Preston Jones, "Quebec and Louisiana: The Civil War Years," *Quebec Studies* 23 (Spring 1997): 73–81; Preston Jones, "Civil War, Culture War: French Quebec and the American War between the States," *Catholic Historical Review* 87 (Jan. 2001): 55–70; and the sections on Stuart Robinson in Canada from Preston D. Graham Jr., *A Kingdom Not of This World: Stuart Robinson's Struggle to Distinguish the Sacred from the Secular during the Civil War* (Macon, Ga.: Mercer University Press, 2002).

4. Philo, "The Civil War in America, and Our Present Difficulty," *United Presbyterian Magazine*, new ser., 5 (Jan. 1862): 3–4.

5. James Gibson (probable author on basis of other American articles signed by him), "The Trans-Atlantic Struggle," *Evangelical Witness* 1 (Feb. 1862): 18. The name of this periodical was changed in 1863 to the *Evangelical Witness and Presbyterian Review*, but I will use the shorter title throughout.

6. "A Voice from Canada," *The Presbyterian; a Missionary and Religious Record of the Presbyterian Church of Canada in Connection with the Church of Scotland* 15 (May 1862): 139.

7. Daniel Duff, letter dated July 28, 1864, *Home and Foreign Record of the Canada Presbyterian Church* 4, no. 1 (Nov. 1864): 12–13.

8. For biographical information, which seems hard to come by, see "Gasparin, Graf Agénor de," in *Religion in Geschichte und Gegenwart*, 3rd ed. (1958; repr., Tübingen: J. C. B. Mohr, 1986), 2:1203.

9. Comte Agénor de Gasparin, *Les États-Unis en 1861: Un grand people qui se relève* (Paris, 1861), translated by Mary L. Booth as *The Uprising of a Great People: The United States in 1861, to Which Is Added a Word of Peace on the Difference between England and the United States*, 2nd ed. (New York: Charles Scribner, 1861); and Gasparin, *L'Amérique devant l'Europe* (Paris, 1862), translated by Mary L. Booth as *America before Europe: Principles and Interests* (New York: Charles Scribner, 1862). The prose in both translations is unusually vivacious.

10. For orientation, see Ramsay Cook on Smith in *Dictionary of Canadian Biography*, vol. 13, *1901 to 1910* (Toronto: University of Toronto Press, 1994), 968–74.

11. Goldwin Smith, *Does the Bible Sanction American Slavery?* (Cambridge: Sever and Francis, 1863).

12. Gasparin, *Uprising*, 72–91, 92–106; Gasparin, *America before Europe*, 381–404.

13. Gasparin, *Uprising*, 44, 61, 63, 68.

14. Ibid., 73, 75–76.

15. Ibid., 75.

16. Ibid., 94 (law and Gospel); ibid., 99–100 (Philemon); and Gasparin, *America before Europe*, 386n (literalism).

17. Gasparin, *Uprising*, 83, 100; Gasparin, *America before Europe*, 383, 391.

18. Smith, *Does the Bible Sanction Slavery?*, 8–24.

19. Ibid., 56, 60.

20. Ibid., 6.

21. Ibid., 88.

22. "Foreign News," *United Presbyterian Magazine*, Nov. 1861, p. 543; "Gift from the British Bible Society to the United States," ibid., Mar. 1862, p. 144.

23. "The Civil War in America," ibid., June 1861, p. 348; "Civil War in America," ibid., Sept. 1861, p. 446.

24. "Foreign," ibid., Oct. 1861, p. 493.

25. "The Civil War in America, and Our Present Difficulty," ibid., Jan. 1862, p. 1; "The Negro Character and the American War," ibid., Nov. 1863, p. 481. The upas tree was, according to legend, devastatingly toxic to anything in its proximity.

26. James Gibson (probable author), "The Trans-Atlantic Struggle," *Evangelical Witness* 1 (Feb. 1862): 17–18.

27. James Gibson, "The American Civil War and Slavery," ibid. 1 (Dec. 1862): 137–39.

28. "American Religious Literature," ibid. 1 (July 1862): 83, 85.

29. "American Christianity – Where Is It?" ibid. 2 (Jan. 1863): 14.

30. James Gibson, "The Past Year," ibid. 3 (Jan. 1864): 1, 2.

31. Philadelphus, "A Nation in Sackcloth," ibid. 4 (June 1865): 143.

32. *The Presbyterian; A Missionary and Religious Record of the Presbyterian Church of Canada in Connection with the Church of Scotland*, which was edited in Montreal, was almost completely preoccupied with affairs in Canada and Scotland.

33. *Home and Foreign Record of the Canada Presbyterian Church* 2, no. 2 (Dec. 1862): 44; ibid. 5, no. 2 (Dec. 1865): 52 (quotation).

34. *Monthly Record of the Church of Scotland in Nova Scotia and the Adjoining Provinces* 7 (Jan. 5, 1861): 12; ibid. 7 (Jan. 19, 1861): 24.

35. Ibid. 7 (May 1861): 119; ibid. 9 (June 1863): 144.

36. For examples of such correspondence, see *Christian Guardian*, Jan. 11, 1860, p. 8; ibid., Feb. 1, 1860, p. 18.

37. "The War in the States," ibid., May 1, 1861, p. 70.

38. Editor, in reply to correspondent, ibid., Sept. 18, 1861, p. 148.

39. Letter on case of escaped slave John Anderson, *Canada Christian Advocate*, Dec. 26, 1860, p. 2; Rev. John S. C. Abbott, "The Barbarism of Slavery," ibid., Aug. 14, 1861, p. 1.

40. Untitled, London *Times*, Jan. 6, 1863, p. 8, col. b.

41. Ibid., col. c.

42. "The Civil War in America," London *Times*, Mar. 23, 1863, p. 9, col. e.

43. Ibid., col. e, col. f.

44. Ibid., col. f, col. g.

45. For orientation, see Quentin Skinner, *The Foundations of Modern Political Thought*, vol. 2, *The Age of Reformation* (New York: Cambridge University Press, 1978), 65–73.

46. On that orientation, see the informative new edition of his letters, mostly sent back from America to the Continent, *Die Korrespondenz Heinrich Melchior Mühlenbergs aus der Anfangszeit des deutschen Luthertums in Nordamerika* [H. M. Mühlenberg's Correspondence from the Initial Era of German Lutheranism in North America], ed. Kurt Aland and Hellmut Wellenreuther, 6 vols. (Berlin: de Gruyter, 1986–2002).

47. J. H. C. Helmuth, *Betrachtung der Evangelischen Lehre von der Heiligen Schrift und Taufe; samt einigen Gedanken von den gegenwärtigen Zeiten* [Consideration of Lutheran Teaching on Holy Scripture and on Baptism; Together with Some Thoughts on Contemporary Times], (Germantown: Michael Billmeyer, 1793), 67.

48. For an overview of Lutheran accommodations to the views of their various

regions, see Robert Fortenbaugh, "American Lutheran Synods and Slavery, 1830-60," *Journal of Religion* 13 (Jan. 1933): 72-92.

49. Paul P. Kuenning, *The Rise and Fall of American Lutheran Pietism* (Macon, Ga.: Mercer University Press, 1988), 97-178.

50. Robert M. Calhoon, "Lutheranism and Early Southern Culture," in *"A Truly Efficient School of Theology": The Lutheran Theological Seminary in Historical Context, 1830-1980*, ed. H. George Anderson and Robert M. Calhoon (Columbia, S.C.: Lutheran Theological Southern Seminary, 1981), 17-18; E. Brooks Holifield, *The Gentlemen Theologians: American Theology in Southern Culture, 1795-1860* (Durham, N.C.: Duke University Press, 1978), 163, 165; and Lester D. Stephens, *Science, Race, and Religion in the American South: John Bachman and the Charleston Circle of Naturalists, 1815-1895* (Chapel Hill: University of North Carolina Press, 2000), 165-68.

51. "Für die Deutschen in Amerika," *Protestantische Kirchenzeitung für das evangelische Deutschland* 7, no. 14 (Apr. 7, 1860): 360; untitled, ibid. 7, no. 35 (Sept. 1, 1860): 862.

52. Untitled, ibid. 9, no. 6 (Feb. 8, 1862): 132. For other expressions of spiritual support for slaves, see "Vereinigte Staaten," ibid. 7, no. 34 (Aug. 25, 1860): 839; untitled, ibid. 7, no. 35 (Sept. 1, 1860): 861.

53. "Ohio," ibid. 10, no. 32 (Aug. 10, 1861): 763-64.

54. Ibid., 764.

55. "Civil War in America," *United Presbyterian Magazine*, Sept. 1861, pp. 445-46; "Nordamerika," *Protestantische Kirchenzeitung* 9, no. 21 (May 24, 1862): 478; Gasparin, *America before Europe*, 392n.

56. James Gibson, "The American Civil War and Slavery," *Evangelical Witness* 1 (Dec. 1862): 139. In the same journal, see also Robert Watts, "The Present Condition of the Northern States," 2 (May 1863): 116; James Gibson, "Christianity on the Battlefield," 2 (Oct. 1863): 269; Philadelphus, "A Nation in Sackcloth," 4 (June 1865): 141; and James Gibson, "Events of the Year," 4 (Dec. 1865): 310.

57. Gasparin, *American before Europe*, 390, 391.

58. D. K., "The American War and Slavery," *United Presbyterian Magazine*, Sept. 1863, p. 392. Such language appears in almost every article devoted to the American conflict in this magazine.

59. See, for example, "General Religious Intelligence," *Home and Foreign Record of the Canada Presbyterian Church* 2, no. 1 (Nov. 1862): 12; untitled, *Monthly Record of the Church of Scotland in Nova Scotia* 7 (May 1861): 119.

60. "The American Churches and Slavery," *Christian Guardian*, June 25, 1862, p. 104.

61. James Gibson, "The Trans-Atlantic Struggle," *Evangelical Witness* 1 (Feb. 1862): 17; Philo, "The Civil War in America and Our Present Difficulty," *United Presbyterian Magazine* 6 (Jan. 1862): 4.

62. "Ohio," *Protestantische Kirchenzeitung* 8, no. 32 (Aug. 10, 1861): 762.

63. "Rather Spiteful," *Christian Guardian*, Feb. 1, 1860, p. 18. A great deal of anti-Roman sentiment could also be found in almost every issue of the *Home and Foreign Record of the Canada Presbyterian Church* during the war years.

64. Untitled, London *Times*, Jan. 6, 1863, p. 8, col. c.

65. James Gibson, "The Trans-Atlantic Struggle," *Evangelical Witness* 1 (Feb. 1862): 17.

66. "The American War and Slavery," *United Presbyterian Magazine* 8 (Nov. 1864): 495.

67. Untitled, *Monthly Record of the Church of Scotland in Nova Scotia* 7 (Aug. 1861): 192; untitled, ibid. 8 (Feb. 1862): 40.

68. "The American War," *United Presbyterian Magazine*, Sept. 1862, p. 440.

69. Robert Burns, "The Aspect of the Times Practically Considered," *Home and Foreign Record of the Canada Presbyterian Church* 4, no. 8 (May 1865): 198–205 (quotation on 201).

70. "North or South? Which?" *Canada Christian Advocate*, Sept. 10, 1862, p. 1.

71. "The Late American Conflict," *Evangelical Witness* 4 (Sept. 1865): 237.

72. Untitled, London *Times*, Jan. 6, 1863, p. 8, col. c.

73. Smith, *Does the Bible Sanction Slavery?*, 96.

74. Gasparin, *Uprising*, 102.

75. Exchange of letters between a Southern women and Child, *Christian Guardian*, Jan. 11, 1860, p. 8.

76. "Nord-Amerika," *Protestantische Kirchenzeitung* 11, no. 18 (Feb. 20, 1864): 179.

77. "The New God – Modern Baal – or the American God," *Canada Christian Advocate*, Oct. 31, 1860, p. 1.

78. Untitled, *Christian Guardian*, Sept. 18, 1861, p. 148; "The 'Times' on Slavery," ibid., Feb. 22, 1863, p. 22.

79. James Gibson, "The American Civil War and Slavery," *Evangelical Witness* 1 (Dec. 1862): 138.

80. Quotation from the reply of the Scottish General Assembly to Southern Presbyterians in *Home and Foreign Record of the Canada Presbyterian Church* 3, no. 1 (Nov. 1863): 22.

81. James Gibson, "The Trans-Atlantic Struggle," *Evangelical Witness* 1 (Feb. 1862): 17.

82. D. K., "The American War and Slavery," *United Presbyterian Magazine*, Sept. 1863, pp. 389–90.

83. "Liberty to the Captive," *Record of the Free Church of Scotland*, Sept. 1, 1863, p. 317.

84. Smith, *Does the Bible Sanction Slavery?*, 29.

85. Gasparin, *Uprising*, 103–4.

86. Untitled, *Protestantische Kirchenzeitung* 7, no. 35 (Sept. 1, 1860): 860.

87. "British Aristocracy and Slavery," *Christian Guardian*, Oct. 23, 1861, p. 167.

88. "Hebrew and Negro Slavery Unlike," *Canada Christian Advocate*, Mar. 6, 1861, p. 2.

89. Gasparin, *Uprising*, 99–100.

90. Smith, *Does the Bible Sanction Slavery?*, 88.

91. Ibid., 5.

92. Gasparin, *Uprising*, 76.

93. See, for explanations, Goldwyn French, *Parsons and Politics: The Role of the Wesleyan Methodists in Upper Canada and the Maritimes from 1780–1855* (Toronto: Ryerson, 1962), 40; Jane Errington, *The Lion, the Eagle, and Upper Canada* (Kingston: McGill-Queen's University Press, 1987); Stewart J. Brown, *Thomas Chalmers and the Godly Commonwealth in Scotland* (New York: Oxford University Press, 1982); and David Hempton, "Noisy Methodists and Pious Protestants: Evangelical Revival and Religious Minorities in Eighteenth-Century Ireland," in *Amazing Grace: Evangelicalism in Australia, Britain, Canada, and the United States*, ed. George A. Rawlyk and Mark A. Noll (Montreal: McGill-Queen's University Press, 1994), 68.

94. On those comparisons, see the outstanding essay by Richard Carwardine, "The Second Great Awakening in Comparative Perspective: Revivals and Culture in the United States and Britain," in *Modern Christian Revivals*, ed. Edith L. Blumhofer and Randall Balmer (Urbana: University of Illinois Press, 1993), 84–100.

95. See especially D. N. Hempton, "Evangelicalism and Eschatology," *Journal of Ecclesiastical History* 31 (Apr. 1980): 179–94; and D. W. Bebbington, *Evangelicalism in Modern Britain: A History from the 1730s to the 1980s* (London: Unwin Hyman, 1989), 78–81, 86–91.

CHAPTER SEVEN

1. See especially John T. McGreevy, *Catholicism and American Freedom: A History* (New York: W. W. Norton, 2003); Patrick W. Carey, *Orestes A. Brownson: American Religious Weathervane* (Grand Rapids, Mich.: Eerdmans, 2004); John F. Quinn, " 'Three Cheers for the Abolitionist Pope!': American Reaction to Gregory XVI's Condemnation of the Slave Trade, 1840–1860," *Catholic Historical Review* 90 (2004): 67–93; and Peter R. D'Agostino, *Rome in America: Transnational Catholic Ideology from the Risorgimento to Fascism* (Chapel Hill: University of North Carolina Press, 2004). These studies build on a number of previous works that explore different aspects of the subject, including Madeleine Hooke Rice, *American Catholic Opinion in the Slavery Controversy* (New York: Columbia University Press, 1944); Benjamin J. Blied, *Catholics and the Civil War* (Milwaukee: by the author, 1945); Joseph D. Brokhage, *Francis Patrick Kenrick's Opinion on Slavery* (Washington, D.C.: Catholic University of America Press, 1955); Anthony B.

Lalli and Thomas H. O'Connor, "Roman Views on the American Civil War," *Catholic Historical Review* 40 (Apr. 1971): 21–41; Walter G. Sharrow, "John Hughes and a Catholic Response to Slavery in Antebellum America," *Journal of Negro History* 57 (July 1972): 254–69; Walter G. Sharrow, "Northern Catholic Intellectuals and the Coming of the Civil War," *New-York Historical Society Quarterly* 58 (1974): 35–56; Judith Conrad Wimmer, "American Catholic Interpretations of the Civil War" (Ph.D. diss., Drew University, 1980); James Hennesey, *American Catholics* (New York: Oxford University Press, 1981), 143–57; Cyprian Davis, *The History of Black Catholics in the United States* (New York: Crossroad, 1990); Kenneth J. Zanca, ed., *American Catholics and Slavery, 1789–1866: An Anthology of Primary Documents* (Lanham, Md.: University Press of America, 1994); and Randall M. Miller, "Catholic Religion, Irish Ethnicity, and the Civil War," in *Religion and the American Civil War*, ed. Randall M. Miller, Harry S. Stout, and Charles Reagan Wilson (New York: Oxford University Press, 1998), 261–96.

2. McGreevy, *Catholicism and American Freedom*, 67; Carey, *Brownson*, 277.

3. See Rice, *American Catholic Opinion*, 31–38, 44–46; on the relative racial tolerance of American Catholics in general, see McGreevy, *Catholicism and American Freedom*, 50, 54–56.

4. Spalding, "Dissertation on the American Civil War," in Zanca, *American Catholics and Slavery*, 211, 212.

5. Quoted in Wimmer, "American Catholic Interpretations," 285 n. 15.

6. *Letters of the Late Bishop England to the Hon. John Forsyth on the Subject of Domestic Slavery* (Baltimore: John Murphy, 1844).

7. I am following the conclusion in Brokhage, *Kenrick's Opinion on Slavery*, 235–43.

8. Hughes, from notes for a speech ca. 1860, in Zanca, *American Catholics and Slavery*, 214.

9. Verot, manuscript sermon, in ibid., 204–7.

10. See Carey, *Brownson*, 264–81; for an overview of Brownson's extensive writings on the conflict itself, see Patrick W. Carey, comp., *Orestes Brownson: A Bibliography, 1826–1876* (Milwaukee: Marquette University Press, 1996), 96–108.

11. *Brownson's Quarterly Review*, Jan. 1857, pp. 89–114, in Zanca, *American Catholics and Slavery*, 137.

12. Carey, *Brownson*, 276.

13. See especially the superb treatment in McGreevy, *Catholicism and American Freedom*, 56–90; and John T. McGreevy, "Catholicism and Abolition: An Historical (and Theological) Problem," in *Figures in the Carpet: Finding the Human Person in the American Past*, ed. Wilfred M. McClay (Grand Rapids, Mich.: Eerdmans, 2006). For recent reflection on changes in Catholic moral theology respecting slavery, see John T. Noonan Jr., "Development in Moral Doctrine," in *The Context of Casuistry*, ed. James F. Keenan,

and Thomas A. Shannon (Washington, D.C.: Georgetown University Press, 1995), 188–204 (with 190–92 specifically on slavery); and Noonan, *A Church That Can and Cannot Change* (Notre Dame, Ind.: University of Notre Dame Press, 2005), 17–123.

14. Quoted in Philip Gleason, *Keeping the Faith: American Catholicism Past and Present* (Notre Dame, Ind.: University of Notre Dame Press, 1987), 44.

15. This paragraph follows D'Agostino, *Rome in America*, 19–45.

16. *A Debate on the Roman Catholic Religion: Held . . . from the 13th to the 21st of January, 1837. Between Alexander Campbell of Bethany, Virginia, and the Rt. Rev. John B. Purcell, Bishop of Cincinnati* (1837; repr., Cincinnati: J. A. and U. P. James, 1851), viii, 311.

17. Quoted in Ray Allen Billington, *The Protestant Crusade, 1800–1860* (1938; repr., Chicago: Quadrangle, 1964), 425.

18. For background, see Margaret Lavinia Anderson, "The Limits of Secularization: On the Problem of the Catholic Revival in Nineteenth-Century Germany," *Historical Journal* 38 (1995): 647–70.

19. McGreevy, *Catholicism and American Freedom*, 28.

20. D'Agostino, *Rome in America*, 32.

21. Gregory XVI, *Mirari Vos*, in *The Papal Encyclicals*, vol. 1, *1740–1878*, ed. Claudia Carlen (New York: Consortium, 1981), 235–41: par. 9 (papal sovereignty), par. 14 (liberty of conscience, free speech), par. 20 (separation of church and state).

22. Quinn, "'Three Cheers for the Abolitionist Pope!,'" 71; this paragraph follows Quinn's illuminating article.

23. For background, see Jean-Paul Bernard and Yvan Lamonde, "Louis-Antoine Dessaulles," *Dictionary of Canadian Biography*, vol. 12, *1891 to 1900* (Toronto: University of Toronto Press, 1990), 252–57; and Preston Jones, "Civil War, Culture War: French Quebec and the American War between the States," *Catholic Historical Review* 87 (Jan. 2001): 68–69.

24. Louis-Antoine Dessaulles, *La guerre américaine: Son origine et ses vraies causes* (Montreal: Le Pays, 1865), 74, 78, 425, 426.

25. For an especially helpful introduction to Dupanloup, see Marvin R. O'Connell, "Ultramontanism and Dupanloup: The Compromise of 1865," *Church History* 53 (June 1984): 200–217.

26. Bishop Dupanloup, pastoral letter, in Zanca, *American Catholics and Slavery*, 123–24.

27. On that circle, with Cochin mentioned throughout, see Barbara Karsky, "Les libéraux français et l'émancipation des esclaves aux États-Unis, 1852–1870," *Revue d'histoire moderne et contemporaine* 21 (1974): 575–90.

28. Augustin Cochin, *The Results of Slavery*, trans. Mary L. Booth (Boston: Walker, Wise, 1863).

29. Ibid., 282.

30. Ibid., 299. A similar conclusion is driven home with similar force on 359n.

31. Ibid., 321, with 304–26 presenting a remarkable array of New Testament texts enjoining servanthood, proclaiming liberty, demanding universal human fraternity, and the like.

32. Ibid., 326–61.

33. Ibid., 347.

34. Ibid., 327, 328.

35. Ibid., 299.

36. Ibid., v.

37. For orientation to nineteenth-century conservative Catholicism, especially as connected to the United States, see Philip Gleason, *The Conservative Reformers: German-American Catholics and the Social Order* (Notre Dame, Ind.: University of Notre Dame Press, 1968); Gleason, *Contending with Modernity: Catholic Higher Education in the Twentieth Century* (New York: Oxford University Press, 1995); and McGreevy, *Catholicism and American Freedom*. For a historiographical explanation concerning why that conservative perspective has been neglected in earlier histories of American Catholicism, see D'Agostino, *Rome in America*, 309–15.

38. As quoted in Jones, "Civil War, Culture War," 62.

39. George Müller, *Der amerikanische Sezessionskrieg in der schweizerischen öffentlichen Meinung* [The American War of Secession in Swiss Public Opinion] (Basel: Helbing und Lichtenhahn, 1944), 135, 138 (with an explanation of this conservative stance, 130–39).

40. For background on this newspaper and its editor during the Civil War, I have relied on Dieter Albrecht and Bernhard Weber, eds., *Die Mitarbeiter der Historisch-politischen Blätter für das katholische Deutschland* [Contributors to the HPB] (Mainz: Matthias-Grünewald, 1990); and the introduction to Dieter Albrecht, ed., *Joseph Edmund Jörg: Briefwechsel, 1846–1901* (Mainz: Matthias-Grünewald, 1988), xxiv–xxxviii. The HPB was collected in two volumes each year, with each volume totaling more than one thousand pages.

41. Joseph Edmund Jörg, "Die beginnenden Sonderbunds-kämpfe der nordamerikanischen Union: Ein politisches Zeitbild" [The First Confederacy Battles of the North American Union: A Contemporary Political Picture], HPB 47 (1861): 270–99; "Der Bürgerkrieg in Nordamerika und der Untergang der Union" [The Civil War in North America and the Downfall of the Union], HPB 49 (1862): 245–79 (dated Feb. 1, 1862); "Der Wendepunkt im nordamerikanischen Bürgerkrieg" [The Turning Point in the North American Civil War], HPB 51 (1863): 211–42 (dated Jan. 21, 1863); "Zeitläufe über Nordamerika, I: Die Umwälzung in der ehemaligen Union und ihre Rückwirkung auf Europa" [Events in North America, I: The Cataclysm in the Former

Union and Its Consequences for Europe], HPB 55 (1865): 476-98 (dated Mar. 9, 1865); "Zeitläufe über Nordamerika, II: Die Geschichte der nördlichen Parteien; der Unterschied der Kriegsführung des Nordens und des Südens" [Events in North America, II: The History of the Northern Parties; the Difference between North and South in Conduct of the War], HPB 55 (1865): 578-604 (dated Mar. 23, 1865); and "Zeitläufe: Der Stand der Dinge in der nordamerikanischen Union und unser Interesse daran" [Events: The Condition of Things in the North American Union and Our Interests Therein], HPB 57 (1866): 548-68. Two of the postbellum reports from the United States are ascribed in Albrecht and Weber, *Mitarbeiter*, to Kuno Damian Freiherr von Schütz zu Hölzhausen, and I am assuming the other two were written by him as well: "Nordamerikanische Correspondenz," HPB 57 (1866): 973-88; "Nordamerikanische Correspondenz," HPB 58 (1866): 448-56; "Die Krisis in Washington and die Zustände überhaupt" [The Crisis in Washington and Conditions Generally], HPB 59 (1867): 132-38; and "Die Wahrheit über die nordamerikanische Union" [The Truth about the North American Union], HPB 59 (1867): 743-55. The review article was by Paul Joseph Münz, "Christentum und Sklaverei" [Christendom and Slavery], HPB 62 (1868): 177-202.

42. J. Margraf, *Kirche und Sklaverei seit der Entdeckung Amerika's, oder: Was hat die katholische Kirche seit der Entdeckung Amerika's theils zur Milderung theils zur Aufhebung der Sklaverei gethan?* [Church and Slavery since the Discovery of America, or: What Has the Catholic Church Done since the Discovery of America Partly to Mitigate and Partly to Destroy Slavery?] (Tübingen: H. Laupp'schen, 1865), 213-24, 217.

43. Jörg, "Die beginnenden Sonderbunds-kämpfe," 271, 279, 289. He repeated the charge of "Terrorismus" in "Zeitläufe II," 581.

44. Jörg, "Der Bürgerkrieg," 260.

45. Jörg, "Zeitläufe: Der Stand," 553.

46. S. zu Hölzhausen, "Correspondenz," 58 (1866): 454.

47. Jörg, "Der Wendepunkt," 215; "Zeitläufe I," 498; and "Zeitläufe II," 592.

48. Jörg, "Zeitläufe II," 592-96.

49. S. zu Hölzhausen, "Correspondenz," 57 (1866): 983; and "Correspondenz," 58 (1866): 451.

50. S. zu Hölzhausen, "Correspondenz," 58 (1866): 455.

51. Jörg, "Der Bürgerkrieg," 263.

52. Jörg, "Der Wendepunkt," 237.

53. Ibid., 237-38.

54. Ibid., 238n.

55. Jörg, "Zeitläufe II," 596-97.

56. Münz, "Christentum und Sklaverei," 179, 197.

57. Ibid., 179.

58. Ibid., 180.

59. Ibid., 202.

60. S. zu Hölzhausen, "Die Krisis," 135–37.

61. For background, see Giandomenico Mucci, *Carlo Maria Curci: Il fondatore della "Civiltà cattolica"* (Rome: Edizioni Studium, 1988), 16–20; Francesco Dante, *Storia della "Civiltà cattolica" (1850–1891): Il laboratorio del Papa* (Rome: Edizioni Studium, 1990), 57–77; and several articles in the *New Catholic Encyclopedia*, 2nd ed., 15 vols. (Detroit: Thomson/Gale for the Catholic University of America Press, 2003): "La Civiltà cattolica" (3:757–58), "contemporary scholasticism" (12:772), "Matteo Liberatore" (8:550), and "Luigi Taparelli D'Azeglio" (13:756). Liberatore and Taparelli were founders of the journal.

62. See especially Lalli and O'Connor, "Roman Views on the American Civil War."

63. "La disunione negli Stati Uniti" [Disunion in the United States], *La Civiltà cattolica* (hereafter CC), ser. 4, 9 (Feb. 2, 1861): 312–24.

64. "Il concetto morale della schiavitù" [The Moral Idea of Slavery], CC, ser. 6, 1 (Feb. 18, 1865): 427–45; "La Chiesa tutrice della libertà in America" [The Church as Guardian of Liberty in America], CC, ser. 6, 1 (Mar. 18, 1865): 662–80; "Lo schiavo negro nell' America" [The Negro Slave in America], CC, ser. 6, 7 (Aug. 4, 1866): 296–313; and "L'abolizione della tratta e della schiavitù" [The Abolition of the Slave Trade and of Slavery], CC, ser. 6, 8 (Oct. 6, 1866): 15–34.

65. "Il Mormonismo nelle sue attinenze col moderno Protestantismo" [Mormonism in Its Connections with Modern Protestantism], CC, ser. 4, 6 (May 19, 1860): 391–413. This last article was identified as written by Cardinal Karl August von Reisach, but the others were published anonymously.

66. "Il concetto," 429.

67. Ibid., 434.

68. Ibid., 437–38; other texts considered were Ephesians 6:5–8; 1 Timothy 6:1–4; Titus 2:9–10; and Colossians 4:1.

69. Ibid., 439–40.

70. Ibid., 440.

71. "La Chiesa," 675.

72. "Lo schiavo negro," 307–8.

73. Ibid., 308.

74. Ibid., 312.

75. "L'abolizione," 31.

76. Ibid.

77. Ibid., 34.

78. For background, see the article on Reisach in the *New Catholic Encyclopedia*, 12:40.

79. "Il Mormonismo," 392–93.

80. Ibid., 393.

81. Ibid., 394.

82. Ibid., 395.

83. Ibid., 396.

84. Ibid., 397.

85. Ibid., 398, 399.

86. Ibid., 399.

87. Significantly, at this point Reisach quoted extensively from the attacks made by J. W. Nevin of Mercersburg Theological Seminary against the American sect system, ibid., 400–402.

88. Ibid., 404.

89. Ibid.

90. Ibid., 408.

91. Ibid., 405.

92. Ibid., 411.

93. Ibid., 412.

94. Ibid.

95. Ibid., 413.

96. Ibid.

97. "La disunione," 317.

98. Ibid., 317–18.

99. Jörg, "Der Bürgerkrieg," HPB 49 (1862): 257.

100. "La disunione," 323–24.

101. Ibid., 324.

CHAPTER EIGHT

1. Orestes Brownson, "Catholicity Necessary to Sustain Popular Liberty" (1845), in *Readings in Church History*, vol. 3, *The Modern Era, 1789 to the Present*, ed. Colman Barry, (Westminster, Md.: Newman, 1965), 151.

Index

McIlvaine, Charles Petit, 78
McInerney, Daniel J., 171 (n. 21)
McPherson, James, 10
Menand, Louis, 9
Methodists, 14, 24, 26–28, 105–6
Miller, Perry, 21
Miller, Randall, 10
Mitchell, Laura, 57, 170 (n. 10)
Moorhead, James, 10
Mormons, 80–81, 121, 145, 150–55
Mühlenberg, Henry Melchior, 109
Mullin, Robert Bruce, 169 (n. 4)
Münz, Paul Joseph, 143–44
Murrin, John, 25

Neander, Augustus, 101
Neumark, Georg, 15
Nevin, J. W., 76, 91, 176 (n. 3), 191 (n. 87)
Noah, 3, 34, 42–43, 46, 56
Noonan, John T., 186–87 (n. 13)
North: conflicts over Bible, 3–4, 36, 38–39;
    negative views from abroad, 114–15, 139,
    140–45, 151–52
Nott, Josiah, 118

O'Brien, Michael, 10, 174–75 (n. 26), 178
    (n. 30)
O'Connell, Daniel, 133
O'Connell, Marvin R., 187 (n. 25)
O'Connor, Thomas H., 190 (n. 62)
Onesimus, 33, 100, 116, 120
Overy, David H., 172–73 (n. 4)

Paine, Thomas, 31
Palmer, Benjamin Morgan, 117
Palmer, Phoebe, 20
Paludan, Phillip, 10, 94
Papal States, 129–30, 145, 147
Paul (the apostle), 35, 37, 38, 60, 69, 71, 116,
    147
Payne, Daniel Alexander, 5, 78
Pendleton, James M., 46–47, 54–55, 83–84

Phillips, Wendell, 133
Pius IX (pope), 90–91, 130, 138, 145
Plymouth Brethren, 123
Polygamy, in Old Testament, 101, 117
Polygenesis, of human race, 69
Pranger, Gary K., 172 (n. 1)
Pratt, Parley, 152
Presbyterians, 14, 24, 27, 93, 102–3, 105
Protestants, American: dominance in
    Civil War era, 13–14; habits of mind,
    17–22; and nation, 25–26, 53; foreign
    Protestant opinions concerning, 96–123;
    Roman Catholic opinions concern-
    ing, 127, 150–54, 157. See also Canada;
    England; Ireland; Germany; Scotland
Providence, 1, 18, 22, 75–94, 163; antitheti-
    cal interpretations of, 4–6, 75–76, 79;
    logic of, 76–77, 93–94; and slavery, 81–
    84; and death of Lincoln, 82, 84–85, 86;
    and Stonewall Jackson, 85–87; Lincoln's
    views concerning, 87–90, 94; foreign
    views concerning, 111–12
Purcell, John, 126, 130
Puritans, 18, 150–51, 153

Quakers, 24, 33
Quinn, John F., 33, 185 (n. 1)

Raboteau, Albert, 175 (n. 28)
Race, 51–74, 81–82, 116, 142, 159–60; and
    biblical interpretation, 33, 39; and
    common sense, 49, 56–73; and Israel in
    Old Testament, 57–60. See also Bible;
    Foreign opinion; Slavery
Raphall, Maurice J., 3–4, 47
Read, Mattie White, 84
Reisach, Karl August von, 150–55
Renan, Ernest, 90–91
Republicanism, 18, 19, 28; and biblical
    interpretation, 23, 40–42; opposing
    slavery, 67–68, 79; supporting slavery,
    79. See also Antirepublicanism